1204
The Unholy Crusade

John Godfrey

Oxford New York Toronto Melbourne

OXFORD UNIVERSITY PRESS

1980

Oxford University Press, Walton Street, Oxford OX2 6DP

London Glasgow New York Toronto
Delhi Bombay Calcutta Madras Karachi
Kuala Lumpur Singapore Hong Kong Tokyo
Nairobi Dar es Salaam Cape Town
Melbourne Wellington

and associate companies in
Beirut Berlin Ibadan Mexico City

British Library Cataloguing in Publication Data
Godfrey, John
1204, the unholy Crusade.
1. Crusades – Fourth, 1202–1204
I. Title II. Twelve hundred and four
940.1'8   D164   80-40298
ISBN 0-19-215834-1

Printed in Great Britain by
Lowe & Brydone Printers Ltd, Thetford, Norfolk

To Tristan and Héloise

Preface

My interest in the Fourth Crusade was first seriously aroused some years ago in Venice, whilst accompanying a party of American students, who spoke much of that strange adventure and were clearly fascinated by the Crusading idea as such. Moral idealism joined with strenuous effort, even with armed conflict, has indeed come to characterize the twentieth century scarcely less than it did the early Middle Ages, and we have seen a revival of the doctrine which justifies physical violence in the service of religion and humanity. My concern with the Crusades broadened and deepened during seminars and lectures on the history of the relations between Islam and the West as a visiting lecturer at the North London Polytechnic; and a factor in strengthening my resolve to delve into the problem of the Latin Conquest of Constantinople was the Annual Summer Conference of the Ecclesiastical History Society, held at the University of Lancaster in 1975, when our theme was the Orthodox Churches and the West. Who could not be moved by the courage, the resilience, the loyalty to age-old traditions, shown by the great Churches of the East, confronted by persecution and outrage?

Many have approached the Fourth Crusade with their views predetermined, and regarding, at the very outset of their studies, the whole venture as obviously criminal. But the study of the Crusades is all too often bedevilled by a reluctance to try to understand the medieval mind. It is easy, for example, to ridicule the early medieval obsession with relics; and yet a man like John of Salisbury (who died in October 1180), greatest scholar of his time, political philosopher, administrator, humanist, and distinguished for his integrity and common sense, had as one of his personal treasures a phial containing some drops of the blood of St. Thomas of Canterbury. The Conquest of Constantinople, to westerners of 1204, far from being a 'crime', was eminently respectable. To us it is otherwise, an event made possible by an amalgam of feudal honour, martial courage, Christian idealism, French vanity, Venetian maritime skill, and human greed. It is a tale of men enmeshed in the toils of their own miscalculations, many of whom were to die 'of love for dreams that were and truths that were not', and is European history's outstanding instance of the dangers which lie in using physical force in the quest of the good.

The present book being intended primarily for the general reader, it is thought unnecessary to load it with extensive references, certainly not to the whole of the vast literature which has come into existence during 'a century of controversy' over the Fourth Crusade. The books and articles cited in the notes and bibliography will indicate the broad nature of the authority on which this account is based, and which, being fairly accessible, might prove a guide to further study by the reader. I thank the friends who have been interested in the book's progress, and particularly Professor Donald Nicol, who read the entire typescript and made many valuable suggestions. Professor Rosalind Hill read the draft of the first chapter, and Dr Ann Williams other parts of the script. Dom Maurus Green, OSB, was helpful in the matter of relics. Of the libraries which I frequented, I found especially useful Dr Williams's Library, Gordon Square, London, with its good Byzantine collection and its efficient staff; and the Library of the Society of Antiquaries of London, whose Librarian, Mr J. H. Hopkins, was a ready source of assistance. The responsibility for errors which remain is naturally my own. I am most grateful to the Oxford University Press for inviting me to write the book, and to the editors for their suggestions and criticisms as the task proceeded. Last but not least my gratitude is due to my wife, whose forbearance and encouragement made the work possible.

Berwick St John   John Godfrey
Wiltshire
1980

Contents

Preface   vii
List of Illustrations and Maps   x

1   Soldiers of the Cross   1
2   Byzantium and Western Europe   11
3   Byzantium and Islam   24
4   The Church Militant but Divided   29
5   The Gathering of the Host   39
6   Venice Looks to the East   56
7   The Affair goes Awry   67
8   The Crusade at Zara   77
9   City of the World's Desire   88
10   The First Siege   101
11   The Die is Cast   110
12   The Storming of Constantinople   121
13   The Great Sack   126
14   A New Empire   134
15   Some Reactions and Consequences   147
16   Byzantium Survives   157

APPENDIXES

I   The Byzantine Emperors 1081–1282   161
II   The Latin Emperors of Constantinople   162
III   Twelfth-Century Doges of Venice   162
IV   The House of Comnenus   163
V   The House of Angelus   164

Notes   165
Select Bibliography   176
Index   179

Illustrations

between pp. 52 *and* 53

1 Enamelled book cover, with Christ in Majesty (British Museum)
2 Innocent III (Mansell-Alinari)
3a Manuel I Comnenus and his wife Maria of Antioch (MS. Gr. 1176, f.11, Vatican Library)
3b Marble roundel of either Isaac II or Alexius III (Dumbarton Oaks Collection, Washington, D.C.)
4a Fulk preaches the Crusade in France (MS. Laud Misc. 587, f.1, Bodleian Library, Oxford)
4b A Crusader takes the Cross (MS. 9081, 99v, Bibliothèque Municipale, Besançon)
4c The text of part of the earliest known Cross-taking rite (MS. B, XI, 10, Trinity College, Cambridge)
4d The Crusaders attack Constantinople by land and by sea (MS. Laud Misc. 587, f.1, Bodleian Library, Oxford)

between pp. 84 *and* 85

5a A military provision cart carrying helmets, cooking-pots, etc. (MS. 638, f.27v, Pierpont Morgan Library, New York)
5b Soldiers in battle, with early thirteenth-century armour and weapons (MS. 638, f.23v, Pierpont Morgan Library, New York)
6 The frontispiece of *Li Livre du Grant Caam*, depicting Venice (MS. 264, f.218, Bodleian Library, Oxford)
7a Pope Alexander III presents Doge Sebastiano Ziani with a ceremonial sword (Print Room, British Museum)
7b A nineteenth-century impression of Acre (From W. J. Conybeare and J. S. Howson, *The Life and Epistles of St. Paul*, Longman, Green, Longman, and Roberts, 1860. Photo: Malcolm Case, Shaftesbury, Dorset)
8a The five domes of St. Mark's (Courtauld Institute of Art)
8b St. Mark's, interior (Courtauld Institute of Art)

between pp. 116 *and* 117

9   One of the oldest surviving views of Constantinople (Bibliothèque
    Nationale, Paris)
10 A tower in the walls of Constantinople (Courtauld Institute of Art,
    copyright Dr Judith Herrin)
11 The tetrarchs Diocletian, Maximinian, Constantius, and Galerius
    (Alinari)
12a Precious glass-ware from Byzantium (Alinari)
12b A Byzantine reliquary of the True Cross (Alinari)

between pp. 148 *and* 149

13 Doge Dandolo crowning Baldwin as emperor, by Aliense (Alinari)
14a Relief of St. Demetrius, from Constantinople (Alinari)
14b Relief of St. George (Alinari)
15 A sculpture in St. Mark's, showing Christ flanked by the Virgin and
    St. John (Alinari)
16 Theodore I Lascaris (1204–22) (Codex Monacensis, MS. Gr. 442,
    Staatsbibliothek, Munich)

Maps

Europe and the Levant *c.* 1190   14
Homelands of the Fourth Crusade   41
The First Assault on Constantinople   103
Constantinople in 1204   103
The Eastern Empire after 1204   139
The Propontis Region   139

Chapter 1

Soldiers of the Cross

On 27 November 1095, at Clermont, north of the Alps, Pope Urban II preached a sermon in which he called for a Holy War, and a great endeavour to deliver Jerusalem from the enemies of Christ. To the assembled crowds of Frenchmen he appealed, 'Christ himself will be your leader, as you fight for Jerusalem, where Christ died for you . . . set out for the Holy Sepulchre, wrest that land from the accursed race, and subdue it to yourselves. Frenchmen, you descendants of unvanquished ancestors, be worthy of the stock from which you come . . . and when you advance to meet the enemy, your cry shall be, God wills it!' Little more than a century later an army of Crusaders launched a full-scale assault, not on Jerusalem but on Constantinople, resulting in its downfall: one of the most extraordinary happenings in European history, the repercussions of which are still with us. How did the movement inspired by Urban lead to the sack of the greatest city in Christendom?

As the conquest of Constantinople in 1204 is best understood when seen in its broad historical setting, we shall, before following the course of the expedition commonly known as the Fourth Crusade, first consider four themes which directly affect the story. A study of the earlier 'holy' wars and Crusades, of the political relationship between Byzantium and the West, of Byzantium's view of Islam, and of the tensions existing between the Roman and Orthodox Churches, will enable us to see more clearly than otherwise the significance of an event which, justly or unjustly, has been called 'the greatest crime of the Middle Ages'.

The idea of Christian soldiering can be said to have begun with Constantine the Great, who, before himself becoming emperor, resolved to free the city of Rome from the oppressive rule of the tyrant Maxentius. Convinced of his need for divine help in so daunting a task, he turned in prayer to the God of his father Constantius (who had been well disposed to Christianity). Thereupon, 'an amazing sign appeared to him from the heavens. . . . About noon, just as the day was starting to decline, with his very eyes he saw the trophy of a cross of light in the sky, above the sun, and with it the inscription, CONQUER BY THIS.' During the following night the 'Christ of God' came to him in a dream with the same sign, and told him to make a likeness of it to use as a protection in all battles with his enemies.[1]

After this incident, which occurred in 312, Christianity changed profoundly in character. The early Church had included a strong pacifist element, many of its members refusing to serve the State whether in peace or war. However, persecution had already for some time been encouraging a more combative spirit, and now from the fourth century onwards the meek and gentle aspect of Christianity was less evident. Early in the fifth century Augustine, greatest of the Christian Fathers, could write that a man who kills in war is not a murderer.[2] The pugnacious temperament grew stronger amongst Christians during the Dark Ages, and one reason for this was that the Church had developed into a great property-owning organization. In anarchic times possessions can only be protected by physical force. Another factor was the conversion of the Germanic peoples. The Roman historian Tacitus, writing about the year 98, had said of the Germans that they disliked peace, and sought glory by violence and war.[3] The Englishman Bede, in his narration of events taking place in 729, observed that the Saracens, laying waste the land of Gaul with miserable slaughter, would shortly receive the punishment merited by their wickedness;[4] and the first outstanding victory of Western soldiers against Islam was in fact that of the Franks at Tours, under Charles Martel, in 732.

Charlemagne, as a Christian ruler, campaigned against the pagan Saxons in northern Germany, forcing them into baptism. The Viking wars of the ninth century stimulated the idea of conflict on Christ's behalf, as did a resounding victory on the river Lech in 955 by the Saxon emperor Otto I, who, carrying his sacred relics with him, halted the advance of the pagan Hungarians. It was the eleventh century, however, an age of religious enthusiasm, that saw the culmination of the martial spirit in Christendom. The sense of faith was strengthened in the period before 1000 by a widespread belief in the Second Coming of Christ. Society was vastly influenced by a spiritual revival associated especially with the Burgundian abbey of Cluny. The papacy increased its prestige. Pilgrimages were much in vogue, and the Crusading idea itself was closely interwoven with that of the sacred journey. In the original sources the Crusader is usually called a 'pilgrim'. There were many who still objected to the use of force as inconsistent with Christianity, but the idea of a man solemnly dedicating himself to be a 'soldier of Christ' spread rapidly, and by the latter half of the eleventh century there was being preached at Rome a doctrine of violence in the service of religion.[5]

The real beginning of the Crusading movement should be seen in the discovery of what came to be known as the True Cross at Jerusalem in 327 by Helena, mother of Constantine. During the course of clearing the site of the rock-cave reputed to be Christ's burial-place, the wood of the crosses on which Christ and the two robbers crucified with him had died was claimed to be found, that of Christ being identified by miraculous means. This event led to the building of the church of the Holy Sepulchre to enshrine the marvellous relic, and the ultimate aim of the Crusaders was always to ensure that this church remained in Christian hands or was accessible to pilgrims. The original building, raised by Bishop

Makarios on Constantine's orders and completed in 335, was destroyed in 614, and has subsequently been replaced by successive churches, with many additions and encumbrances. The climax of the whole complex was the *anastasis* or Resurrection at the west end, enclosing the 'tomb' of Christ. To pray in this church was the most sublime act of devotion to which any Christian could aspire. The earliest extant mention of the Finding or 'Invention' of the Cross is by Cyril, bishop of Jerusalem, about 350, in Lenten lectures to his catechumens delivered in the Holy Sepulchre church. He said that fragments were already being cut off and scattered far and wide, to Constantinople, Rome, and elsewhere.[6]

By the time the Muslims, during the triumphant progresses which followed the preaching of the Prophet Muhammad, captured Jerusalem in the seventh century, most of the Cross had been divided and distributed amongst numerous churches. The cult of the Veneration of the Cross spread quickly throughout Christendom, producing amongst its fruits the famous hymns of Venantius Fortunatus, *Pange lingua* and *Vexilla regis*, 'Sing, my tongue, the glorious battle', and 'The royal banners forward go, the Cross shines forth in mystic glow'. The poet here was inspired by the arrival of a piece of the True Cross for Queen Radegunde's monastery at Poitiers in 569.[7] These hymns were probably known to the Anglo-Saxon who composed the haunting verses called the *Dream of the Rood*, with their theme that *Crist waes on rode* (Christ was on the Rood). Seventh-century England became studded with carved crosses of which many fragments survive. The entry in the *Anglo-Saxon Chronicle* for 885 tells how Pope Marinus sent King Alfred a fragment of the Cross, and it was perhaps this fragment which eventually found its way to Flanders and is now enshrined in the cathedral of SS. Michel and Gudule in Brussels, with the inscription, 'Rood is my name, once, trembling, and wet with blood, I bore the Mighty King'. The cult of the Cross had a principal centre in Constantinople, but many portions of the True Cross were to arrive in the West. In 1109 Ansau, precentor of the Holy Sepulchre church, sent a fragment to Paris cathedral, and in 1174 Amalric I, king of Jerusalem, presented a piece to the monks of Grandmont. Probably no greater gift could be made to anyone than a piece, however small, of the wooden framework on which Christ had died. By the twelfth century Constantinople was acknowledged to be the chief repository of surviving fragments. The Crusader was by definition a soldier of the Cross; the church of the Holy Sepulchre was the centre of his aspirations; and the acquisition of relics (especially Cross-fragments) one of his driving motives.[8]

The Crusades, as conventionally understood, were the result of the emergence into history of the Seljuks, so named from their tribal ancestor and a branch of the Turkish peoples who had swarmed over the Volga into the steppe-lands north of the Black Sea. Under two brothers, Tughril Beg and Chagri Beg, they had invaded and occupied Persia, and had recently abandoned an animistic form of religion in favour of Islam; Tughril Beg (1038–63) now set up a Sultanate alongside the Abbasid Caliphate of Baghdad. Though fierce soldiers, they were appreciative of men with fine minds, and Tughril Beg's nephew and successor Alp Arslan (1063–72) had as his vizier or principal minister an able Persian, Nizam-al-Mulk, who founded institutions for higher education at Baghdad, Nishapur, and other places, the so-called Nizamiyah universities. Nizam gathered around him a circle of enlightened intelligentsia, including the poet and astronomer 'Umar al Khayyām, and the mystic philosopher al-Ghazzali, who was to Islam what Thomas Aquinas was to be to Catholicism.

Set on conquest, Alp Arslan invaded Armenia, and on 19 August 1071 annihilated the Byzantine army at Manzikert. The Seljuks poured into Asia Minor and took Nicaea. Marching south into Syria they defeated the Fatimids of Egypt, who controlled the Holy Land. Jerusalem fell, the great Byzantine city of Antioch was lost, and even Constantinople was threatened.

The danger to Christendom was recognized by Pope Gregory VII, who in 1074 proposed an expedition which would save the Byzantine capital from the Turks. It was Gregory's scheme which first really gave to the Crusading idea a positive form. Gregory's hope was that his expedition might be followed by a Council aimed at settling the differences between the Catholic and Orthodox Churches. His project came to nothing, but the West meanwhile received news of the Byzantine defeats and especially of the Turkish capture of Jerusalem. The city had in fact been in Muslim hands for centuries, ever since it had been taken in 638 by the Caliph 'Umar during the first age of Arab expansion, though the traditional habits of Christian pilgrimage to the sacred sites had, on the whole, been respected. Such pilgrimage now became much more hazardous, particularly as the old route through Asia Minor was disturbed by the less civilized conditions which followed the end of the long period of Byzantine rule in that region.

In 1094 the emperor Alexius I Comnenus called on Western Christendom to help him regain the lost imperial territories. In response, Pope Urban II raised the matter the next year in a Council at Piacenza, at which were present messengers from Constantinople trying to recruit for the depleted Byzantine army. It was after the Piacenza appeal that Urban preached his sermon, in November 1095, calling passionately for the liberation of the Holy Land. Urban stressed that as their earthly reward the warriors of Christ would have the gains naturally resulting from a war of conquest.[9] Popular preachers followed up the theme, dwelling on the iniquity of places associated with the life of Christ being in Muslim hands. The deliverance of the Holy Places is the central idea of the Crusading writers, and of course this made excellent recruiting material. Though the broader aims of the Crusading movement were never to be related to Palestine alone, but included all Syria and even the lands to the north and to the south, the Holy War never settled down to the recovery of the vital territories of Asia Minor, which would have made the future of the Byzantine Empire, and indeed of Europe itself, secure from further Turkish assaults.

In considering the conditions under which the Crusades took place, three important factors have also to be borne in mind. The Magyars had recently been converted to Latin Christianity, making possible a direct land journey from the Danube to the outposts of the Empire in Bulgaria (annexed by Byzantium early in the eleventh century). Secondly, the hitherto superior position of the Muslim naval forces in the central and eastern Mediterranean had been undermined by the rise of the Italian merchant cities. Pisa and Genoa had taken Corsica and Sardinia from Islam, and Venetian ships dominated the Adriatic. And thirdly, after the death of the Sultan Malik Shah in 1091 there was civil war amongst his sons, and the Seljuk Turks were divided, the local emirates in Asia Minor and Syria quarrelling violently.

There was a preliminary excursion consisting largely of an unruly mob which, after making a bad impression on the Byzantine people by its undisciplined behaviour, was cut to pieces by the Turks. The First Crusade proper then set out, in 1096, to make its way through the dense forests of the Balkans, known to medieval travellers as the 'Bulgarian forest'. The principal leaders were Godfrey, duke of Lower Lorraine, who was accompanied by his brother Baldwin, at the head of the men of northern France; Bohemond with his Normans from Apulia, and his nephew Tancred; and Raymond of St. Gilles, count of Toulouse, with a force of knights from Provence. There was also Robert of Normandy (son of William the Conqueror). With Raymond went Adhémar, bishop of Le Puy, composer of the supremely beautiful plainsong melody in the hymn *Salve regina*, and whose cathedral was a popular centre for pilgrims who came to pray before its famous black statue of the Virgin. As papal legate he was regarded by many Crusaders as virtual leader of the enterprise, and in the campaign ahead was personally to participate in some of the fighting. This was a feature of the Crusades which baffled the Byzantines, who were shocked when they saw amongst the Latins the very bishops and priests bearing weapons or riding into battle. There was of course some opposition in the West also to the idea of clergy carrying arms, and during the Crusades there would be frequent exhortations that they confine themselves to their spiritual functions. Nevertheless, many clergy were to insist on being actively engaged in the armed struggle, and in 1119, after the disaster known as the Bloody Field, near Aleppo, when a force of Norman troops was annihilated by the Turks, the clergy at Antioch were given a dispensation to bear arms, and, with the merchants, were put to guard the battlements.[10]

The strong French and Norman participation in the First Crusade is noticeable. Urban II himself was a Frenchman and knew only too well how to arouse the enthusiasm which has so long characterized his countrymen. It is difficult to judge just how far these first Crusaders were impelled by genuine religious motives: though Godfrey was largely sincere, Bohemond was prompted mainly by the ambition to carve out a territorial dominion for himself, and Raymond, the oldest of the leaders, also probably had in mind a domain on which he could settle down. Amongst the rank-and-file soldiers, materialistic motives sometimes came to predominate over spiritual ones, or became intermingled with them.[11] The men tended to be unruly, not hesitating to seize from the native Byzantines whatever provisions they needed. The various contingents eventually assembled at Constantinople, where Godfrey's troops took to plundering one of the suburbs until forcibly stopped by the Byzantine army. The emperor Alexius, by now rather alarmed at the monster which he had introduced into his Empire, was determined to obtain oaths of fealty from the leaders as well as promises that they would restore to him ex-Byzantine territories which they might conquer during their progress. Here he had a limited success. Raymond positively refused the oath, proudly declaring that Christ alone was his Master, this sincerity much impressing Alexius.

The emperor agreed that the Crusaders should have access to the purchase of provisions. But he was uneasy over the intentions of the leaders, especially Bohemond, who in previous years had fought as an open enemy of the Empire in Greece and Thrace. Anna Comnena, the emperor's daughter, who was later to write the valuable history *Alexiad*, which covers the period 1069–1118, says of Bohemond that he coveted Constantinople's riches. She writes that in appearance he was impressive and charming – with something savage and horrible in his glance.[12] She refuses to believe, however, that all the Crusaders were merely venal, and acknowledges that some were true Christian soldiers, 'marching in complete simplicity to worship at Christ's tomb'. The emperor firmly refused all help to the Crusaders on their forthcoming perilous march through Seljuk-dominated Asia Minor unless they swore fealty to himself, and in the end even Raymond gave way. In summary, we can hardly think that the first of the great Crusading armies had done much to help forward the cause of Graeco-Latin goodwill. Although an actual assault on Constantinople during this First Crusade was never seriously proposed, the plundering and looting by the soldiers while advancing through the Empire had created a popular Byzantine hostility towards the West which was to be permanent. Fulcher of Chartres, a cleric with the army, writes of the emperor's unwillingness to allow the Crusaders inside the capital in groups of more than about half a dozen, for fear of what they might do to it. Fulcher enthuses over the wealth of Constantinople, not least over its store of relics.[13]

In May 1097 the army crossed the Bosphorus, to the immense relief of the Byzantines. Imperial troops marched with the Crusaders, who helped them to recover Nicaea, though the emperor annoyed his allies by refusing them leave to sack the city, and by treating his Muslim prisoners of war honourably. Next, the Crusaders defeated the Turks at Dorylaeum, largely without Greek assistance, but heartened by the message passed through the ranks, 'Stand fast... trusting in Christ and the victory of the Holy Cross. Today, please God, you will all gain much booty.'[14] They were led in the battle by the composer of *Salve regina*, Adhémar of Le Puy. Antioch was taken, the Crusading leaders writing to Urban with the good news. They told how they had routed the Turks but could not overcome the heretics, such as Greek and Syrian Christians, and appealed to him to come and join them in person, so that by his authority heresy might be destroyed.[15] Finally, in July 1099, came the crowning mercy, the capture of Jerusalem. The Holy City was taken with a savagery which was not contrary to the rules of contemporary Western warfare and did not deter the victors from making a solemn procession of thanksgiving afterwards, to sob with joy as they prayed at the Saviour's Sepulchre. The Temple was captured by Tancred, his horsemen riding through blood which splashed to their knees and bridle-reins. The few Saracens who survived the accompanying massacre were compelled to carry out the corpses from the city, and a vast heap was made and burnt, the stench pervading the air for months.

The result of the campaigns of the First Crusade was that four small Latin States were established. Godfrey's brother Baldwin obtained the county of Edessa, to be the least Latin of the four, some of the Crusaders settling down almost at once to marry Eastern wives and Baldwin himself marrying an Armenian. More important was Bohemond's acquisition, Antioch. The emperor Alexius, after promising to help Bohemond in the Antioch campaign, had withdrawn before the fighting was over. The desertion was an unfortunate event in the history of the relations between the Empire and the Crusaders, and something which the latter never forgot.[16] Bohemond repudiated his oath of fealty to Alexius; and in 1100 he was formally invested as prince of Antioch by the papal legate. He went home to start a recruiting campaign in France and Italy, spreading the allegation that the emperor was a traitor to the Holy War. Returning, he attacked the imperial port of Durazzo and invaded the mainland, but was defeated and forced by the emperor to swear allegiance in respect of the Antioch principality. It is a measure of the extent to which both Antioch and Edessa remained within the Byzantine sphere of influence that their coins continued to be struck in Greek form and with Greek letters.

The third Latin State, Tripoli, was small and throughout the twelfth century remained virtually subject to the Jerusalem kings; but it included the famous castle of the Hospitallers, Krak des Chevaliers. The most important State was of course that of Jerusalem itself, with Godfrey as its first ruler, though he did not take a royal title and styled himself Defender of the Holy Sepulchre. He died after a short rule, in the summer of 1100, and in the words of Fulcher's Chronicle, 'went to Heaven with the archangel Michael coming forward to greet him'. He was succeeded by Baldwin, who became the first crowned king. At its largest extent, the Latin kingdom of Jerusalem included Western Palestine, Lebanon as far north as Beirut, some lands east of the Sea of Galilee, and a piece of territory south-east of the Dead Sea. But the interior heartland of Syria was never conquered.

Although these States, collectively known as Outremer, 'the land beyond the sea', were outposts of Western Europe, they developed characteristics which differentiated them sharply from the homelands. Consciously Christian, they nonetheless soon acquired, through daily contact with the original inhabitants, a sense of tolerance for which the men of Outremer were condemned by their compatriots at home. The broad mass of native Syrians remained Muslim, and the Westerners, besides developing feelings of respect, intermingled and intermarried with them. The States of Outremer constituted a society dedicated to war, but the martial spirit of many of the Latin residents in fact declined, and there was a constant need of reinforcements from the West, leading to the employment of mercenaries; and as time went on an increasing amount of the real soldiering was done by the Military Orders.[17]

Outremer was dependent for its existence on the maintenance of contact with Europe, and this made vital the possession of the Syrian coastal towns, whose conquest was in turn made possible by the help of Italian fleets. For assisting with the capture of Jerusalem, Pisa secured a quarter in Jaffa. Genoa obtained concessions in Antioch. Prominent amongst these Italians, after a hesitant start, were the Venetians, who took part in the siege of Sidon in 1110 and played a decisive role in the capture of Tyre in 1124. Italian city-republics which provided naval help to the Crusaders in this way were always interested in securing commercial advantages in return. A market-place, street, or warehouse in a captured port or town, free of dues or taxes, would be demanded, and the Italian merchants invariably made sure that their quarters were ruled by their own officials. Although it would be a great mistake to assume that motives of piety were totally absent from Italian minds, it is a fact that the ships of Genoa, Pisa, and Venice were never provided to the Crusaders for purely idealistic or religious reasons.

The naval power of the Italian cities was of paramount importance to the Crusading movement, ships serving as transports for Cross-soldiers and their provisions. The Italians, moreover, had banking and credit facilities to offer; and from the start of the Crusades the nimble-witted Italian merchants realized that a door had been opened to new sources of wealth. The Crusading States did maintain some war-galleys on their own account, but at this juncture in the history of medieval Europe the Western nations tended on the whole to have a poor sense of the importance of sea-power. Their soldiers were brave, but had lost the superlative sea-craft which had distinguished the recently ended Viking Age, and the great days of Portuguese and Spanish seafaring lay well ahead. English sailors played some part in the Crusades, but generally it was the Italians who dominated the maritime scene. Even the warlike Normans seem to have used their vessels mainly as transports rather than warships. The Italians thus quickly gained commercial benefits from the success of the Crusaders. It did not matter much to them if their trading partners were non-Christians, and by the early years of the twelfth century they were already trading with Egypt.

During the earlier decades of the twelfth century the Latin States in the East maintained their position fairly satisfactorily, and were seen as an integral part of the Christian establishment. To the West European the maintenance of

Outremer now seemed as natural as the founding of abbeys and the building of cathedrals. Fighting continued in Syria, but this tended to be of the normal type found in almost any Western country, and most of these petty wars were not 'religious'. Relations were poor with Alexius Comnenus, whom the Crusaders regarded as half-hearted in his devotion to the Holy War, especially as he maintained official diplomatic contacts with the Turks. There were skirmishes with the Muslims, but it remained to the Crusaders' advantage that during these years they had to deal with a collection of small and independent emirates, not a strong and united Islam. The situation changed dramatically, however, when in 1144 Zangi, the atabeg of Mosul on the Tigris, who was increasing his power over Muslim rivals, in the course of his campaigns captured the Frankish stronghold of Edessa. This had never been much more than an outpost, but its fall caused immense alarm in the West, and the result was the Second Crusade.

Queen Melisende, regent for her youthful son Baldwin III, king of Jerusalem, sent an urgent appeal to Pope Eugenius III for help from the West. Louis VII, king of France, solemnly took the Cross at Vézelay, and the influential Cistercian Bernard preached the necessity for a new expedition. The Hohenstaufen emperor Conrad III was reluctant to leave Germany, but on the remonstrances of Bernard joined the Crusade. During 1147 the armies assembled. But meanwhile the Byzantine emperor Manuel, after some energetic campaigning against the Turks, arranged a treaty with them, agreeing to a twelve years' truce, thus causing intense indignation in the West. The Second Crusade took the overland route through the Balkans, both Germans and French robbing and molesting the native inhabitants on the way. Even Conrad's nephew, the future Frederick Barbarossa, is alleged to have destroyed a Byzantine monastery and slaughtered the monks.[18] Many ordinary, unarmed pilgrims accompanied the armies, and the troops themselves were drunken and ill-disciplined. Odo de Deuil, a French monk with the army who afterwards wrote the best account of the Second Crusade, remarks that the Byzantines 'were judged not to be Christians, and the Franks considered killing them a matter of no importance'.[19] Arriving at Constantinople, the Crusaders looted the suburbs. On this occasion there was a definite proposal to attack the capital, and when King Louis was taken on a tour of the city by the emperor, members of the French party could not help noticing the weakness of some of the towers and fortifications.[20] The anti-Greek faction was led by a fiery Cistercian, Godfrey, bishop of Langres, who tried to persuade the French leaders to storm the city, saying that 'Constantinople is Christian only in name, not in fact'. But a more humane prelate, Arnulf of Lisieux, used his good offices with Louis VII to ensure that this aggressive proposal came to nothing.

It was a relief to Manuel when the Crusaders were all safely over the Bosphorus, after a delay in or around Constantinople of about three weeks. The French and Germans made their way partly by the coastal roads of Asia Minor and partly by sea to Syria, squabbling with the residents over the question of provisions. After an unsuccessful siege of Damascus the Crusade broke up. Its members dispersed, embittered over a failure which they regarded as due to the lack of imperial support, if not to positive connivance with the Seljuk Turks on the part of the Byzantines. At home three great churchmen, Suger of St. Denis, Bernard, and Peter the Venerable, were shocked by the absence in Byzantium of enthusiasm for a Crusade on which so much store had been set and which seemed so obvious a Christian duty. Very significant is the indignation of the highly respected Peter the Venerable, abbot of Cluny, the greatest of the religious houses in France. Although interested in Oriental studies and responsible indeed for commissioning the earliest Latin translation of the Koran, he was an ardent advocate of the Holy War and wrote much against the Saracens. He was regarded by his contemporaries as a model of Christian gentleness and moderation, and was no friend of the stern-minded Bernard.

The three men, Suger, Bernard, and Peter, made no secret of what they wanted – a direct military assault on Constantinople. Pope Eugenius III would not back them, but from now on there was an atmosphere in the West, particularly amongst the French, of outright hostility towards the Byzantines, and a feeling that one day they would have to be subdued by the true servants of Christ. In his account of the Second Crusade, Odo de Deuil (who succeeded Suger as abbot of St. Denis, the Benedictine abbey near Paris) bewailed its lack of will to attempt the capture of Constantinople.

Chapter 2

Byzantium and Western Europe

An important element in the events leading to the conquest of Constantinople lay in the attitudes of Byzantium itself to the warrior States of Western Europe, attitudes which developed in course of time into outright hostility. These feelings were to become deeply engrained, after being rekindled by a serious encounter which took place in 1081, the first year of the reign of Alexius I Comnenus, and had a lasting effect on subsequent developments.

Some years earlier, in 1059, the Norman adventurer Robert Guiscard had vowed himself the pope's man, in return for papal recognition of his seizure of the Byzantine territories in southern Italy, Calabria and Apulia. Rome saw the possibility of regaining her old authority in southern Italy, lost to the Byzantines long before. In 1071 Robert captured the Apulian coastal town of Bari, centre of the imperial administration in Italy, in so doing bringing to an end five centuries of Byzantine rule in the peninsula.[1] But Robert's aims were wider, and he had the recent and spectacular success of the Norman William in conquering the powerful English kingdom to encourage him. His years in southern Italy had made him well acquainted with the excellences of Byzantine civilization, and he now decided to make Byzantium his own. In 1081 he therefore invaded the mainland of the Empire, the Balkans and Greece, and defeated the imperial army at Durazzo, despite resistance by the Venetian fleet fighting on Byzantium's behalf and a stubborn stand by Alexius's recently acquired Anglo-Saxon contingent. The Normans advanced eastwards to threaten Constantinople, but were repulsed in 1083 and forced to withdraw from the Balkans.

It was a narrow escape for the great city, and it is significant that this attempt to subdue the Eastern Empire had obtained the explicit approval of Pope Gregory VII, who regarded himself as spiritual ruler of all Christendom. Some indication of the fate from which Constantinople had been saved by its victory of 1083 can be gathered from the ironical sequel of the following year. Marching north to help his papal lord against the Western emperor Henry IV, Guiscard drove off the German invaders of Italy but could not prevent his own troops from inflicting on the city of Rome one of the worst sacks in its history.

The First Crusade had followed these ominous events; and then Bohemond prince of Antioch (Robert Guiscard's son), resentful of the way in which Alexius had allegedly deserted him at Antioch, became an implacable foe of the Empire, and he inherited his father's ambition to conquer Constantinople. In 1106, in Chartres cathedral, with Paschal II's approval, he called on the West to join him in a Holy War against Byzantium, and this led to an invasion of Epiros (the modern Albania), accompanied by a papal legate. The Normans were driven back by Alexius, but there was mounting anger in Constantinople; a second papal campaign had been launched against the Orthodox Empire.

The Empire itself was short of military manpower, and it was also tending to become weaker at sea. The imperial economy was unsound; for the first time in centuries the unit of currency, the gold bezant, was falling in value. Despite this, after the First Crusade, the Empire had recovered much of its old security, while the danger of being overwhelmed by the Seljuks had receded, and but for the necessity of confronting the Norman attack from the West, Alexius I might well have been able to concentrate on his Eastern frontier with decisive results. As it was, much of Asia Minor was regained, including the Black Sea coastlands as far east as Trebizond, and the recovery was maintained under his son and successor John II Comnenus (1118–43), who held the Seljuks in check though he did not regain the vital Anatolian inland plateau.

The Byzantine revival continued under John's son Manuel I Comnenus (1143–80), under whom there was also a marked tendency for the Empire to draw closer to the West. Manuel, whose mother was Hungarian, himself first married a Bavarian wife, Bertha of Sulzbach, and then a Latin, Maria from Antioch. He was on good terms with the Hohenstaufen emperor Conrad III, whose wife Gertrude was Bertha's sister. Unfortunately for his Empire, Manuel seriously neglected the fleet; and ships of the Italian city-republics, including Venice, were increasingly drawn into the Byzantine naval service in return for commercial concessions. The Second Crusade had, meanwhile, soured relations between East and West, and Manuel tried to forestall any Western aggression by landing Byzantine troops in Italy in 1155. They were soon forced out, but Byzantium had shown something of its old strength and there was a real chance during these years of driving the Seljuk Turks out of Asia Minor. But Manuel preferred to come to terms with them. The anonymous twelfth-century Byzantine writer known as the Manganean poet refers to Manuel's fighting with the Turks, and also to the visit of the Sultan Kilij Arslan to Constantinople in 1146. Manuel showered gifts upon him: 'you heaped on him precious cloths and gold-woven carpets, also garments woven in the imperial workshops, you enriched him with pearls and precious rings for his fingers.'[2] Manuel's overriding worry being aggression from Western Europe aimed at the capture of Constantinople, he tried to cultivate good relations with the West, but he could not prevent a series of attacks by Roger II of Sicily, who temporarily occupied Corfu and ransacked Thebes. Roger's son William I sacked Corinth, and showed his audacity in 1156 by sailing a fleet of forty ships right to the walls of the Byzantine capital.

Next, Manuel formed an alliance with Amalric, king of Jerusalem since 1162, and made gifts to the Holy Sepulchre and other Palestinian churches.[3] Amalric was uncle to Henry II of England and Anjou, and it was widely felt at this time that such a family connection made it a matter of honour for Henry to come to the aid of the threatened Jerusalem kingdom. Henry did not repudiate the obligation, and sent annual sums of money to the Military Orders at Jerusalem to be held by them on his behalf. Taking the offensive against the Muslims, Amalric led several expeditions aimed at conquering Egypt, and in these was supported by Manuel, who was able to commit one hundred and fifty warships to the effort. This combined military operation was to be the last attempt at co-operation between Byzantines and Latins in the Crusading movement, and though the campaigns were unsuccessful, they did demonstrate to the Crusaders that the conquest of Egypt was a not impossible task for a powerful army. The able and energetic Amalric died in 1174.

The Byzantine Empire still flourished under the later Comneni,[4] but as a result of Manuel's westernizing policy many Latins had found positions of authority for themselves in Constantinople, and they tended to wear an air of self-assurance, the arrogance of the Venetians being especially disliked. The Byzantines were proud people, conscious of the glories of their past, and they resented the presence of foreigners introduced to reinvigorate the ailing Empire. Venetian and other Italian merchants had long lived in Constantinople and elsewhere in the Byzantine world, but by the second half of the twelfth century they were putting down strong roots. By this time there may well have been about 20,000 Venetians, and twice that number of other Italians, in the Empire,[5] and the significance of these numbers will be grasped when it is borne in mind that the population of the city of Venice itself was perhaps little more than 60,000; so the Venetian Republic clearly had a huge stake in Byzantium. So strong did resentment against foreigners become in the Empire that by 1171 Manuel felt he had to make some attempt to appease public opinion, and he did so by suddenly arresting all Venetians in the Empire and seizing their property. It was a fatal blunder.

Meanwhile, storm-clouds were gathering in the East. The Sultanate of Iconium had consolidated its position, virtually unhindered by Constantinople; and then all hopes of a Byzantine recovery in Asia Minor were shattered by an overwhelming defeat of the imperial army by the Seljuks at Myriokephalon in the Phrygian highlands, on 17 September 1176. The Turks themselves suffered heavy casualties in the fight, which took place in a blinding sandstorm, but as a result of their triumph they were established in what was to be their homeland, and they remain there to this day. Englishmen, serving as members of the Varangian Guard, played a valiant part at Myriokephalon, and Manuel was later to tell the English king Henry II, 'I am pleased to think that a number of those great men of yours were with us'.[6]

In 1179 the emperor made a final gesture towards the West by marrying his daughter Maria to Rainier of Montferrat, and his son Alexius (II) to Agnes, daughter of Louis VII of France and sister of the future Philip Augustus. Manuel

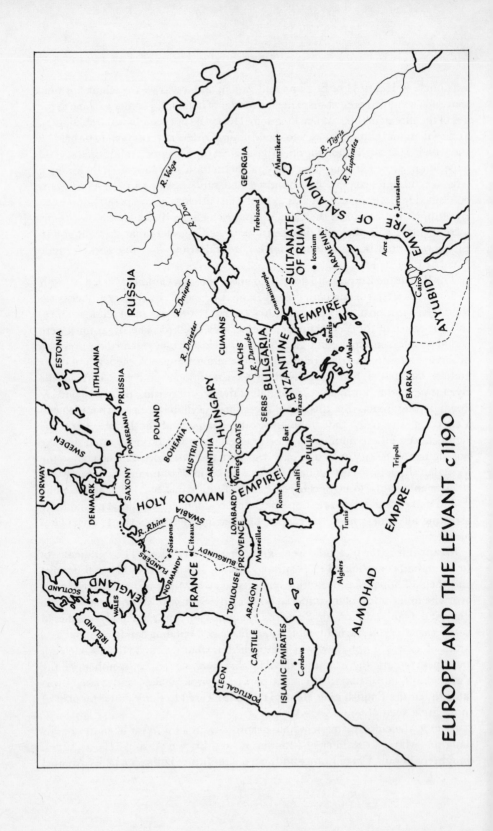

EUROPE AND THE LEVANT c.1190

ended his reign in the autumn of 1180, retiring to a monastery shortly before his death. With the passing of Manuel, said the contemporary Byzantine scholar Eustathius of Thessalonica, 'darkness covered the land, as with an eclipse of the sun'.

The new ruler was the recently married eleven-year-old Alexius II, with his mother Maria of Antioch (Manuel's widow) as regent, assisted by an aristocratic lover. Under this regime numerous privileges and tax concessions were showered on the nobility and country landowners; and the monasteries, too, were highly favoured. All this caused resentment throughout the middle classes and the populace, as well as frustration amongst the civil servants responsible for balancing the imperial accounts. The government continued to turn for support to the many Latins resident in the capital, and discontent grew, finding a focus in the empress's stepdaughter Maria and her husband Rainier of Montferrat. Disorder broke out in the capital in 1181, the Byzantine crowd for the first time in a century becoming almost uncontrollable.

A new figure now appeared on the scene in Andronicus Comnenus, governor of Pontus and a member of the imperial family, who in April 1182 stirred up the mob, causing it to abandon all order and reinforcing it with retainers of his own. The mob's targets were the Latin merchants with their families, and the clergy serving them. There were now few Venetians left in the city as a result of Manuel's drastic action against them a few years before, but in the foreign merchants' quarters on the southern shore of the Golden Horn were many Genoese and Pisans. Some of these, warned of the impending attack just in time, managed to escape the coming fury and scramble aboard the Italian ships lying in the harbour. But most were still in their homes. The Byzantine mob rampaged through the city looking for Westerners, slaughtering men, women, and children indiscriminately. In their blind rage some rioters even burst into the hospital of the Knights of St. John and butchered the sick in their beds. Churches packed with refugee Westerners were set on fire. Cemeteries were attacked, dead bodies being dug out and hacked to pieces. The Latin clergy especially attracted the seething, pent-up anger of the Byzantine mob. The papal legate in Constantinople, Cardinal John, who had been sent a year or two earlier by Alexander III to discuss with Manuel the possibility of Byzantine support for a new Crusade, was decapitated and his head tied to the tail of a dog which was then let loose in the streets. It is said that when Cardinal John was urged to seek safety he refused to flee, with the words, 'I remain here by orders of Pope Alexander and in the cause of the Church's unity'. More than four thousand Latins who escaped the slaughter, both men and women, were sold as slaves to the Turks.[7]

Many Latins, however, managed to evade the Byzantines. Besides those who had shown the foresight to get aboard their ships in the harbour, there were others who hurriedly joined them once the slaughter started. It was a sizeable fleet of vessels packed with refugees which now sailed over to the Isles of Princes in the Sea of Marmora, and the fugitives vented their bitterness on the monasteries of the neighbouring islands, looting and setting them on fire. As news of the massacre spread, there was a general exodus of Italian merchants from the various provincial towns of the Empire. On hearing of the outrage Pope Lucius III wrote to discover the truth of it, and there was a total break between the papacy and Byzantium for several years. A direct attack on the Empire by Pisa and Genoa was scarcely possible, but the two cities now unleashed a campaign of piratical attacks on the Empire's shipping. Their sailors proceeded to terrorize the Aegean islands, causing immense damage, more than balancing the losses of the merchants in Constantinople. The Italian traders had been jolted into realizing that they were not merely resented but loathed by many Byzantines, and that when in due course they returned to Constantinople their economic position would have to be buttressed by political power. And should the Byzantine emperors prove unable or unwilling to provide the necessary protection, the possibility of direct Latin rule over the city might have to be considered. The forces making towards a complete Latin occupation of Constantinople were thus steadily growing.

With the disastrous defeat by the Turks at Myriokephalon in 1176, and the breakdown of relations with the West which followed the massacre of 1182, the outlook for the Empire was menacing. These years also saw the beginning of the collapse of Byzantine authority in the Balkans. After Manuel's death, Bela III king of Hungary took, or rather regained, northern Dalmatia and many towns, including the port of Zara, and though a Byzantine army marched against the Hungarians, it failed to dislodge them.

Meanwhile, after the Latin Massacre, the Empire's government was taken over by the man who had largely inspired the rioting, Andronicus Comnenus. The Princess Maria and her husband Rainier, who had shown themselves dangerously adept at manipulating the mob, were quietly removed, and Maria of Antioch, the late emperor's second wife, was also murdered. Her son Alexius II was forced to sign her death-warrant. Andronicus had himself crowned to rule jointly with Alexius, in September 1183, and then the young man was strangled.

An orgy of terror against the nobility followed. Andronicus had always held the Westernized courtiers of Manuel in contempt, and in this he knew that he had the people behind him. Some nobles were blinded or put to death on the merest suspicion of disloyalty, and some prudently fled abroad, these including Alexius Angelus, a future emperor, who found safety with the hospitable Saladin of Egypt. Many took refuge with the Turks in Asia Minor, others in Syria, others with Western European nobles. Spies were everywhere in Constantinople, and the aristocracy lived in dread of arrest. Yet Andronicus was an able ruler. The status of professional civil servants was raised and administrative corruption was for a time stamped out. Provincial governorships were not put up for sale as before, but the most suitably qualified men were appointed. The historian Nicetas likened Andronicus to a centaur, a cruel man with some virtues, part man, part beast.[8] Nicetas's brother Michael Choniates, archbishop of Athens, praised Andronicus with enthusiasm, as being someone who would root out the poisonous weed of Latinism.[9]

But though Andronicus had obtained power by exploiting the popular hatred of Latins, it is not clear how far he himself was actually anti-Western. Earlier in his life he had been in exile in the Latin kingdom of Jerusalem, and must have been familiar with Latin ways, but he had also been a guest at Muslim courts. Though the survivors of the massacre had mostly left the city, some had remained, and the emperor had an official Latin interpreter, a certain Pisan, Leo Tuscus. The Venetians had not been greatly affected by the massacre, and Andronicus was anxious for their naval help in the event of the expected retaliatory attacks from the West. He therefore allowed the Venetians to reopen their quarter in the city, and restored their commercial privileges. A strong Venetian embassy was sent by Doge Orio Malipiero to discuss these matters, one of its members being a future doge, Enrico Dandolo. Some sort of an agreement was concluded on this occasion, though Andronicus did not succeed in obtaining any promise of naval support. He fully realized that Constantinople's economic prosperity largely depended on the Italian merchants and their ships, the Byzantine fleet being now very depleted. But Andronicus's reconciliation with the Latins had the effect of angering the hitherto adoring city mob.

The Latin Massacre was by any standards an atrocity, which it is impossible to justify, even when allowances are made for the likelihood that the stories told by the refugees to William of Tyre, who recorded them, gathered additional colour on their passage from Constantinople to Syria. The massacre naturally aroused great anger in the West, and it was widely felt that war against Byzantium was now more than ever necessary. Effective revenge, however, actually came not from the north Italian merchant cities at all but from Norman Sicily, at the time ruled by William II. The Normans themselves had no important commercial links with Constantinople, but there was a century-old tradition of warfare between the Mediterranean Normans and the Empire, and it so happened that William II had a personal grudge against Byzantium. In 1172 Manuel had promised him the hand of his daughter Maria, but had failed to fulfil his pledge at the last moment, almost literally leaving the bridegroom standing at the altar. William, like his Norman forebears Robert Guiscard and Bohemond, now planned an outright invasion. During the earlier part of 1185 he assembled a large though motley army, composed not only of regularly paid mercenaries but of freebooters from many countries serving only for the promise of loot. Even pirate ships were included in the fleet. In the summer the expedition arrived at Thessalonica, the second city of the Empire, famous for its annual fair which attracted merchants from as far away as Flanders. On 24 August Thessalonica fell after a brief siege, and there followed a wholesale sack, in which the inhabitants were treated with extreme brutality. William's army included some of the most uncouth types of men, who despised the refinements of Byzantine culture. The Orthodox clergy especially drew the derision of William's ruffians, who broke into churches while worship was in progress and mockingly parodied the chanting of the priests.

The fall of Thessalonica convinced the emperor that an assault on Constantinople itself was imminent, and the unusual savagery of the Western army was a warning of what might be in store for its inhabitants. The Norman army began its march on the capital. Andronicus strengthened the city's defences, and even made approaches for help to Saladin, sultan of Egypt and Syria. But again the Byzantine mob ran amok, and again Andronicus became suspicious of the nobles. Amongst those whose arrest he ordered was a distant cousin, Isaac Angelus, who managed to find sanctuary in the great church of St. Sophia. The crowd rallied round Isaac, and when the emperor called on his guards to disperse the rioters they refused. Isaac was hastily crowned emperor and Andronicus fled. In the accompanying confusion the mob seized the opportunity to loot the imperial palace, and churches were pillaged of their relics and icons. Andronicus was captured on the Black Sea coast, just on the point of making his escape by ship to Russia. According to Robert de Clari (the Picardy knight who after returning from the Fourth Crusade dictated his account to a scribe), Andronicus managed to put out to sea but his vessel was driven back by a storm. He took refuge with his companions in an inn and hid behind the wine-casks, but was discovered by the innkeeper's wife, who told her husband. The upshot was that the fugitive was handed over to the authorities, and nobles and people co-operated in putting Andronicus to a lingering death in Constantinople, with hideous cruelty, on 12 September 1185.[10]

Isaac II Angelus (1185–95) stopped the advance on Constantinople of William II's army, though he was convinced that in due course there would be yet another attempt on the Byzantine capital from the West. He tried to keep on good terms with the Latin world, marrying his sister Theodora to Conrad of Montferrat, who was put in command of the imperial army. Isaac himself married a Latin, Margaret of Hungary, and allowed the Italians in his capital to have their own churches.[11] There was a crisis in 1187 when the Western troops serving in the army became insubordinate, and also another popular upsurge of resentment against the Italian merchants. Conrad departed to visit the Holy Places and fight the Saracens in Palestine, disillusioned with his assignment in Constantinople.

Meanwhile in the world of Islam a brilliant leader, Saladin of Egypt, had overthrown the Fatimid dynasty and become sultan. Annihilating the Latin forces at Hattin near the Sea of Tiberias on 4 July 1187, his army had overrun Palestine and taken Jerusalem on 2 October. A notable feature of Saladin's occupation of the city was the consideration shown to Christians, quite the opposite to the savagery which had marked the Crusaders' entry into Jerusalem in 1099. Saladin refused to destroy the Holy Sepulchre church, though urged to do so by his advisers; he merely closed it for three days. Only Tyre among the cities of the former Latin Outremer now remained in Christian hands.

The fall of Jerusalem shocked Western Christendom, and it led directly to the Third Crusade, headed by Frederick Barbarossa of Germany, Philip Augustus of France, and the English king Richard I. By now the Crusading idea had lost its early freshness and spontaneity, and there had to be intensive efforts to gain recruits. Criminals and social misfits were by the twelfth century being encouraged to expiate their sins or shortcomings by taking the Cross. It had, for example, been laid down at the Second Lateran Council in 1139 that men guilty of arson should serve for a year in Palestine; and murderers and other violent offenders were often sentenced to fight in the Holy Land. There was also the now well-established privilege of 'essoin', whereby those absent on pilgrimage (which technically included Crusading) were granted a stay in any legal proceedings which might be pending against them.

Frederick Barbarossa was the first to get his army on the move. He took his Germans along the overland route, which meant marching through the Balkans and the Empire. In 1188 he formally asked permission to lead his forces through the Byzantine Empire and to buy necessary provisions on the way. The emperor Isaac II Angelus agreed but was alarmed at the prospect, and unknown to Frederick negotiated for help from Saladin. Isaac had earlier been a guest of the Sultan, and had made no attempt to conceal his delight on hearing of his former host's capture of Jerusalem, even sending formal congratulations. The Orthodox community in Jerusalem, which exceeded the Latins in number, may well have been a decisive factor in weakening the city's resistance to Saladin, who as his personal adviser on Christian affairs had at his side an Orthodox cleric.[12]

Saladin himself did not relish having to confront a formidable new Crusading alliance of English, French, and Germans. He and the emperor therefore exchanged expensive gifts and came to an understanding, Isaac agreeing to put all possible obstacles in the path of Frederick's army. When in the summer of 1189 Frederick's envoys duly arrived in Constantinople to announce the approach of the Crusading army, they were seized and put in prison by Isaac, a positively hostile act. At the same time, Isaac granted official approval for Islamic worship in the mosque built in Constantinople by Muslim merchants.

Advancing through the Balkans in 1189, the Germans met with guerrilla opposition from the peasantry and bandits, roads were often blocked, and Isaac refused to sell food as promised. Frederick could not bring himself to believe that Isaac, the Most Christian Emperor, was responsible for these delaying tactics, until he actually had to fight and rout some regular imperial forces. Isaac's attitude was due to a genuine dread that Frederick was aiming at the capture or at least the plunder of the capital, and in view of the three previous Western attempts to march on Constantinople his feelings are understandable. In this fear he was encouraged by the patriarch of Constantinople, Dositheus, a bitter opponent of Crusaders. Convinced that Frederick's troops would wreak havoc in the city, the patriarch proclaimed in advance a general absolution for all murderers of Crusaders. Frederick settled down for the 1189–90 winter in Thrace, while his troops foraged for food and devastated the surrounding countryside, and then in view of Isaac's obstructing tactics decided that Constantinople would have to be reduced before he could cross the straits.

Frederick sent a summons to his son Henry to gather ships from the north Italian cities, including Venice, and join his father for a siege of Constantinople. It would be a combined land-sea operation, the Italian galleys attacking the sea walls while Frederick mounted an assault by land.[13] Frederick's real objective was to proceed with the Crusade in Syria, though the idea of taking and sacking Constantinople on the way was probably not uncongenial to his troops.

Isaac realized that it would be difficult to stop the advance and, shaken by the depredations of the German troops, came to an agreement with Frederick at Adrianople to help his army in its passage over the straits. He also agreed to provide markets for the purchase of food. Frederick had thus by his persistence brought to nothing the combined scheme of Isaac and Saladin to wreck his expedition, but the view, stubbornly held throughout the greater part of the twelfth century in the Western world, that Byzantium was no friend of the Holy War against Islam was still further reinforced. From now on Crusaders made a point of avoiding the passage through the Empire, taking the sea route instead. And the fact that Isaac had actually been in alliance with Saladin convinced many Latins that the Eastern Empire might be regarded as a legitimate object of military assault. Byzantium, men thought, was at heart sympathetic to Islam. Saladin in the event had given little real help to Isaac in the attempt to hinder the Germans, but the mere existence of an understanding between the two men had caused grave harm to Latin-Greek relations, and must be regarded as an ingredient in the complex of motives, miscalculations, and accidents which was to produce the catastrophe of 1204.

Frederick was a great soldier, clearly destined to emerge as leader of the Third Crusade. He took his troops across the Bosphorus, but on 10 June 1190 was drowned while trying to swim a swiftly flowing river, and with his death his army melted away until relatively few Germans were left to continue the campaign. The French and English expeditions were of comparatively little concern to Byzantium as they did not take the overland route and were not therefore seen as a threat to Constantinople. In the spring of 1191, however, Richard with his English forces took and occupied Cyprus, at the time in a state of rebellion against Constantinople. Richard first placed Cyprus in the care of the Templars, later handing it over to a former king of Jerusalem, Guy de Lusignan, and it was to remain a Crusaders' stronghold for many centuries, long outliving the Frankish colonies in Syria. A former province of the Byzantine Empire had thus been unceremoniously annexed.[14] The measure to which the island had earlier been Byzantinized can be gathered from the fine twelfth-century fresco paintings still to be seen in its churches.

Richard's army (about half of which was actually English) duly arrived in Palestine by sea. It joined Philip's army in an attempt to aid the titular king of

Jerusalem by besieging Saladin in Acre. The two kings did not co-operate well, but the city surrendered on 12 July 1191, Richard massacring his 2,700 captives.[15] By mid-summer of 1191 the French king was tired of crusading, and was also in ill health. He returned to France, leaving the bulk of his French troops behind to continue the fight. The command was left effectively in the hands of Richard, who went on with the campaign, and though his army was conglomerate, with English and Normans, Bretons and men of Anjou, Flemings and French, native Syrian Franks, Templars and Hospitallers, organized into appropriate battle-groups, he defeated Saladin at Arsuf and relieved Jaffa. Richard came within sight of Jerusalem, but realized that he could not take it and did not even begin the attempt. He had, moreover, by now adopted the view of native Franks that the real objective of the Crusaders should be Cairo. He arranged a five-year truce with Saladin; pilgrims were to be allowed free access to Jerusalem and Acre, and the other Syrian ports would remain in Christian hands. Immediately after the signing of the treaty, selected Englishmen went into Jerusalem unarmed to pray at the holy shrines; the French, whom Richard thought had been insufficiently active in the fighting, were refused permission. The pilgrim parties were led by Hubert Walter, bishop of Salisbury, who was honourably received by Saladin, and the bishop was able to arrange that a small group of Latin clergy remained to say mass at the Holy Sepulchre and look after the shrines of Nazareth and Bethlehem. It was a solid if limited success for the Crusaders. But when the emperor Isaac heard of the arrangement he protested at what he regarded as an infringement of the rights of the Orthodox Church. Saladin rejected the protest, and the earlier friendly relations between the two men cooled, though they were still in formal alliance.

The policy of Isaac II Angelus was to keep the nobles at court, entrusting the administration of the Empire to professional bureaucrats. In traditional Byzantine style, Isaac ruled the Church as a department of State, but though he appointed to bishoprics he did not interfere in doctrinal causes. He restored monasteries and beautified them with mosaics; but, writes Nicetas (who did not like him), he was known to rob churches, even taking the gems from crosses and book bindings to be made into necklaces, and helping himself to sacred vessels for use on his dining-table.[16]

The islands and coastal districts of the Empire continued to be troubled by Genoese and Pisan pirates, and it was in an attempt to make the Italians forgive the 1182 Latin Massacre that Isaac restored the old customs concessions of the Genoese and Pisans, with the result that the merchants returned and trade was resumed. Large cash payments were made to the Venetians in compensation for past injuries; and money was paid to the Seljuks in return for peace in the East. But Isaac's main concern in his reign was a general uprising in 1186–7 by the Slavonic Bulgarians of the central Balkans and the Latin-speaking Vlachs (ancestors of the modern Romanians) of Macedonia. Bulgaria had been part of the Empire since about 1018, and during the intervening period the Balkans had been comparatively quiet, through the steadying influence of the many Greek-speaking minority communities and a ruling imperial hierarchy of Byzantine officials and clergy. But now there was serious unrest. The insurrection of 1186 was led by two brothers, the mountain chieftains Peter and Asen, who themselves were Vlachs. As a result of the rebellion an independent State of Bulgaria was again established, with Asen as king. The Cumans also were involved in the revolt, as military auxiliaries of the Vlach-Bulgarians. As a people the Cumans are a puzzle, for though Turkish-speaking they were blond and blue-eyed. Horse-riding nomads from the plains of south Russia, they seem never to have been interested in forming themselves into a regional State.

Largely as a result of these Bulgarian campaigns Isaac drained the imperial treasury dry, and with not only the bulk of Asia Minor but now the Balkans nearly gone, the Empire was greatly reduced in size. There was also much popular ill feeling over the compensation being paid to the Italians for the 1182 massacre, and an opposition party developed, centring around the emperor's brother Alexius, of whom Isaac was personally very fond. During his final campaign against the Vlachs Isaac was seized and blinded, in April 1195. It was an undeserved fate for a ruler who has sometimes been blamed as idle and incompetent but who in fact was a vigorous campaigner, taking a prominent part in the fighting himself. He had a deep concern for government and its problems, and it was not his fault that through the failure of preceding emperors to regain the vital recruiting-grounds of Asia Minor, and the steady decline of the central authority throughout the century, the Empire was now approaching a point of grave weakness.

Isaac was succeeded, in 1195, by his brother Alexius III, the only one of five brothers, great-grandsons of Alexius I Comnenus, who had not been blinded. In his anxiety to make his position secure Alexius distributed money and privileges wholesale, and Nicetas says with sarcasm that if requested he would even have granted the right 'to till the sea, or to sail over the land'.[17]

Meanwhile in the West Frederick Barbarossa had been succeeded as German emperor by his son Henry VI, a ruler with immense ambitions. By virtue of his marriage to the Norman princess Constance, Henry had inherited the kingdom of southern Italy and Sicily, and on Christmas Day 1194 he was crowned king of Sicily in Palermo. The Norman kingdom, which had been a source of so much trouble to Byzantium, was now part of the German Empire. The prospect for Constantinople was indeed alarming. Early in 1195 Henry VI sent messages to Isaac demanding the cession of the Byzantine lands taken by William II of Sicily during his Thessalonican campaign. He also asked for Byzantine naval help in the great Crusade to Palestine which he was planning and probably envisaged as likely to make him triumphant in the East as well as the dominant ruler of the West. Henry took the Cross and formally proclaimed his Crusade at Easter in 1195. Soon afterwards he arranged the marriage of his brother Philip of Swabia to a Byzantine princess Irene, daughter of the recently deposed emperor Isaac. This was an important move, linking the Western emperor with the dynastic interests and quarrels of Byzantium. By the marriage, Henry had created for himself the role of protector of the deposed Eastern emperor's children, and a ready excuse for aggression against Constantinople when the need should arise. In 1196 Henry demanded huge sums of money from the new emperor Alexius III, who in order to pay had to levy a special tax known as the Alamanikon (German tax), besides resorting to plundering the imperial tombs.

The advance guard of German Crusaders arrived in Syria in 1197, sailing from ports in Sicily and southern Italy. But though a large fleet was certainly assembled, we have no evidence that Henry VI intended at this juncture an assault on Constantinople. It was enough, at least for the time being, to obtain money from Byzantium by the mere threat of force. In the event Henry's Crusade came to nothing, as he died at Messina of a fever, still a young man, in September 1197. We shall never know his real intentions towards the Byzantine Empire.

Under Alexius III the Byzantine campaigns in the Balkans continued, and with some success. By a series of victories during 1200–2 the Vlach-Bulgarians, under their king Kalojan (younger brother of Peter and Asen, and ruler since 1197), were held back after advancing dangerously close to the capital.[18] Thrace was effectively recovered for the Empire, and this was a solid gain for Alexius. In Asia Minor he remained on the defensive, and continued his predecessor's policy of buying peace from the Turks.

Otherwise, the tale of these years is one of decadence. In public administration there was much corruption, an example of this being the spiriting away by the man entrusted with the fleet, Michael Stryphnos, of money intended for the maintenance of ships. So serious indeed was the decline of the imperial navy that when the Fourth Crusade arrived in the Bosphorus there would be scarcely twenty old ships to oppose the efficient Venetian fleet; not many years earlier the Empire had been able to put more than a hundred vessels to sea against the Normans. The army was more effective, perhaps indeed an improvement on that of recent years; but despite its successes against the Bulgarians it was to be completely outmatched by the new Crusading force soon to arrive from Western Europe: that fateful event towards which so many influences and circumstances had been moving during the twelfth century.

Chapter 3

Byzantium and Islam

It is fundamental to our understanding of the Fourth Crusade to realize that Byzantium had close relations with the Islamic world, and these constitute the third theme which we have to consider. The Byzantine-Muslim connection was one which the Crusaders found hard to comprehend, and for which they could not forgive their Greek brother-Christians. The Frankish residents of Syria had indeed come to live on good terms alongside their Muslim neighbours; but Outremer was an outpost, and little more, of Western Christendom. In the homelands of the Franks the creed of Muhammad was held in almost universal detestation. Islam was the enemy of Christianity, and Muhammad an agent of the Devil about whom absurd fables could be told. What the Christians of Western Europe and the Muslims did have in common was the conception of the Holy War, known to Islam as the *jihād*. The early Arab conquests had been made under the guise of religion, though there was an intermingling of spiritual and material motives, which indeed characterized both Crusade and *jihād*.[1] But the Byzantines, though they had a long military tradition, were never to regard warfare as 'holy'. Thus when the emperor Nicephorus II Phocas (963–9) wanted his soldiers who had been slain in warfare with the Muslims to be proclaimed martyrs, his patriarch retaliated by citing Letter 188 of the fourth-century Father Basil of Caesarea, which recommended that anyone who killed in war should refrain from communion for three years.

Almost from its birth Islam was in contact with the Eastern Empire, the Arabs sweeping over Syria and Palestine between 635 and 638, and bringing Byzantine rule to an end in Egypt. Relatively small armies, not countless hordes, achieved these victories, made possible largely by the sympathetic attitude of the Syrian and Egyptian peoples to the invaders. During the seventh century all northern Africa came under Islam's sway, though the Arabs failed in 718 in an attempt to take Constantinople, and fighting continued between them and the Empire for many generations.

But there were also friendly contacts, and Byzantium made substantial contributions to the creation and advancement of Islamic civilization.[2] Besides the formal missions between Constantinople and Baghdad and Cairo, trading connections were maintained by Byzantine merchants with the Arabs now occupying former imperial provinces. Constantinople itself was the main commercial link between the Levant and Europe, though this was less pronounced after the First Crusade, which made possible direct contact between Western Europe and the Eastern Mediterranean ports. It was from this time that the commercial prosperity of Constantinople began to decline, Italian ports such as Venice and Genoa becoming the main intermediaries between East and West.

Although Byzantium was linked to Western Europe by a common, though differentiated, Christianity, it shared with the Islamic world a culture which until the twelfth century made much less impression on the West. It was a culture which looked to classical Greece for its ultimate forms. In Greek-speaking Byzantium this culture found a natural home, but it also strongly influenced the Muslim world. There was a constant tradition of interchanging scholarship and artistic craftsmanship between Byzantium and Islam, of which an instance is the successful request made by the 'Ummayad caliph of Cordoba, al-Hakim II (961–76), to Constantinople for the services of skilled artists to decorate the Great Mosque of Cordoba with mosaics. A tenth-century patriarch of Constantinople, Nicholas Mysticus, writing to the emir of Crete, could describe the Arabs and Byzantines as the two powers of the Universe, living as brothers though different in religion. Arabs visiting Constantinople were given official precedence over the Franks at the emperor's table. The emperor Romanus III (1028–34) maintained excellent diplomatic relations with the Fatimid caliph in Egypt, and he was allowed to restore the Church of the Holy Sepulchre.[3]

But with the establishment of the Sultanate of Iconium in Asia Minor by the conquering Seljuks in the eleventh century, the tradition of friendship had become dimmed. At the time of the Third Crusade, it is true, the emperor Isaac II was in alliance with Saladin of Egypt, but the old tolerant relationship, though interspersed with periods of fighting, between Byzantine and Arab, kindred spirits with an appreciation of beauty, mysticism, and intellectualism, was now overshadowed by the bitter conflict between Latin Christian and Turkish Muslim which largely constituted the Crusades. But the Byzantines, though the Turks had half destroyed their Empire, were never really committed to the Christian Holy War. Their commercial and cultural contacts over a long period had been too close for them to regard Islam as an implacable foe, and this conciliatory attitude of mind was to characterize Byzantium for long after the Fourth Crusade.

From the religious viewpoint, Byzantium was not at first particularly alarmed by the Arab phenomenon, some theologians tending to regard Islam as yet another Christian heretical sect which the Orthodox Church might expect in due course to tame or absorb. One such scholar was John of Damascus in the eighth century, first a Christian tax-collector serving the 'Ummayads at Damascus and then a monk, who thought critically, though not harshly, of Islam because it rejected the doctrine of the Trinity. The Byzantines had much experience of Christians who were unsound in their view of the nature and being of God; and the Monophysite form of Eastern Christianity, prevailing in Egypt, not only helped to prepare the way for the triumph of Islam as a political power but contributed to the formation of Islam as a religious faith. In course of time Christian thinkers were to develop a critical view of Islam, having in mind the explicit denial of the Christian Trinity which occurs in the Koran: 'God is alone and eternal. He neither begets nor is begotten, and there is none equal to Him.'[4] There was also much criticism of Islam because of practices such as polygamy and the veneration of the Ka'aba with its black stone at Mecca.

In 1178 there was a controversy which illustrates very well the ambivalent attitude of Byzantium to Islam. In that year the emperor Manuel clashed with the Church, ordering it to revise the authorized rite for reception of Muslim converts to Christianity, by deleting a clause in which converts anathematized the 'God of Muhammad'. Orthodox churchmen, led by Eustathius, archbishop of Thessalonica, objected to this demand, and the emperor agreed to a compromise. Converts would simply be required to renounce 'Muhammad and his teaching', not his God. The controversy pointed to the existence of two different Byzantine approaches to Islam. Strict churchmen tended to look upon the latter as a form of paganism; but the more tolerant men, who were especially prominent in government circles, recognized Muslims as worshipping the same God as Christians.[5] Byzantine satirists poured scorn on Islam, particularly for its doctrine of sensual delights in the hereafter; and despite the many specific contacts, it is doubtful whether the Orthodox ever really understood the inner nature of Islam. But by the twelfth century Byzantium and Islam were beginning to draw closer together again, a tendency which infuriated the Latin West.

Islam, like Christianity, was a divided religion. At an early stage in the great Arab conquests in the seventh century, the election of 'Alī as caliph, or deputy of the Prophet, in succession to 'Uthmān had created a schism which remained permanent. Under the Abbasids of Baghdad the Islamic culture attained its greatest heights, but these rulers failed to hold Islam together. A number of Islamic States arose out of the eventual disintegration of the Abbasid empire and amongst these was the Fatimid dynasty of Egypt. The religious basis of the latter's power was the species of Islam known as Isma'īlism, tending to neo-Platonism in its philosophy and tolerant of many religions, but with a socially radical strain which made it particularly acceptable to the poor and oppressed. The unorthodoxy of the Fatimids made them unpopular with the rest of the Islamic world, though they nevertheless were to rule for two centuries (969–1171).

Egypt was much in the minds of the Crusading leaders, who knew the importance of capturing it if they were to defeat Islam, though it was not easy for the rank and file to be convinced that to win dramatic victories in Syria and Palestine, and capture places famous in Bible story, was in the long term of secondary importance. The Crusading States of the Holy Land were vulnerable, always liable to be caught in a war of two fronts – Egypt in the south and Iraq in the north. Egypt during the whole of the Crusading age was a great power in its own right, and free of an earlier dependence on the Abbasids of Baghdad. Egypt was wealthy and prosperous, largely through her extensive trade, notably in India and the Far East by way of the Red Sea. During the Fatimid rule, Egypt under its caliphs dominated all northern Africa as far west as Morocco, and much of Arabia. The Fatimids created out of the ancient capital of Fustat a virtually new city which they called 'the Victorious', al-Kahira (Cairo). They traded extensively with Europe, and the rising standards of a Western Europe emerging from the Dark Ages led to a demand for luxury commodities, encouraging, in their turn, Venice and other Italian city-republics to trade with Egypt. Carpets were brought back from Alexandria in return for northern goods such as timber. The Fatimid power, however, suffered an eclipse in the later years of the eleventh century, when there were several years of famine and much indiscipline in the largely mercenary army, and it was from the weakened Fatimids that the Crusaders were able to take Jerusalem in 1099.

The Fatimid caliphs of Cairo were supplanted in 1171 by Saladin, a devout son of Islam but a man devoid of religious 'enthusiasm', with no sympathy either for deviant movements such as Isma'īlism or for freethinkers. Under him both Egypt and Syria came within the fold of orthodox Islam. He built up a vast Empire, known as the Ayyubid (from his father Ayub), covering the entire area from Mesopotamia to Tunisia, and including the sacred Muslim cities of the Arabian peninsula. Such strength enabled Saladin to inflict his crushing defeat on the Crusaders in 1187 at Hattin and retake Jerusalem. Of this great Muslim Ayyubid Empire, Egypt was the pivot and centre, and would have to be a major target in any future Crusade. Saladin was careful to foster the already existing trade connection with the Italian cities; and he was helped in this by the growth of anti-Western feeling in Byzantium. The Western merchants made increasing use of the Egyptian ports; there was, for example, in Alexandria a strong Venetian colony, with two *fondaci* or warehouses. The very last thing the Venetians, Genoese, and other Italian merchants wanted was to see their new and valuable links with Ayyubid Egypt destroyed by Crusading attacks. This trafficking with an infidel people was sternly disapproved of by the papacy and indeed was to be explicitly condemned (without effect) by the Fourth Lateran Council of 1215, convened by Innocent III. The plain fact was that by the close of the twelfth century the prosperity of Venice depended on Constantinople and Egypt. In the Byzantine capital the danger to this prosperity lay in the hostility of the native inhabitants to the Latin businessmen in their midst; in Egypt the haunting possibility for the Venetians was that a Crusading invasion might ruin all. It is a realization of these factors which helps us to appreciate the reasons for the forthcoming diversion of the Fourth Crusade from Egypt to Constantinople.

When Saladin died, early in 1193, his lands were divided between his many sons. Of the latter, the most important were al-Afdal, who took over Damascus; al-Aziz, who declared himself sultan of Egypt; and al-Zahir, with a separate

State in Aleppo. The unity created by Saladin was thus shattered, and his sons fell to fighting amongst themselves, the opportunity which existed after the end of the Third Crusade to drive the Franks right out of Syria being lost to the Saracens. The world of Islam recovered its cohesion just before the Fourth Crusade, however, and the quarrels between Saladin's sons were halted by their uncle, Saladin's brother al-Adil, who resumed his brother's dominion over Egypt, Syria, and Mesopotamia, and proclaimed himself sole sultan. He reigned from 1202 to 1218, which was to be a time of friendly relations with the Franks in Syria.

There are said to be few sights more impressive than that of a Muslim congregation a prayer. The monotheism, fostered in the first place by the illimitable expanse of the desert, itself breeds a sense of brotherhood which is not easily found in any other religion. The overriding sense of a loving God is evident in the words with which every Sura of the Koran opens, 'In the name of Allah, the Compassionate, the Merciful', also often used by a Muslim before any important undertaking. 'Do not our hearts become tranquil in remembering God?' asked the Muslim in times of trouble. Possessed with the idea of the unity of God, he would say, 'Praise be to God, who has no Son', on passing a Christian church. Islam owed much of its success to the miracle of the Koran, which Arabists tell us has a hypnotic effect on those who hear it read aloud in the original, with its rhythms and cadences.[6] Famous as scientists and philosophers, Muslims were also poets, taking as their themes the battlefield, love, flowers and gardens, the call of the huntsman, the rollicking of the tavern, the charm of the countryside. Their poetry could be mystical too. 'O my Joy and my Desire and my Refuge, my Friend and my Sustainer and my Goal. Thou art my Intimate, and longing of Thee sustains me.'[7]

But the Latins of Western Europe were for the most part unimpressed by the achievements of Muslim civilization. Islam presented a challenge which they had to accept, not an opportunity for social and cultural contact. It was intolerable that the holiest sites of Christendom should be in the custody of unbelievers. By the close of the twelfth century three major attempts had been made towards the Christianization of the Sacred Land. Yet still there sounded in Jerusalem itself the call of the minaret, 'God is the most High. I witness that only God can be worshipped. Muhammad is his prophet.' To the Latin Christian this was little short of blasphemy, and the apparent indifference of the Orthodox to the Muslim occupation of Jerusalem, where Christ suffered and died, disgraceful and unforgivable. It was small consolation that in Palestine Latin priests were permitted to mutter the words of the mass and attend to their shrines. The Western Church was interested above all in power, and was prepared to go to almost any lengths to attain this objective.

Chapter 4

The Church Militant but Divided

In the twelfth century the chief influence in European society was unquestionably the Christian religion, organized in a vast complex of dioceses and parishes, monasteries and other institutions. There was as yet no sign of any decline in its power, and in theory the Church was one. Between the West and the East, however, were many differences and points of rivalry, and these constitute yet another factor which affected the actions of the Crusaders. In the Western Church the mass was recited in Latin, whereas in the Orthodox Communion the vernacular was allowed. Whereas the Latin mass was crisp and to the point, Orthodox worship was leisurely, and depended for much of its effect on dim churches lit by candles and lamps, their dancing shadows evoking life from the mosaics and frescoes on the walls around. Byzantines were comparatively little interested in exterior decoration, like that of the great Gothic cathedrals fast arising in Western Europe during the years around 1200. In the East the interior icon was all-important. There had been a vigorous campaign from 726 onwards under the emperors Leo III and Constantine V to destroy all religious pictures and substitute a non-representational art of pure ornament, such as that of flowers and scrolls. But by the middle of the ninth century the icon had been restored, to remain a permanent feature of Byzantine religion.

By far the most important issue between the Latin and Orthodox Churches, however, was that of the universal jurisdiction of the papacy, and it was this which caused the development of the schism. It is difficult to say just when the latter began, and in any case there had been from early times differences of character and temperament between the two Christian worlds. In the East the emperor's will had the force of law, and his authority extended over the Church; but in the West matters were different, largely because the old imperial authority collapsed during the Dark Ages and the Church stepped into the vacuum. While the Byzantine Church, under the protection of State patronage, was able to devote its genius to mysticism and the contemplative life, the Latin Church had the busy task of caring for a barbaric society and insensibly acquired a paternalistic habit of mind. It is a mistake to think that the Byzantines rejected the papacy, and probably from as early as the fourth century they acknowledged the primacy of Rome.[1] But they believed that the ultimate authority in the interpretation of the Faith lay not with the Roman or indeed any other single

Church, but in oecumenical councils. For long there was rivalry between Rome and Constantinople, though no sense of clearly defined schism, and the essential unity of the Church held firm.

The importance of the celebrated addition to the Nicene Creed, 'and from the Son', has been over-emphasized. The clause itself was not included in the original creed of Nicaea drawn up in 325, and the trouble arose when some Latin churches, referring to the Holy Spirit, began to add to the clause 'who proceedeth from the Father' the words 'and from the Son'. The addition became widespread in the Carolingian period about 800, and was given particular force by the custom of regularly singing the Nicene creed at the principal Sunday mass, a practice largely due to the influence of the Englishman Alcuin, adviser to Charlemagne.[2] Not, however, until the early part of the eleventh century did the Roman Church as a whole accept the additional clause. The objection of the Eastern Church to the clause was less on theological grounds than through its strict adherence to the principle that no alteration or addition to so fundamental a formulary as the Creed should be made except by an oecumenical council, and not by the unilateral action of a single Church or patriarchate.

During the tenth century the peace between Greek and Latin Christendom was generally well kept, but everything changed in the 1040s, when the Normans began the conquest of the then largely Byzantine territory of southern Italy. The Western Church was being swept by a reform movement emanating from the abbey of Cluny and other centres, and the confidence of the Latin church was growing. The southern Italian provinces taken by the Catholic Normans were now brought within the jurisdiction of the papacy, which set about introducing Latin usages in place of the long-familiar Greek ones. In retaliation the patriarch of Constantinople, Michael Cerularius, turned his attention to the Latin churches established in the capital for the use of Western merchants, ordering them to adopt Greek customs, and when these churches resisted he closed them, towards the end of 1052.

The crisis found the pope, Leo IX, ill and tired, and he handed the matter over to Cardinal Humbert, a man who combined natural arrogance with an intense personal dislike of Byzantines. In 1054 Humbert went to Constantinople with two other legates, and while they were there the pope died, on 15 April. The three men now had no legal standing, as legates could not speak on behalf of a dead pontiff, and Leo's successor Victor II was not to be appointed for several months. Nevertheless, on 16 July 1054 Humbert strode with his fellow legates into the church of St. Sophia and deposited on the altar a papal bull excommunicating the patriarch.[3] As there was no pope at the time, the bull was invalid, and in any case it contained a list of quite unfounded accusations. A few days later Humbert and his fellow legates were in their turn excommunicated by a Greek synod, though care was taken not to implicate the papacy or the Latin Church generally in the excommunication – just as Humbert for his part had directed his anathemas against the patriarch and not the Orthodox Church as such.

The affair was not taken seriously by official circles in Constantinople, as it was uncanonical, and the famous incident of 1054 does not mark the point of separation between Orthodoxy and Catholicism, as commonly supposed, though it did lead to much bitterness.[4] As it happened, the patriarch Cerularius himself was deposed soon afterwards by his own emperor for the effrontery of starting to wear the purple buskins, the distinctive mark of the imperial office. One feels that the *cause célèbre* of 1054, though far-reaching in its effects, was a clash between two arrogant personalities rather than a decisive encounter between two great Churches.

With the pontificate of Gregory VII (1073–85) the papal claims to supremacy took a step forward, though the Eastern Churches hardened in their view that only an oecumenical council could decide doctrinal matters and that the supreme government of the Church lay with the five historic patriarchates, which besides Rome and Constantinople included Alexandria, Antioch, and Jerusalem. This combination constituted the 'five-fold strength of the Church' – and could be regarded as Christendom's 'five senses'.[5] The Catholic and Orthodox Churches were, however, still not in formal schism, and Pope Urban II, the great protagonist of the First Crusade, went out of his way towards the close of the eleventh century to conciliate the East. In 1098 he held a Council at Bari, his aim being to reconcile the Greek churches of southern Italy to Latin rule, placating them by giving them permission to use the Orthodox liturgy. A remarkable indication that openly recognized schism had still not arrived early in the twelfth century is a request made by Peter the Venerable, abbot of Cluny, asking the patriarch of Constantinople to reopen and restore a certain disused Cluniac priory, which suggests that he recognized the authority of the Orthodox patriarch over Catholic churches and monasteries within his jurisdiction.[6]

However, during the twelfth century the forces making for schism began to have more positive effect. Although the emperors Alexius, John, and Manuel had themselves no wish for enmity with Rome, the Church of Constantinople was deeply conscious of its venerable traditions. The honorific primacy of Rome was still not denied, but the unruly conduct of Crusading soldiers passing through Byzantine territory had left a bad impression.[7] The colonies of Italian merchants were arousing fears in the Empire that its trade was being usurped. For the first time Byzantine churchmen were meeting their Latin counterparts in large numbers and at close quarters, and they did not like what they saw. The Byzantines were especially horrified by the sight of bishops and priests bearing weapons. East and West were steadily becoming estranged, though the ecclesiastical leaders of both sides were still reluctant to admit that the unity of the Church was in the process of being broken. Odo de Deuil, the monk-historian, told how Louis VII on his way to the East with the Second Crusade paused to celebrate the feast of St. Denis (9 October). Hearing of this, the Byzantine emperor sent a contingent of his clergy to participate in the Latin service. The Franks were deeply moved by the beauty of the Greek singing. 'The mingling of voices, the heavier with the light, the eunuch's, namely, with the manly voice (for many of them were eunuchs), softened the hearts of the Franks. Also, they gave the onlookers pleasure by their graceful bearing and gentle clapping of hands and genuflexions.'[8] But Odo's Chronicle gives us the impression that he himself so hated the Byzantines that he doubted whether they really deserved to be called Christians at all.

The failure of the Second Crusade brought matters to a head. It was widely felt in the West that the campaign would have succeeded if there had been full support from Byzantium, and the idea was now increasingly mooted of a Holy War against Byzantium itself and of its forcible subjection to the papal see. The death of the westernizing emperor Manuel in 1180 accelerated the deterioration of East-West relations, and this was followed by the outrage of the massacre of the Latin merchants in 1182, which seemed to justify to the West its right to rule all Christendom. Although it is not possible to point to any specific date marking formal schism, it would appear that by the closing years of the twelfth century there was a realization on both sides that the Catholic and Orthodox Churches had virtually separated. There were still many contacts. Thus the Amalfitans were maintaining a Latin monastery on Mount Athos at least as late as 1196; and in 1199 Innocent III had to write to the Latin clergy of Constantinople telling them not to administer the rite of confirmation to children, after the Greek manner.[9] But the differences which for centuries had existed between the two traditions were now more consciously recognized, because of the commercial and Crusading contacts which had brought West and East to know each other better. If anything was really responsible for the split between the Latin and Greek Churches, it was that movement of Westerners towards the Levant which was so striking a feature of the eleventh and twelfth centuries.

In the final decade of the twelfth century the great power and the ambitions of the Western emperor Henry VI had the effect of drawing the papacy and the Byzantine Empire closer together, in their mutual interest, after some years of animosity which followed the Latin Massacre of 1182. Pope Celestine III and the emperor Alexius III tried to re-establish good relations. Then after the death of Henry VI in 1197, Celestine III also died, and he was succeeded by Innocent III.

The man elected by the cardinals as their new pope, on 8 January 1198, was their youngest member, at the time thirty-seven years old. Giovanni Lotario was of a noble Italian family, the Conti, his father being Trasimondo of Segni and his mother Clarina. Lotario was born at Anagni, though little is known of his childhood. He studied theology in Paris under Peter of Corbeil; and during his time as a Paris student he visited England, a pilgrim to the tomb of Thomas Becket at Canterbury. He later studied canon law at Bologna, where his teachers included Uguccio of Ferrara. Returning to Rome, he became a canon of St. Peter's, and the election of his uncle Paul, bishop of Palestrina, to the pontificate as Clement III (1187–91) was favourable to his career.

When barely thirty, Lotario was promoted by his uncle to the cardinalate, his titular church being that of SS. Sergius and Bacchus, which he at once proceeded to restore and beautify. The church, now vanished, was in the Forum, close to the arch of Septimius Severus. There has been a tendency to see Innocent as primarily a canonist, a man interested above all in law, order, and power, but there was also a spiritual side to his character. During his period as cardinal Lotario did not participate much in public life, and was drawn rather towards study and meditation. He wrote amongst other treatises the *Contempt of the World*, which is monastic in tone and suggests that if Lotario had been left alone he might in due course have fulfilled his life in professed 'religion'. In his first year as pope he was in fact to recognize a new Order founded for the purpose of ransoming Christians in Muslim captivity. He also placed a newly founded brotherhood of the Holy Spirit in charge of a hospital which he established on the site of the old English or Saxon School. Situated between St. Peter's and Ponte Sant' Angelo, this is known today as Santo Spirito in Sassia.

On electing Lotario the cardinals knew that the dignity of the papacy would be safe in his hands. In his inaugural sermon he stated in uncompromising terms his view of the Roman Church and the papal office. The Church is founded on an unshakable rock, and the successor of St. Peter stands between God and man.[10] There is no pride more impressive than that of the man who is both aristocrat and ascetic. Innocent, in the final analysis, thought in terms of authority and power, attributes to be used for the salvation of man from eternal doom.

Within a short time of his consecration Innocent was at his desk writing to the archbishop of Ravenna reminding him that the Church was only truly free when it accepted that the Roman See had full power in spiritual and material concerns.[11] Wherever the new pope looked he saw division and confusion, sovereigns with a low conception of their duty to their subjects, the Latin and Orthodox Churches now in a state of practical separation, the Catholic Church itself threatened by heresy, Islam still in control of the places most sacred to Christendom. It took only a few months to confirm Innocent in his conviction that he was God's instrument for the correction and reformation of all men, and for the reinvigoration of Christendom. In October 1198 he drew his famous analogy of the sun and moon as representing the relationship between the spiritual and earthly power. 'The Creator of the universe set up two great luminaries in the firmament of heaven, the greater light to rule the day, the lesser light to rule the night. In the same way . . . he appointed two great dignities, the greater to bear rule over the souls, the lesser to bear rule over bodies. . . . These dignities are the pontifical authority and the royal power.'[12]

Innocent became concerned in the quarrels of the great families of Rome, he himself building the stronghold known as the Torre dei Conti, the stump of which is still in the Forum area. He asserted his authority in the Patrimony of St. Peter, the lands of the Italian seaboard between Tuscany in the north and the Sicilian kingdom in the south. Eventually he was to obtain recognition of his feudal overlordship by many kingdoms – Sicily, Aragon, Portugal, Hungary, England. Quite early in his pontificate, meanwhile, he was intervening in political affairs, putting the doctrine of supremacy to the practical test; and he was convinced that he was at the head of the entire Christian world, as Vicar of Christ and successor of St. Peter. It cannot be a reproach against him that he held to a belief which is after all not far removed from that of the reformed Roman Church of today; the Second Vatican Council has declared that 'in virtue of his office, that is, as Vicar of Christ and Pastor of the whole Church, the Roman pontiff has full, supreme, and universal power over the Church'.[13]

Innocent made himself guardian of the late Henry VI's infant son, the future emperor Frederick II. He claimed the right to examine and approve the claims and qualifications of an emperor-elect before consecrating him. During civil war in Germany between the Hohenstaufen Philip of Swabia (Henry VI's brother) and the Welf Otto IV of Brunswick, the pope supported Otto. He was never to care much for Philip, and the interests of the Hohenstaufens were not in line with those of the papacy and of Italy. The Byzantine emperor Alexius III also was ill-disposed towards Philip, not least because the latter's wife Irene was daughter of Isaac II whom he had deposed. Innocent and Alexius therefore had at least an aversion in common. But there was a more particular reason for drawing Innocent towards Alexius. The pope was anxious to recover for Christendom the Holy Places of Palestine, and had set his heart on a great new Crusade. He regarded Byzantine help as essential for this project. He was also determined to achieve a positive reconciliation between the Orthodox and Latin Churches, to extinguish for ever the smouldering animosity between them, and effectively to make them one great Communion under papal supremacy. To these two ends Innocent made a number of calls for Alexius's help, but was invariably rewarded with noncommittal answers.

In his very first year as pope, during the summer of 1198, Innocent called on Alexius III to bring the Byzantine Church into subordinate communion with Rome, and make a resolute effort to place the strength of his Empire behind the cause of the Holy War. About the same time Innocent also wrote to the patriarch of Constantinople, John Camaterus, urging the claims of papal supremacy.[14] Alexius's reply to this call, written in February 1199, was that both the deliverance of the Holy Places and reunion would indeed come, in God's own time. The patriarch replied expressing some scepticism about the papal claims to supremacy; and Innocent retorted uncompromisingly, late in 1199, that 'by divine ordinance Rome is the head and mother of all Churches'.[15] The patriarch rejoined by asking 'where in the gospels does Christ say that the Roman Church is the head and mother of all Churches?' He maintained that amongst the five great patriarchal Churches, Rome had the primacy of honour not on account of Peter's presence there but because Rome was the first imperial capital.[16] The pope also wrote, towards the close of 1199, to Alexius III, rebuking him for his dilatoriness in attempting a Crusade on behalf of Jerusalem.

During 1200 there were further exchanges between Innocent and Alexius. The emperor now brought up the argument, so traditional in Byzantine thinking, that the Church was dependent on the secular authority. In the East it had always been regarded as part of the emperor's duty to protect the Church, and though he had no authority to make doctrinal changes it was normal for him to preside over her Councils. Innocent would have none of this, and declared that the pope's duty included the rebuking of secular rulers and that the latter held no authority over the Church and her officers. This particular exchange highlights one fundamental difference between the Latin and Greek ecclesiastical positions. The idea known as 'caesaro-papism', implying the subordination of the Church to the State, accepted by many Byzantines,[17] would have been quite impossible in the Latin Church after her spectacular successes in the Pope-versus-Emperor controversy relating to the appointment and investiture of bishops in the eleventh and twelfth centuries.

During the early stages of his pontificate Innocent was not only in direct communication with Constantinople, largely over the union issue, but also busy with his idea of a decisive Crusade which would free the Holy Land from Islam. There was, of course, no question in his mind about the rightfulness of war as such. War was justified by God's law, and supported by the scriptures and Fathers. According to the canon lawyers a war was just if it had a worthy object and intention, and a valid authority behind it, such as the Church or a sovereign ruler. Violence was an allowable way of achieving a good end. A new Crusade was now especially necessary in view of the death of Henry VI, who had intended a campaign to subdue the Holy Land and had formally taken the Cross. It was only natural that Innocent should call on Alexius III to join the cause, and one of his first acts on becoming pope had been to write also to Aymar, Latin patriarch of Jerusalem, telling him that a fresh Crusade was to be launched and asking for an increase in fasting and prayer. A report on conditions in Palestine would be welcome. Aymar replied with the requested information, though he was unenthusiastic over the prospect of another Crusading expedition. The pope also wrote to the bishop of Lydda, and to the Templars and Hospitallers, asking them to keep him informed about the situation in Palestine.

Innocent formally published his plan for a 'sacred war against the Saracens, for the recovery of the Holy Land', in a general letter to the Western archbishops as early as August 1198, ordering them to inform their diocesan bishops.[18] He wrote bitterly of the Muslims who, boasting of their victories over the Latins, were mockingly asking, 'Where is your God? We have violated your sacred places – let your God now arise and help you.' Innocent entrusted two cardinals with the superintendence of the project: Soffredo, who was sent to discover what help might be forthcoming from Venice, and Peter Capuano, who was the effective head of the new Crusade in the pope's eyes. Peter Capuano, a native of Amalfi (not of Capua as might be assumed from his family name), arrived in France towards the end of 1198, and proclaimed the papal Crusade at an assembly of

French bishops held in Dijon. At this gathering the bishops promised a contribution of a thirtieth of their revenues to the undertaking. The two most powerful sovereigns of the West, Philip Augustus of France and Richard of England, veterans of the Third Crusade, would be unlikely to rally to the new call, as they were quarrelling over lands which had been seized by Philip from Richard while the latter was absent from his kingdom. In January 1199 Peter Capuano was able to persuade the two kings to cease squabbling, though a few weeks later Richard was in any case dead.

There was scarcely any response to the Crusading call from the crowned kings of Europe, the only kingdom to respond formally being Hungary. The Hungarian king Bela III had previously taken the Cross but had been unable to go to the Holy Land. He died in 1196 and was succeeded by his elder son Emeric; to his younger son Andrew his bequest was a large sum of money and the Crusading obligation. Andrew squandered the money on personal pleasures, and also unsuccessfully contested the throne with his brother. It was Emeric who was persuaded by Innocent III to take the Cross. There was further discord between the brothers, and eventually Andrew was to succeed Emeric on the latter's death in 1205. Emeric was actually to take no part in the Fourth Crusade, though in the pope's eyes he formally belonged to it. In due course Andrew (II) was to fulfil the vow bequeathed to him by leading a force to the Holy Land during 1217–18, as a contingent of the Fifth Crusade. Andrew was father of Saint Elizabeth of Hungary, who was to renounce court and family life for austerity and charitable work.

Philip Augustus was not interested in Innocent's project. He had been Crusading before and wanted no more of it, and in any case was in trouble with Innocent over the question of a divorce from his Danish wife Ingeborg. The German king Philip of Swabia was busily engaged with his bitter rival Otto of Brunswick. John of England, Richard's successor, was just beginning a struggle with Philip Augustus over his continental possessions, and in English history textbooks 1204 is in fact important not as the year of the conquest of Constantinople but of the loss of Normandy, Maine, and Anjou. Mindful, doubtless, of the powerful contribution made by England to the preceding Crusade, Innocent did indeed persevere with John. In a letter of 27 March 1202 he was to remind him of an injunction laid on him by the archbishop of Canterbury (Hubert Walter, himself an ardent participant in the Third Crusade) to provide a hundred English knights to serve in the new Crusade for one year. There is no evidence that this contingent was ever sent.[19]

Near the end of 1198 Innocent launched a general money-raising campaign, intending the following March as the date for the start of the actual expedition. He made it known that the papacy itself was donating a tenth of its revenues, and asked all churches and monasteries for a fortieth of theirs. There was the usual indulgence, every participant in the Crusade being promised remission of former sins. The estates of those taking the Cross would be under the protection of St.

Peter during their owners' absence. This was by now a customary guarantee – it had been stated in specific terms by the First Lateran Council in 1123. Sometimes the task of keeping an eye on the estate or property of an absent Crusader would be entrusted to the diocesan bishop, sometimes to a specially appointed official known as a 'conservator'. Crusaders who needed to borrow money to enable them to set out, declared Innocent, were absolved of any requirements as to interest. This also was standard Crusading practice or was in process of becoming so, and obviously made it difficult for Crusaders to raise money from prospective lenders. Jewish moneylenders who pressed their claims were to be forbidden any further commercial dealings with Christians.

Never had a Crusade been preached and planned with such methodical and whole-hearted papal backing, and yet the appeal met with a disappointing response. One reason for this is that Innocent had not been pope for long, and had hardly had sufficient time to make the undoubted force of his personality felt throughout Europe. Some men, such as the minnesinger Walther von der Vogelweide, appear to have thought the new pope too young to be taken seriously. Popes as a rule were experienced and venerable men. Another cause of the relatively poor response was the spread of heresy in Western Europe, now so grave that devotion to the Catholic Church was being undermined. Though heresy, steadily growing throughout the twelfth century, was at its strongest in Provence and Lombardy, it was also firmly rooted in the traditional Crusading territories of northern France and the Rhineland.

By the autumn of 1199 there was still no army in being, and Innocent renewed his efforts to reawaken the old Crusading zeal. During December 1199 and January 1200 letters were sent to all parts of the Catholic world, and by the closing weeks of 1199 Innocent's efforts began to be solidly rewarded. Christians who did not take the Cross, he declared, must contribute to the funds, though a concession was made in the case of the Cistercian, Carthusian, Premonstratensian, and Grandmontine religious Orders, which instead of the stipulated fortieth were asked for a fiftieth of their revenues. The attempts to raise money were intensified. There was to be in every church a collection chest with three keys, one of which should be held by the parish priest, one by a pious layman, and one by the diocesan bishop. The main purpose of the chests would be to assist indigent knights in their passage to the Holy Land; the proceeds of the papal taxes were intended rather for Crusaders already in Palestine and for expenses such as repairs to castles. The granting of financial help to Crusaders had been a feature of the Third Crusade, the so-called 'Saladin tithe' being levied in 1188 to pay for it. The clergy, however, appear to have responded lukewarmly to Innocent's financial appeal, and the historian Gerald of Wales complained of the money-raising activities of a papal envoy Philip, sent at the beginning of 1200 to England to arrange the collection of the fortieth from the clergy.

The strongest objectors to the Crusading levy were the Cistercian monks, who at first flatly refused to pay even the specially reduced rate of a fiftieth. The opposition of some abbots reached the point where they actually tried to persuade men to renounce Crusading vows already taken. Amongst Cistercian abbots who are known to have received the summons from Rome to produce money are Ernald of Rievaulx in Yorkshire, and Martin of Pairis in Alsace. The latter, unlike many, excelled himself in enthusiasm, and became a fervent preacher of the Crusade, going to Citeaux, the mother-house of the Order, for formal permission to accompany the coming expedition. There was an angry quarrel between Innocent and the Cistercian Order over the Crusade, though by the summer of 1201 the differences were resolved, the abbot and chapter of Citeaux itself sending a substantial contribution of 2,000 marks, on behalf of the Order as a whole, as an earnest of its support. The pope accepted this as exempting the Cistercians from any further payment. The Chapter General which met in September 1201 saw the Order fully committed to the enterprise, though for many years successive Chapters General would still be struggling to get individual abbeys to pay their share of the 2,000 marks.

Innocent must have been relieved to secure the support of the powerful Cistercians. And indeed he clearly expected that the clergy and religious would play an important role in the expedition. There had in earlier times been some qualms about clerical participation in warfare, and Urban II had tried to insist that monks or priests who wanted to go on Crusade should first obtain the approval of their abbot or bishop. Innocent III had doubts about the propriety of clerks or monks accompanying Crusading expeditions, but in 1201 ruled that they might do so provided it was clearly understood that they went in the capacity of preachers or chaplains. The Crusading monk was a familiar figure. The standard rule had always been that a monk should spend his whole life within the bounds of his religious house, but Crusading was an exception to this requirement and monks had been present in all the Crusading armies from 1095 onwards. In the Fourth Crusade the Cistercians especially were to play an influential part, thus fuelling a criticism increasingly being levelled against members of the Order by the closing years of the twelfth century, that they were becoming over-occupied with secular concerns.[20]

Chapter 5

The Gathering of the Host

A prominent feature of the Church's life in the years preceding and following 1200 was itinerant preaching, the result of a genuine and deep-seated enthusiasm for Catholic Christianity; and Geoffrey de Villehardouin begins his Chronicle by mentioning a preacher who was causing an especially great stir. 'In 1198, when Innocent was pope of Rome, Philip king of France, and Richard king of England, there was in France a certain holy man, Fulk of Neuilly.' The parish of Neuilly held by Fulk lay between Paris and Lagny-sur-Marne. Fulk himself was a cleric of dissolute life who underwent a religious conversion, and, ashamed of his ignorance of theology, attended lectures in Paris, after which he decided that personal residence on his benefice, amongst his flock, was of less importance than making his voice heard by a wider audience. From about 1195 he entered on a series of general evangelistic tours, preaching in churches and market-places, and on village greens, and he carried his message to Flanders, Normandy, Champagne, and other regions of Western Europe, including the Île de France, the royal domains centred on Paris. A fervent denouncer of sin, he was particularly virulent in his attacks on prostitutes, for whom he founded a penitentiary convent near Paris, and on moneylenders.

After these preaching campaigns Fulk appeared at the Cistercian Chapter General in 1198. It was customary for the sessions of the Chapter General, always held at Cîteaux, to open on 13 September, the vigil of Holy Cross day, and on this particular occasion the pope had asked the abbots present to pray for the forthcoming expedition. Fulk himself took the Cross at this Chapter and at once displayed fiery enthusiasm to preach the Crusade. He asked the Order to appoint monks to help him in his preaching, but this was refused. Not only Villehardouin, but Robert de Clari and other sources speak of Fulk's preaching activities, and it is clear that he was an influential 'revivalist' figure in contemporary religious life. In a famous rebuke to Richard I of England, during the last year of the latter's life, he is said to have called on the king 'to give in marriage his three evil daughters, pride, avarice, and luxury'. In an equally spirited reply the king said he would send his daughters to those who would welcome them: 'I will give my pride to the Templars, my avarice to the Cistercians, and my luxury to the bishops.'[1]

News of Fulk reached Rome, and Innocent III was quick to recognize the potentialities of a persuasive orator. It was this same genius for spotting the effective popularizer of Christianity that a few years later was to lead Innocent to give his official approval to St. Francis. On 5 November 1198 the pope wrote to Fulk in terms which implied authorization to preach the Crusade. The English chronicler Ralph of Coggeshall dwells on Fulk's success, saying that he claimed to have personally given the Cross to 200,000 people.[2] Writers of the time were fond of vast, round numbers, often quite incredible, and Ralph was using the words 'ducenta millia' as meaning 'a very large number'. Like many clergy and preachers, Fulk combined a 'passion for souls' with skill in the art of fund raising, and the money which he collected he entrusted to the Cistercians at Cîteaux. For the remaining three or four years of his life Fulk would remain wholly devoted to the Crusade.

It was after commissioning Fulk as a Crusade preacher that Innocent sent to France his legate Cardinal Peter Capuano, towards the end of 1198, to urge men to take the Cross. Some did commit themselves, and it is certain that during 1199 the idea itself of a great new Crusade was widespread in northern France; but if any place can be pinpointed as the birthplace of the Crusading army destined to cause such a sensation in history, it is the castle of Écri – the modern Asfeld-la-Ville in the Ardennes, on the river Aisne.

The lord of the castle, Tibald, count of Champagne, with his wife Blanche of Navarre, was holding a tournament there at the start of Advent in 1199.[3] An innovation of the eleventh century, the institution of the tournament was now at its height, and served as an excellent training exercise for 'chevaliers', men to whom the noblest activity in life was a fight on horseback. Tibald was the son of Mary, countess of Champagne, who had died not long before, and she herself was daughter to Louis VII of France and Eleanor of Aquitaine. Mary's court at Troyes, where Tibald must have spent much of his boyhood, was a centre of chivalry and the cult of knightly love. Perhaps as a youth Tibald knew the poet Chrétien de Troyes, a protégé of Mary's court, who wrote in the spirit of the Arthurian romances. In Chrétien's *Erec and Enide* that knight is chided who allows attachment to wife and family to take precedence over glory on the battlefield. Aged twenty-two, Tibald was now full of enthusiasm, and with him at the tournament was the twenty-seven-year-old count Louis de Blois. The two men were closely related: not only were their fathers brothers but their mothers sisters. Tibald's older brother Henry de Champagne, now dead, had taken part in the Third Crusade and had stood before Acre. He had been one of the last Christian rulers of Jerusalem. Moreover, Tibald and Louis were nephews of Richard of England, and men would know that they were grandsons of that great woman Eleanor of Aquitaine. Were the two young men stirred by the thought that it might be their role to take up the task which their famous uncle had been forced to leave half-completed? Richard himself had died at Chinon only six months earlier, from a wound received during a minor skirmish with a rebel vassal in the Limousin. If he had survived, it would have been difficult to envisage anyone else as the leader of the new Crusade.

HOMELANDS OF
THE FOURTH CRUSADE

R. Elbe

BRUNSWICK

Magdeburg •
Halberstadt •

Bruges •
• Ghent
FLANDERS
Béthune •
St. Pol • • Loos
Amiens • • Corbie
Boves • • Nesles
Compiègne •
Montmorency
• Paris
Montfort •   • Neuilly
Friaize •
Villehardouin •
Frouville •   Orleans •
Angers •   Blois •   • Bracieux
Chinon •

R. Rhine

Limburg •

• Katzenellenbogen

Avesnes •
• Bouillon
• Ecri
Soissons •

LORRAINE

CHAMPAGNE   ALSACE
Bar-le-Duc
Brienne •   • Hagenau
• Joinville
Troyes •   Langres •   SWABIA
Clairvaux •
• Champlitte

• Vézelay
• Citeaux
• Autun
• Cluny

AUVERGNE

BURGUNDY

R. Seine

R. Loire

ALPINE
ALPINE   RANGE
LOMBARDY

Le Puy •   • Pavia   Venice •
• Turin
• Piacenza

MONTFERRAT
PROVENCE

Marseilles •

During the Écri tournament both Tibald and Louis took the Cross, and many others followed suit.[4] We do not know that this was directly as a result of Fulk's preaching, and there is no evidence that Fulk was actually at the tournament, though this has been a conventional view of historians in modern times.[5] We can dismiss from our minds romantic notions of Fulk appearing like some medieval Telemachus in the arena, calling on the combatants to put their weapons to worthier uses. The fact is that Tibald and his companions took the Cross, and as a result the chivalry of France began to declare itself. The Crusade was also preached in western Germany, the main propagandist here being Martin, abbot of the Cistercian house of Pairis in the vale of Orbey, in Alsace. He failed to arouse any really popular enthusiasm, and was less successful than Fulk in inspiring the nobles.

The taking of a Crusading vow was no light matter, and it is difficult for the twentieth-century mind to grasp the sense of sanctity which attached to an oath in the early Middle Ages. The vow as such was regarded as part of natural law, and therefore inviolable. From the start of the Crusading movement there had of course been men who had lapsed, a notable case in the First Crusade being Count Stephen of Chartres and Blois, who, losing heart during the siege of Antioch, had returned home in 1098. So badly had he been received, not least by his grim wife (a daughter of William the Conqueror), that he had gone back to Palestine, there to complete his vow by praying in the Holy Sepulchre church and dying shortly afterwards in battle. There were many who took the Cross in a state of temporary enthusiasm, or even when they were in their cups, and later felt sorry for it. Fulcher of Chartres claimed that the armies of the First Crusade totalled only a tenth of all those who had actually taken the vow.[6] Defectors were in theory liable to excommunication, and the First Lateran Council in 1123 laid down that such men were to be refused admission to any church.

In essence, 'taking the Cross' was an undertaking to make a journey to the Holy Sepulchre church in Jerusalem, as a member of an armed expedition marching under papal supervision. A Crusader wore the Cross, at first rather informally, usually by sewing a small cloth cross on to his shoulder. No liturgical rite of Cross-taking is known for the First and Second Crusades, though one survives which seems to have been in use in connection with the Third. This earliest known text of a Cross-taking rite is in an Ely pontifical (the book of rites and ceremonies performed only by a bishop) of the latter years of the twelfth century, now in the library of Trinity College, Cambridge.[7] No elaborate ceremonial accompanied the rite, which consisted simply of the blessing and presentation of the Cross: 'Lord, bless this ensign of the holy Cross, that it may help forward the salvation of thy servant.'

By Innocent III's time the original spontaneous enthusiasm had declined, and there was a tendency for the role of Cross-soldier to be increasingly regulated by ecclesiastical prescriptions and obligations. He was still a 'pilgrim' (and is so referred to consistently by Villehardouin), though often with a less fervent sense of the Holy Sepulchre as the goal of his journey. Earlier, the solemn vow, made in the presence of witnesses before a person in holy orders, had been binding, and enforceable in the church courts. But by about 1200 there was a greater readiness to grant dispensations, for such causes as the poor fighting qualities of the devotee, or his financial inability to fulfil his vow. It was now possible to commute a Crusading vow by paying the expenses of some other Crusader. However, the vow as such was substantially intact, and in some respects even more stringent. For instance, Innocent decreed that a man might take the Cross without his wife's approval, which was something new. One remarkable provision, adopted from the old Roman law on votive obligations, was that an unfulfilled vow was hereditary and could be bequeathed by a man to his heir, and was enforceable by confiscation of inherited property. Only the pope or someone specifically authorized by him could dispense from the Crusading vow.[8]

Amongst high-ranking men who responded to the call were Simon de Montfort, lord of Montfort and Épernon since 1181, and Renaud de Montmirail, the brother of Henry, count of Nevers. The Champagne region produced, besides Tibald himself, Count Gautier de Brienne and Geoffrey de Villehardouin. Geoffrey had been born about 1150, the son of Vilain de Villehardouin, a man with lands in the neighbourhood of Troyes, Villehardouin itself being a village on the banks of the river Aube. By becoming marshal of Champagne in 1185, Geoffrey would assume duties which included the easing of quarrels between barons and making the necessary arrangements in the event of war. It is possible that he was himself a veteran of the Third Crusade, and it is likely that he had much to do with the mustering of the Crusaders following Innocent's call to arms. We infer that Geoffrey was not an especially devout man, from the lack of interest in the Church and papacy which is a feature of his Chronicle, and it is perhaps this factor which explains the failure of many more recent historians to appreciate the pietistic motivations and ecclesiastical background of the Fourth Crusade.

Those who took the Cross also included Geoffrey of Joinville, on the Marne, near Villehardouin. He was seneschal of Champagne, an office with largely ceremonial duties. His family had a strong Crusading tradition and he was joined in his vow by his brother Robert. Both these men were subsequently to defect, Robert to Apulia under Gautier de Brienne, and Geoffrey to Syria, where he was to be killed in battle in 1203. Geoffrey would be long remembered in his native land as a valiant soldier of the Cross, his shield hanging in St. Lawrence's church at Joinville. The Champagne contingent included Garnier de Trainel, bishop of Troyes, who had already in 1198 taken the Cross, obtained a papal dispensation, and now, impelled by the motives of militant Christianity, made his vow again. There was a good response in the territories controlled by Louis, count de Blois; and also in Fulk's old principal preaching-ground the Île-de-France, where those who came forward included the bishop of Soissons, Névelon de Chérisy. From the Île-de-France came also an old soldier of the Third Crusade, Matthew de Montmorency, with his nephew Guy, well known as a singer of popular lays.

Enthusiasm for the Crusade was strong in Flanders. In Bruges, on Ash Wednesday, 23 February 1200, Baldwin the ninth count of Flanders and sixth count of Hainault opened his Lenten devotions by taking the Cross.[9] Now twenty-eight years old, he had been count of Flanders since 1195, and though a feudal vassal of the French king, Philip Augustus, had given support to the two English rulers Richard and John in their wars against France. He was fond of warfare and had recently fought Philip with great energy, forcing him in January 1200 to make territorial concessions to Flanders. He was an uncomfortable neighbour for the French king who would not be sorry to see him go. Baldwin was also a patron of poets, and his piety is revealed by the many charters to monasteries which he issued between February 1200 and his actual departure on Crusade in April 1202. Most favoured by him were the Premonstratensians, but he was also attracted to the Cistercian abbey of Loos, whose abbot Simon was later to figure prominently in the Fourth Crusade. Baldwin's initial intention was to be absent on Crusade for three years.

He was joined in taking the Cross by his wife Mary, Tibald's sister. Baldwin had married her when she was twelve and he fourteen, after a betrothal in early childhood. In the event she did not join him when he set out in 1202 as she was awaiting the birth of a child, but remained at home as his regent. It was nearly two years after his departure before she eventually set out for the East, leaving her two young daughters behind.

The Cross was also taken by Baldwin's brother Henry, and his nephew Thierry, bastard son of Philip of Alsace, count of Flanders, who had crusaded in Palestine in 1177. Amongst others were Baldwin's relatives William, chief magistrate of Béthune, and William's brother Conon, a popular and established member of the school of musician-poets known as *trouvères*. Conon was an articulate speaker, and as such was to be of immense value to the Crusaders as a negotiator. Conon and William were the sons of Robert, who had died at the siege of Acre in 1191, and Conon, who was now about fifty years of age, had himself been present with his father in the Third Crusade. His Crusading songs show the conventional mingling of religious fervour with sadness at being obliged to leave behind one's beloved.[10] The Flemish contingent included the governor or castellan of Bruges, Jean de Nesles, and Renier de Trit; and there was also Jacques d'Avesnes, whose father of the same name had led the Flemish battlegroup in Richard Lion-Heart's army, dying a hero's death at Arsuf, his body being found surrounded by dead Saracens on the field after the battle. The Flemish element in the new Crusading army now assembling was strong, and during the spring of 1200 the town of Bruges was undoubtedly a busy recruiting centre, alive with interest in the Holy War.

After the Ash Wednesday Cross-taking by the leading men of Flanders in 1200, many lesser lords and knights committed themselves, men such as Count Hugh de St. Pol in Picardy, his near relative Peter d'Amiens and Count Geoffrey du Perche (cousin of Louis de Blois). In the contingent of Peter d'Amiens was a certain knight Robert, a vassal whose fief included Clari (the modern Cléry-lez-Pernois). Robert de Clari was accompanied by his brother Aleaumes, a priest, who was to prove to be one of the heroes of the campaign. Peter d'Amiens also brought with him a clerical brother, Thomas, a canon of Amiens cathedral.

Throughout 1200 there was a slow but steady response to the great call, and the prospects of a substantial army were improving. Very noticeable is the absence of any active participation by the crowned sovereigns of Western Europe, such as had marked the Second and Third Crusades. This probably suited Innocent's idea of a Crusade, as rulers like Philip Augustus and Richard Lion-Heart could not have been easy men with whom an autocratic pope might co-operate, and in any case the presence of two or more kings in an army told against unity of command and direction. Still less did a man with Innocent's sense of order and discipline want an untrained rabble. Upper-class and middle-ranking soldiers, with their respective contingents, feudal in outlook and generally steadfast in their loyalty to the Church and the Holy War, were well fitted for the role of pope's men. Meanwhile, Tibald, count of Champagne, was regarded by general consensus as leader of the enterprise. Though very young, he was at the heart of French chivalry, and above all nephew of the great Richard of England.

The assembling and organizing of the army was to proceed along customary Western medieval lines. At the start of the Crusading era, fighting forces had been broadly divided into *milites*, that is the mounted troops, and *pedites* or foot-soldiers. But by the closing years of the twelfth century the institution of knighthood had developed considerably, becoming a matter of birth, ceremony, and formal profession. The knight was now a 'gentleman'. He was not, however, the only mounted warrior, as there was also the mounted sergeant, 'serjans à cheval', in addition to the sergeant on foot. The sergeants did not in any way correspond to the sergeants of modern armies, but were tenants below the status of knighthood on a lord's estate, owing him military service by virtue of the land which they held. The knights and sergeants represented the offensive strength of a Western army of this period.

Armour was now heavier than previously. The hauberk was in two pieces, a chain-mail tunic reaching to the knees, and a chain-mail garment resembling a closely-fitting pair of trousers. There was usually a hood covering the neck and head; and carried by a strap over the right shoulder was the shield of wood, elm being especially favoured, covered with leather, and kite- or oblong-shaped, though smaller than a century before. Over the hauberk was worn the surcoat, which protected the mail from sun and weather, and also, by the time of the Fourth Crusade, displayed the armorial bearings of the wearer, especially necessary with the frequent displacement of the old nasal helmet by a new protective piece for the head known as the helm. This was a large cylindrical helmet with a slit for the eyes, and small breathing-holes. The ordinary foot-soldiers, as indeed some of the mounted sergeants, were by this time beginning to wear a round helmet not unlike the famous 'tin hats' of the British armies of the two World Wars. The chief weapons of the mounted troops by about 1200 were the lance and sword, the former being bigger and heavier than the earlier spear (which could be thrown as a missile). In feudal armies the main tactical advantage was the cavalry charge, though the Fourth Crusade was in the event to offer little scope in this respect. There was nothing the Saracen or Byzantine feared more than the initial charge of a Frankish force of mailed cavalry; this was the moment when the Western knight thrilled to the joy of battle. But there were always many foot-soldiers, armed with spears and bows, their main functions being to break up or at least hinder an enemy cavalry charge and to serve as a protecting wall for their own cavalry. On the march it was usual for the foot-soldiers to precede the mounted troops.

There is not much evidence as to how military expeditions were fitted out and supplied at this time, though we know that each knight and sergeant would be expected to produce his own weapons and personal equipment; the time had not arrived when kings or central governments equipped their armies. If maritime transport had to be contracted, each man would be called on to pay his fare. He received no wages, but could hope for booty. A captured city, especially if it had put up a stiff resistance, might expect to be looted, and the massacre of prisoners and even non-combatants was not contrary to the rules. As for food and provisions, it was the usually accepted practice for an army, if necessary, to live off the country. Fulcher of Chartres, writing of the First Crusade, describes food looted from farms as 'gifts of God's mercy'. Warfare for the peasant or citizen meant utter misery, but it was regarded nonetheless as a fact of life. Crusaders were soldiers dedicated to Christ, but the elimination of poverty and wretchedness from men's lives was not seen in the Middle Ages as one of the functions of Christianity.

An army in early medieval Western Europe was usually small by modern standards, 20,000 men constituting a sizeable force, divided into battle-groups or divisions. The commanders would have no 'staff', and there does not generally appear to have been much sense of any strategical approach to a campaign. Problems were confronted as they arose, and particular situations reacted to, and this attitude must constantly be borne in mind when following the course of the Fourth Crusade. Commanders tended to be opportunists rather than men actuated by grand designs. In the divisions would be the barons, each bringing his knights and sergeants with him. Villehardouin names almost a hundred leading men as being members of the assembling forces, though there are probably some whom he has missed or forgotten. Perhaps Peter d'Amiens's baronial contingent, with its ten knights and sixty sergeants, was not untypical.

The idea of the Crusade was safely launched and a promising start had been made in recruitment, but it was necessary for the participants to decide what to do next. Accordingly, two conferences of the Crusaders were held, in the spring and summer of 1200. The first was held at Soissons, the seat of bishop Névelon, which appears to have served as the headquarters of the Crusade during this preparatory period. The subjects for discussion at Soissons were the date on which the expedition should set out and its actual destination. Both matters were deferred, as it seemed that the army so far was too small for any serious plans to be laid. Perhaps a fair estimate is that about 10,000 men had been sworn, though more were expected. In two months' time another conference was held, a larger gathering at which all the nobles who had taken the Cross were present. It did not meet in Soissons, however, but in Compiègne, twenty-five miles to the west. Why was there this change in location for the second conference? The question raises a consideration which has commonly been overlooked by students of the Fourth Crusade.

Compiègne was not the seat of a bishopric as was Soissons, though it did have an abbey containing one of the most important relics in France, an ancient shroud of Christ. It is possible that this shroud was one seen in Jerusalem by the seventh-century Gallic bishop Arculf, who was later to visit Iona during the abbacy of Adamnan to whom he spoke of the shroud, which was also mentioned some years later by Bede. Compiègne abbey, which possessed its shroud from the later years of the ninth century, may well have acquired it from the East through the agency of the Carolingian emperors. The fact is that from about 900 onwards it attracted large streams of pilgrims and devotees. What more natural than that Christ's armed pilgrims, about to embark on the most solemn and perilous journey, should make a preliminary pilgrimage here, and fortify their resolution in the proximity of such a relic? In effect, therefore, the conference at Compiègne took place in the context of a dedicatory pilgrimage.[11]

But despite such an inspiring location, there was much argument at Compiègne, and again no agreement was reached.[12] A committee of six was therefore appointed, with full delegated authority, confirmed by sealed charters, to make all the necessary arrangements for getting the Crusade into motion. The six men were to negotiate as though they themselves were the very barons, who agreed unreservedly to abide by whatever arrangements they made. Two delegates each were nominated by Tibald, Baldwin, and Louis de Blois. One of Tibald's nominees was Geoffrey de Villehardouin, marshal of Champagne; and it is the fact that Geoffrey was close to the seat of authority which makes so valuable the Chronicle which he subsequently produced.

Naturally, it was taken for granted at this stage that the purpose of the expedition was to fight Islam and regain the Holy Places. The question at issue was how this might best be done, and particularly how the army was to get to the Levant. The six delegates discussed the matter, and agreed that an approach should be made to Venice, where 'they might hope to find a larger number of ships than at any other port'.[13] The important factor here is that the traditional overland route through the Balkans and Asia Minor was now too hazardous owing to the decline of the power of Byzantium. The Vlachs and Bulgarians had made conditions for Balkan travel very dangerous; and since the Myriokephalon disaster the Byzantine Empire had lost most of Anatolia to the Turks, keeping a precarious hold only on the coastlands. A Crusading force which attempted the old land march would run the risk of arriving in Syria, from the north, too battered to be of much use. The difficulty experienced by Frederick Barbarossa in getting his Germans through the Balkans and Asia Minor was fresh in men's minds. The only forces of the Third Crusade to fight effectively in the Holy Land had been those of the English and French, who arrived by sea. The six delegates were sure to know, too, that in the Second Crusade Louis VII, after his army's bitter experiences in getting across part of Asia Minor by the coastal route from Constantinople, had been forced eventually to hire ships from the Byzantines to enable them to complete the journey to Syria by sea.

It is likely that the Crusading leaders had already decided in principle on a sea voyage rather than a land journey, and of course they were not entirely without ships. Baldwin, count of Flanders, one of the three principal leaders at this stage, had a fleet, but only large enough to transport his own Flemish troops. A sea-borne expedition for the Crusade was necessary not least because of the increasingly held view that the right place to attack the infidel was in Egypt, which was both his principal power-base and the area where he might be brought to a decisive battle. The Crusaders must have longed to do to the Turks what the Turks themselves had done to the Byzantines at Manzikert and Myriokephalon. The nature of the land in Egypt, without mountains or forests (the bane of the Balkans as far as Crusading armies were concerned), would make a guerrilla type of resistance difficult. Richard of England had accepted the 'Egyptian' doctrine on abandoning his Palestine expedition, and this fact was bound to carry weight with his young nephew Tibald, the acknowledged leader of the new campaign. Villehardouin does not say that the barons actually decided to attack Egypt during their Compiègne discussions, and it appears that this was simply one of the various alternatives brought forward, the final resolution to make for Egypt being made by the Committee of Six. Certainly it was the Committee which took the fateful decision to approach Venice for the provision of ships, as is stated specifically by Villehardouin, himself one of the six. 'After talking it over among themselves they agreed unanimously' that Venetian transport would be necessary.[14]

The delegates, Geoffrey de Villehardouin, Milon de Brébant, Conon de Béthune, Alard Maquereau, Jean de Friaize, and Gautier de Gaudonville, set out on horseback,[15] their arduous and tedious journey doubtless enlivened by songs from the trouvère Conon de Béthune. Crossing the Alps by way of the Mont Cenis pass in the depth of winter, they arrived in Venice, after many delays, very early in the spring of 1201.

They were received hospitably by Enrico Dandolo, Doge of Venice since 1193. Dandolo was a shrewd man, accustomed to think with care about any proposal put to him, and when he was told that the letters of introduction carried by the envoys empowered them to act fully at their own discretion on behalf of Tibald,

Baldwin, and Louis, three of the most influential magnates of Western Europe, his attention was at once alerted.[16] The Crusaders had made their first and fundamental mistake, in fact, in giving an open-handed commission to the delegates to act for them (though this would be in accordance with general Western practice at the time), the chief barons ratifying their decisions in advance. To Dandolo this must have seemed almost too good to be true.

The delegates addressed the doge: 'We respectfully ask you to convene your Council tomorrow, so that we may put before it our lords' proposals.' But Dandolo prevaricated and insisted on waiting four days, as being the minimum time in which he could summon his Council. The delegates artlessly agreed, and Dandolo probably used the time for an intensive sounding of views amongst leading Venetians, not necessarily only those on the Inner Council. The Council would therefore be mentally and psychologically prepared when they met the six visitors. The meeting was duly held on the fourth day, in the doge's palace, and the delegates delivered their message. 'The great barons of France have taken the Cross, to avenge the insult offered to Our Lord and to retake Jerusalem . . . in God's name have pity on Outremer, and provide us with a fleet of war vessels and transports.' They promised that the necessary conditions would be fulfilled and the expenses borne. According to the interview as recorded by Villehardouin, who was present in person, the doge demurred, and said that the barons were asking Venice to support what was clearly going to be a great undertaking. He and his Council would need a week in which to consider it.[17] In his mind was probably the capability of the Arsenal, the state-controlled shipyard, to take on the work of constructing the necessary fleet. There were unlikely to be any insuperable difficulties, for the Arsenal was an efficient institution, well stocked with timber and maritime spare parts, and accustomed to producing vessels to order for specific purposes.[18]

After a week the delegates again met the doge in his palace, and there was a long discussion, Villehardouin saying that it was impossible to include in his account everything that was said;[19] a disappointment because it would be interesting to know more. Why did the envoys not receive a prompt and straightforward answer to an unambiguous request? One suspects that not only did Dandolo skilfully and patiently lead them to the admission that they would find the Venetian transports quite indispensable, but also that he adroitly flattered them to the point at which they convinced themselves that their Crusading army was going to be very large and imposing. He then put his offer (subject to the final approval of the Republic) to the six envoys. The Venetians would construct transports sufficient for 4,500 horses and 9,000 squires, as well as for 4,500 knights and 20,000 foot sergeants with their equipment. The formal contract would include food enough for the whole army over a period of nine months, and fodder for the horses. The fee was to be five marks for each horse and two marks per man. The ships would be available for one year, dating from the day on which the expedition set sail from Venice. The total cost was put at 85,000 silver marks (the mark was not strictly a coin, but an 8 oz. weight of gold or silver). Over and above this, the Republic would add to the expedition fifty armed warships, on condition that it took half of all conquests (territories or booty). It was essentially a business deal, precise, practical, and aimed at profit.

The envoys said they would discuss the offer and give their reply the next day. Such haste in deciding a matter of immense importance compares unfavourably with the long care and deliberation on which the Venetians had for their part insisted. The envoys decided in favour of the contract after talking it over during the evening, and gave their acceptance to the doge on the following morning. The six men had thus committed the Crusading leaders and barons to the financing of an enormous fleet, before being quite sure that the Crusading army would be large enough to justify it. At the Soissons conference in the previous year there had been misgivings over what was considered the slow rate of recruitment. And yet it could have been none other than the envoys themselves who suggested, or who were gently coaxed into suggesting, the figure of 33,500 men, on the assumption that eventually this number would assemble in Venice. As in the end nothing like this number was to appear, we must conclude that the envoys calculated badly, or did not allow for the large numbers of Crusaders who might be expected not to turn up at all. This miscalculation was to prove fatal, and the saddling of the Crusade with the burden of paying for an unnecessarily large fleet goes far to explain the forthcoming chain of events. Yet nowhere in Villehardouin's narrative is there as much as a hint that possibly he and his colleagues had acted thoughtlessly in assenting to so big a commitment.

Indeed, Villehardouin almost gives the impression that he believes the Venetians to have been outwitted. On the day after that of the envoys' acceptance of the proposals, Dandolo met his Great Council, some forty men, and quietly and patiently brought them round to the scheme.[20] This suggests some scepticism in the Great Council, doubts being felt concerning the ability of the barons to pay for the ships. Dandolo must have shared these doubts. But were there other schemes and possibilities already turning in his mind? He perhaps guessed that the envoys had seriously miscalculated, or realized that he had tricked them, and was sufficiently informed about the northern French to know that they would be unlikely to raise at this stage an army of well over 30,000 men. He could turn the envoys' mistake to his own advantage.

The consent of the people still had to be obtained, and, in the true spirit of an Italian city-republic, the *arengo* or popular assembly was called out. Thousands of excited people thronged St. Mark's basilica – 'the finest church in existence', says Villehardouin. A mass of the Holy Spirit was sung. The doge then invited the delegates from the West to ask the people for approval of their proposals. At the request of his colleagues Geoffrey de Villehardouin was the spokesman. He declared that they came from the greatest barons of France, and called on the Venetians to join with them in regaining Jerusalem. 'Help us to avenge the injury done to Our Lord!' The assistance of Venice, he said, was essential because of its maritime strength. The crowd was deeply moved, and a great shout went up, 'We consent! we consent!' Says Villehardouin, 'Such was the uproar that it seemed as if the earth was shuddering.' Dandolo then spoke, urging the Venetians to support the scheme. The intention that the expedition should in the first instance make for Cairo was not mentioned, and the impression was maintained that the aim of the Crusade was simply to recover Outremer.[21] The formal agreements were signed and sealed by the representatives of both sides on the following day, in late March or early April 1201. The destination of the expedition was left vague, Egypt not being specifically mentioned in the treaty.[22]

Messengers were next sent to Innocent III for his approval of the compact, which was given with some reservations. Villehardouin claims that the pope gave his 'very willing' approval, 'mult volentiers'.[23] But actually Innocent was none too happy about any arrangement made with Venice, whose whole-hearted commitment to the Holy War he distrusted, and whom he suspected of ulterior designs. He would have preferred Genoa and Pisa to have provided the Crusaders' transport. In granting his approval, early in May, he was significantly insistent that the Crusade should never turn its attack on Christians, except such as might obstruct its journey, or when there was some other reasonable cause, and then only by leave of the papal legate accompanying it. In view of these qualifications the Venetians on their part decided to take no notice of the papal confirmation of the treaty. But in fact by his saving clause, that Christians should not be attacked except when there was a 'just and essential reason', Innocent had left the door ajar for Crusaders in the final analysis to disregard their strict vows to fight only Muslims, should they ever consider it absolutely necessary.[24]

The great Crusade as planned by Innocent was never envisaged as an expedition arranged in this way by French lords and Venetians, acting independently of the Church's authority. But Innocent was a realist, and thankful that after the somewhat lukewarm response to his initial call, plans were now taking positive shape and a force was in being which he could accept as his army. On 5 May 1201 he wrote to the English bishops advising them that Englishmen who had taken the Cross must now prepare to join the army of the counts of Flanders, Champagne, and Blois.[25] We do not know of any Englishmen who did so, though of course the argument from silence is always dangerous. It is quite possible that some individual English knights did make the Channel crossing to join the Flemish and French, though significantly Villehardouin does not include amongst the numerous names which he gives those of any Englishmen. Innocent also wrote to the French bishops, and on 8 May he wrote to the clergy of Venice, calling on them to give financial help to the Crusade.

The envoys arranged that the Crusading army should assemble in Venice by mid-summer (on St. John Baptist's day, 24 June) of the following year, 1202, by which time the promised ships would be ready. Meanwhile their construction had to begin, so the envoys raised a loan of 2,000 silver marks in the city and paid this money in advance to the doge, as an earnest of their good intentions.[26] On the basis of great expectations, the six men had virtually sold the baronage of crusading France and Flanders to the merchants of Venice.

After handing over the initial payment, the Franks left Venice and arrived at the Lombard city of Piacenza. Here Villehardouin and Alard Maquereau separated from their companions and made their way straight home to France, while the other four broke their journey to visit Pisa and Genoa a little further south, to explore the possibilities of finding help for the Crusade in those regions also. In view of the comprehensive and substantial assistance negotiated with Venice, it could not have been ships that they wanted from the Pisans and Genoese. Indeed, according to Robert de Clari, the six delegates had already asked Genoa and Pisa, unsuccessfully, for transport before approaching Venice.[27] It is difficult to understand what the four men might have been now seeking. The Pisans and Genoese would not easily have been persuaded to join a venture in which they would be allies of their deadly rivals, the Venetians. It is possible that the six delegates had heard of an interest in the Crusade being shown by Boniface, marquis of Montferrat. Boniface's brother Rainier had been married to the emperor Manuel's daughter, receiving Thessalonica as his personal estate. Boniface therefore had strong family connections with the East, and it might be that he saw in the forthcoming Crusade a means by which he could now secure Thessalonica for himself. The delegates may have wanted to learn more about Boniface's ideas on the Crusade.

While crossing the Alps through the Mont Cenis pass into Burgundy, Villehardouin met a group of men who had taken the Cross and were making their way into Italy. One of them, Count Gautier de Brienne, was taking the chance offered by the journey to ride down to Apulia to assume possession of some lands belonging to his wife, daughter of Tancred the last Norman king of Sicily, whom he had married recently. The party, which included Robert de Joinville, expressed their delight on hearing from the envoy of the agreement reached with the Venetians, and assured him that they would join the army as soon as it assembled at Venice. In the event they failed to do so and, writing many years afterwards, Villehardouin records his regret, as they were good men and brave soldiers.[28] The incident causes us to wonder just how much of the original enthusiasm had waned and how many vows had quietly been forgotten during the delegates' absence in Italy. In this particular case Innocent III was actually aware of the circumstances and had given his approval to Gautier's expedition. Count Gautier, who was popular in knightly circles, attracted many adventurous young men to his side, and it was while on his way to join him that Francis of Assisi heard at Spoleto the call to more spiritual enterprises. In the autumn of 1201 Gautier de Brienne duly achieved his aims in southern Italy.

Meanwhile Villehardouin arrived home in Champagne, where he was met by a critical situation. At Troyes the leader of the army, Count Tibald, was ill and depressed. When he was told of the treaty arranged with the Venetians, so improved did his spirits become that he even went out riding, something he had

1. Enamelled book cover, with Christ in Majesty. Limoges, late twelfth century. The stern and militant side of Christianity is made evident.

Within the painted fresco, the following inscriptions appear:

Innoceti   .PP. III.

✠ INNOCENTIVS EPS SERVVS SERVORV DI. DILECTIS FILIIS IOHI PRIORI ET FRI
SPECV BEATI BENEDICTI REGLARE VITA SERVANTIBVS IN PAP III. INTER HOLOC
VIRTVTV NVLLV MAGIS EST MEDVLLATV QVA QD OFFERTVR ALTISSIMO DE PING
CARITATIS. HOC IGIT ATTENDENTES. CV OLI CAVSA DEVOTIONIS ACCESSISSEM AD LOCV
VRE QVE BEATVS BENEDICT SVE CONVERSIONIS PRIMORDIO CONSECRAVIT. ET IVENISSEM VOS IN
INSTITVTIONE IPIVS LAVDABILITER DNO FAMVLANTES. NE PRO TEPORALIS SVBSTENTATI
SPIRITVALIS OBSERVANTIE DISCIPLINA TORPERET. APOSTOLICV VOBIS SVBSIDIV IMP
IMPENDENDV. SPERANTES QD IDE BEATISSIM BENEDICT NRE DEVOTIONIS AFFECTV
ET PRECIB APVD PIISSIMV PATRE ET IVSTISSIMV IVDICE COMMDABIT. VRE ITAQ
NECESSITATIB PVIDERE. SEX LIBRAS VSVALIS MONETE VOBIS ET SVCCESSORIB V
CAMERA BEATI PETRI SINGVLIS ARNIS PCIPIENDAS CONCESSIM. DONEC IDALINO CER
VOBIS ESSENT VTILITER ASSIGNATE. STATVENTES VT EA QVE ADSVSTENTATIONE VR
SVEVISTIS PCIPERE DE MONASTERIO SVBLACEN. VOBIS ETSVCCESSORIB VRIS P
MINIME NEGARENTVR. POSTMODV AVTE CV REVERSI FVISSEM ADVRBE QVOSD
VRIS AD NRAM PRESENTIA DESTINASTIS HVMILITER IMPLORANTES. VT CONC
IPSA IN ALIQVO CERTO LOCO DIGNAREMVR PPETVO STABILIRE. DE QVO PRET
SEX LIBRAS PCIPERE VALERETIS. DOS IGITVR HABITO FRATRV NRORV CONS
ASSENSV. IA DICTAS SEX LIBRAS VOBIS ET SVCCESSORIB VRIS PCIPIENDAS SI
ANNIS DE ARNVO CENSV CASTRI PORTIANI CONCEDIM ET CONCESSIONE IPSA
PRIVILEGIO CONFIRMAM. NVLLI ERGO OMNINO HOMINV LICEAT HANC PAGINA
CONCESSIONIS ET CONSTITVTIONIS INFRINGERE VEL EI AVSV TEMERARIO
IRE. SIQVIS AVTE HOC ATTEPTARE PRESVPSERIT. INDIGNATIONE OMNIP
ET BEATORV PETRI ET PAVLI APOSTOLORV EIVS SE NOVERIT INCVRTVRAME

2. Innocent III. Not a true likeness, but the youthfulness of the pope at the time of his accession is clear. Church of St. Speco, Subiaco.

3a. The swarthy Manuel I Comnenus and his wife Maria of Antioch.

3b. Either Isaac II or Alexius III is shown in this marble roundel of a late twelfth-century Byzantine emperor.

4a. Fulk preaches the Crusade in France; an illustration from Villehardouin's *Conquest of Constantinople*.

4b. A Crusader takes the cross.

4c. The text of part of the earliest known cross-taking rite, from the Ely Pontifical, written in England in the twelfth century.

4d. The Crusaders attack Constantinople by land and by sea, from the Bodleian copy of Villehardouin's narrative.

not attempted for some time. But he died shortly afterwards, on 24 May 1201. There is no knowing what calibre as a fighting leader Tibald might have shown had he survived, but he was certainly in the finest tradition of French chivalry. He was respected and highly regarded by all, and his unexpected death came as a blow to the venture.

In an attempt to find a new leader, an approach was made to Eudes, duke of Burgundy, though he was not amongst those who had taken the Cross. His father Hugh had participated in the Third Crusade, and Eudes himself was later to be one of the Albigensian Crusaders. His ancestors had fought the Moors in Spain. He was a powerful nobleman with an exceptionally strong following of knights,[29] but he declined the offer of the leadership, as did Count Tibald of Bar-le-Duc, cousin of the deceased Tibald.

A further conference was therefore held towards the end of June at the Soissons 'headquarters', those present including Baldwin of Flanders and Louis de Blois, and it was decided, after much argument and difference of opinion, to write to Boniface, marquis of Montferrat. Villehardouin told the conference, 'If you were to invite him to join us and take the Cross, and assume the position of the late count of Champagne, with full command of the army, I can assure you that he would accept your offer without a moment's hesitation.'[30] These words make it perfectly clear that Villehardouin himself knew of an ambition in this direction on Boniface's part. And indeed Boniface did not need much persuading to accept the invitation. He was one of the most notable men of Western Europe, and a good soldier. He was 'well connected', a cousin of the king of France, Philip Augustus, who indeed was himself in favour of the appointment. Boniface came of a Crusading family, his father William having died in the cause of the Holy Land. Of his brothers, Rainier had been the ill-fated son-in-law of the Byzantine emperor Manuel, while Conrad, after a period as commander of the imperial army under Isaac II, had become a Crusader in Palestine and ultimately titular king of Jerusalem.

Boniface was more experienced than the other leaders, being about fifty years old, though he himself had never served on Crusade. One has the impression that in thinking nostalgically, in middle age, of his family connection, he was suddenly fired with an interest in Eastern affairs. But though a man of high chivalry, a lover of troubadours and the courtly life, he did not regard Crusading in a religious light. The inclusion of Boniface in the Crusade was in some ways an original move, by introducing a north Italian element which widened the scope of the army's composition, but it dealt a blow to its unity of spirit, based as this was in the first instance on the baronage and knighthood of northern France and Flanders. Moreover, the house of Montferrat was on close terms with the Hohenstaufens, and this would not endear Boniface to the pope, who disliked Philip of Swabia and indeed began to have his first serious misgivings as soon as the marquis of Montferrat joined the Crusade.[31]

Boniface duly arrived at Soissons in August 1201, calling on Philip Augustus of

France in the course of his journey, and at a meeting of the barons held in the gardens of Notre Dame abbey he agreed, after some demur, to become the leader.[32] 'He gave way to their entreaties, and assumed command of the army.' At once Névelon, bishop of Soissons, accompanied by Fulk of Neuilly and two Cistercian monks in Boniface's own company, escorted him into the abbey church, where they made him a Crusader by attaching a cross to his shoulder. On the very next day Boniface left Soissons, telling the barons to begin their final preparations. Their general point of assembly would be Venice.

Making his way to Burgundy, Boniface took the opportunity to attend the annual Chapter General of the Cistercian Order at Citeaux, on 14 September.[33] Not only numerous abbots, making their obligatory attendance, but also barons and lesser lay-folk were thronging the place (sixteen miles south of Dijon) for this great annual occasion in French social and ecclesiastical life. Fulk was there, still busily urging men to leave all for Christ and his Holy Sepulchre. Whereas three years earlier, at his appearance at the 1198 Chapter, Fulk had been unsuccessful in gaining Cistercian support for his preaching, this time he secured for the Crusade the services of several abbots. Guy, abbot of Vaux-de-Cernay near Paris, vowed his support, as did Simon abbot of Loos in the Tournai diocese, and Peter abbot of the Piedmontese house of Lucedio. Simon was to attach himself to the contingent of Baldwin, Peter to Boniface. But despite these encouragements there was already some decline in the earlier enthusiasm, even amongst the Cistercians. Evidence for this is that the 1201 Chapter ordered the abbot of Citeaux to enquire into the matter of some lay brothers or 'conversi' from the Orleans house of La Cour-Dieu, who had taken the Cross and then returned to their abbey. A little earlier, in June, the pope had written to Cistercian abbots in general, ordering them to ensure that all men who had taken the Cross should faithfully fulfil their vows, a reference no doubt to men on their monastic estates or within their areas of influence.

Although it would be a vast exaggeration to say that Citeaux was the power-house of the Fourth Crusade, the Chapter General of September 1201 does mark an important point in the mounting of the enterprise. Several Cistercians were to go with the Crusade, and the Chapter of 1202 would decree that abbots with the army were to be exempt from the normal requirement of attendance at annual Chapter. Not only abbots but ordinary monks also went. The names of such men are not usually preserved, but we do know of two Clairvaux brethren, Hugh and Artandus, who were subsequently to return laden with relics from Constantinople.[34]

One result of this concentrated enthusiasm in September 1201 at the Citeaux Chapter was the accession to the Crusade of many noble Burgundians. About the same time Gautier, bishop of Autun, took the Cross, bringing into the movement a useful force of knights from Auvergne. Knights from Provence were also joining the Crusade, receiving their crosses and solemn benedictions from the priests; there was no man who did not realize that once he had left for the Holy War the chances were heavily against his ever seeing his home again. There also seems to have been a strong family element in the enlistment, brother joining brother and son joining father.

After the Cistercian Chapter, Boniface did not return at once to Montferrat but made his way to Germany to the court of Philip of Swabia, his feudal lord and personal friend. The purpose of the visit must almost certainly have been to discuss the forthcoming expedition, perhaps with a view to securing more German recruits. The court at this time was at Hagenau in Alsace, and here Boniface was to spend most of the winter of 1201–2. What designs, if any, were to be formed at the Swabian court during these months we shall never know, but there are grounds for suspicion that Boniface was harbouring ambitious thoughts; and the fact that on being elected commander-in-chief he so quickly made for the Hohenstaufen court, instead of busying himself personally with the organizing of the army, is significant.

Chapter 6

Venice Looks to the East

Venice had its origins in the old Roman mainland province of Venetia, with its many fine cities, notably Aquileia;[1] and when the entire region suffered during the barbarian invasions of the fifth century, it was on the sandbanks or *lidi* off the Adriatic shore that the men who fled from the Goths and Huns found safety. The refugees at first expected their exile to be temporary, but as the prospect of a return to their mainland home receded, a State of Venice gradually emerged, a second Venetia living on and protected by the sea. Cassiodorus, minister of the Ostrogoth king Theodoric early in the sixth century, noted the propensity of the Venetians for seafaring. The Venetians owned many vessels, which 'fear not the stormy winds. They come home safely to port, nor do they ever founder, they who time after time set sail from shore.'[2]

With the collapse of the Western Roman provinces and the rise of a distinctively 'Byzantine' Empire, Venice tended to look eastwards. In his sixth-century Italian wars the emperor Justinian made use of Venetian ships to transport Byzantine troops, and in 584 the emperor Maurice, worried by the Lombard invasion of northern Italy, formally recognized the Venetian State and took it under his protection. The early lagoon settlements thus became part of the Eastern Empire, and early Venetian history was to be powerfully influenced by the spirit and culture of Byzantium.

Each of the small communities, such as Torcello, Burano, Heraclea, Rialto, was ruled by its elected tribune. There were attempts at federation, but it was not until late in the seventh century that real unity of the islands was achieved, with an overall *dux* subject to the emperor at Constantinople. The first *dux*, Paulo Lucio Anafesta, who came from the now vanished Heraclea, was elected in 697, the Venetian Republic making its earliest formal treaty, with the Lombards, during his rule. The connection with Constantinople was meanwhile maintained, and Venice supported the emperor Leo III in the iconoclastic campaign which angered Rome. In the eighth century the Republic acquired one of the less attractive habits of Byzantine political life, a predilection for blindings, and three doges in succession were overthrown by their enemies and deprived of their sight. In 814, during the dogeship of Angelo Partecipazio, the seat of government was finally established in the island known as Rialto, on which the present city stands.

There have been romantic notions about the freedom-loving Venetians, and Wordsworth in bewailing the extinction of the Republic many centuries later could call Venice 'the eldest Child of liberty'. But in fact the Venetian Republic was not, save in its very early stages, 'democratic', and though the dogeship had settled down by the eleventh century as an elective, not an hereditary, office, it was the aristocratic merchant families which were to become the ruling factor in Venetian society. From one or other of these families the doge was invariably chosen.[3] But during the twelfth century the powers of the doge came to be circumscribed, theoretically by the 'commune' but in reality by the inner and greater Councils, which certainly existed by about 1185. Nonetheless, the doge was a splendid figure. In early days, for example, for his headdress he wore only a plain circlet of gold, but this had been elaborated into a bejewelled golden crown by 1200. The famous *corno* or ducal cap came into use only during the thirteenth century, and it is not known to have been worn by Enrico Dandolo. After 1204, in imitation of the Byzantine emperor, the doge wore red shoes. It was in the thirteenth century that the colourful processions made familiar by the paintings of Gentile Bellini first became part of the Venetian scene, and the doge came to be regarded as the symbolic centre of the Republic and guardian of the State relic, the body of St. Mark. The *arengo*, or popular assembly, was convened on certain occasions, especially when some highly important matter affecting the Republic was under discussion.

The fortunes of Venice were from the start founded on that natural element which today threatens to destroy them, the sea. The islands were difficult to conquer from the mainland, and throughout their history the men of Venice retained that feeling for independence from foreign interference which often characterizes seafaring peoples. At first the Venetians found a livelihood by fishing, but their ambitions grew and it was to Venice's advantage that the ancient city of Aquileia, like Ravenna, was in decline. The latter, formerly the headquarters of the Roman Adriatic fleet, by medieval times had a silted harbour. Venice eventually won control of the Adriatic by defeating the Arabs, and by the year 1000 had established a line of trading stations along the Dalmatian coast, at Zara, Veglia, and other ports. A reason for the Venetian Republic's success was that more than any other State it understood the importance of geography in politics and commerce. The Venetians were to develop an unerring eye for good harbours, trade routes, and strategic islands. They always knew just how much of an area it was necessary to occupy, and they were not interested in conquest for its own sake. The islands of the lagoons themselves were largely unproductive of food, most of which had to be imported, and it was by commerce that the Republic lived.

The Venetians crossed the Alps to transact business with the rising merchants of Germany, but it was especially seaborne traffic which interested them, the more so as they tended to look eastwards rather than to the west or north.[4] The Republic traded with Alexandria and regarded the Egyptian connection as vital.

The Syrian ports, and Cyprus, became increasingly accustomed to Venetian merchants and their warehouses or *fondaci*. In Constantinople, Venice was already well established by the tenth century, and it was then that she began the process which eventually was to oust the Byzantines from the carrying-trade between East and West. During the eleventh and twelfth centuries the Venetians founded trading settlements throughout the Eastern Empire, outstripping other Italians despite strong opposition from Pisa and Genoa, and maintaining an independent attitude to Byzantium itself. They were in a secure position at Adrianople, a hundred miles north-west of Constantinople. In the immediate sea-approaches to the Byzantine capital, Venetian merchants were actively engaged at Abydos and Rodosto, and on the western coast of Asia Minor they were at Sardis, capital of the ancient kingdom of Lydia. With other Latins, they had their own quarter in the great Macedonian port of Thessalonica. The Venetians had footholds in many towns and ports in the Greek peninsula, and also in such islands as Euboea, Andros, and Lemnos. Venetian traders had early sailed to the Black Sea and the Sea of Azov, an area which few other Italians were to reach until after 1204. The Venetian colonial Empire was beginning to take shape.

Though by the twelfth century Venice was a great commercial centre, she did not produce much on her own account, the only significant exports being glass and brocaded work. There was some local production, but it was above all as middlemen and entrepreneurs that her citizens excelled, dealing in such commodities as English woollens destined for the East and oriental silks on their way to the markets of Western Europe.

The formal relationship with the Byzantine Empire lasted until about the year 1000, and in artistic matters Venice's affinities remained with Byzantium. In her Church loyalties she was Catholic and Western: her liturgical rite was of the Roman family, not the Orthodox. A striking instance of Venetian Romanism occurred in the twelfth century, during a famous quarrel between Frederick Barbarossa and Pope Alexander III. Frederick proclaimed an anti-pope of his own, Victor IV, but Venice brought her naval forces to the support of Rome, with decisive results. The emperor and Alexander met personally in St. Mark's in Venice during 1177 to settle their differences, and to mark this visit and the resulting 'Pactum' of Venice the pope presented Doge Sebastiano Ziani with a ceremonial sword. In recognition of Venetian loyalty Alexander III formally invested the Republic with the lordship of the seas, a status which was symbolized by the annual ceremony known as the 'Espousal of the Adriatic'. The ceremony itself was still older, going back to a series of sweeping victories by Doge Peter Orseolo II over Adriatic pirates around the year 1000, and the establishment of Venetian influence along the Dalmatian coast with its valuable ports, such as Zara. These successes had justified the doge in assuming the title 'dux Dalmatiae', but the official recognition by the papacy of the claim and the ceremony which symbolized it were of high value to the Republic and, moreover, had the effect of keeping her closely within the Catholic fold, though the Venetians were to maintain an independent attitude to the papacy. The ceremony, which took place annually on Ascension Day, included the sailing out to sea by the doge in his State barge, later known as the *Bucentaur,* and culminated in his casting a ring into the waters, reciting the words, 'we espouse thee, O Sea, as a sign of our lasting dominion over thee'.[5]

The Venetians prized their trade with the Eastern Empire, not least because of the civilized traditions which formed the background to Byzantine affairs. The Empire maintained a sound coinage, and this was a matter of immense importance to men of business. The earliest chrysobull (golden bull), or formal document, granting a commercial concession to Venice was to Doge Peter Orseolo II, from the emperor Basil II in 992. Peter sent his elder son to be educated at the Byzantine court, and then saw him married to the emperor's great-niece. The Venetian Republic long maintained excellent relations with the Byzantine Empire, and there was a succession of chrysobulls which usually stipulated that Venetian vessels should be available as imperial transports when needed, and which had the result, unforeseen by the Byzantines, of increasing Venice's maritime power. When Alexius (1081–1118) was toiling on almost every front to save the Empire from destruction, the Venetian navy came to his help in his fight with Robert Guiscard's Normans at Durazzo, and there was a joint Byzantine–Venetian victory near Corfu. Alexius rewarded Venice in a treaty of May 1082, with important commercial concessions. The Venetians were granted the right of trading throughout the Empire duty-free, as well as being given a quarter in the capital, with shops, wharves, and churches. This agreement put Venice in a strong position, enabling her to undersell the local Byzantine merchants, who had to pay the duties, even in their own markets; and the grounds of future bitterness were thus created. As part of this agreement, the emperor also promised a payment of twenty pounds of gold annually to St. Mark's, Venice.

The great church of St. Mark symbolizes more than anything else the uniqueness of Venice. The first church on or near the site, dedicated to St. Theodore, was replaced by a new church to receive the body of St. Mark, smuggled out of Alexandria in 829 (though it was not until 1063 that the present church was begun). The acquisition of St. Mark's body signalled the liberation of Venetia from effective Byzantine overlordship, as she now had her own trophy or palladium. St. Theodore, a Byzantine religious hero, had been replaced by a New Testament or 'apostolic' saint. Nevertheless, the basilica of St. Mark, when it came to be built in its existing form, was Byzantine in style. Modelled on the church of the Holy Apostles at Constantinople, it was of cruciform plan with five cupolas supported by columns and aisles around the arms of the cross. The main structure of St. Mark's was completed in 1094, when the relics of St. Mark were formally deposited in it. The Western emperor Henry IV came in person to see the newly consecrated church and to venerate the relics. The building has a broadly based structure skilfully planned to sustain the thrust of the cupola vaulting, and the architect must almost certainly have been either a Byzantine himself or a Venetian trained in the schools of Constantinople.

St. Mark's was the chapel of the doge, who himself nominated the ecclesiastical head of the church, known as the *primicerius*, and in due course (in 1296) the doge's name would even be inserted into the canon of the mass. For its construction St. Mark's owed much to Doge Domenico Selvo (1071–84), who introduced Byzantine craftsmen to work on it as well as using precious building materials from the Levant, such as marble and porphyry. As one stands in St. Mark's today one realizes that it is an essentially Byzantine building, not a Western church with some Byzantine details. The so-called iconostasis of red marble is a fair example of an early medieval Byzantine screen, though the bronze figures of the Virgin and Apostles surrounding it would not normally have been seen in an Orthodox setting. The present screen was actually made towards the close of the fourteenth century, and behind it is the high altar enshrining the body of St. Mark; most of the church's mosaics, though Byzantine in character, are also later than the eleventh and twelfth centuries.

By the close of the twelfth century, however, there already stood in their present position on the quayside, close to St. Mark's, the two columns made by Niccolò dei Barattieri in the 1170s. They are now crowned by representations of the two patron saints of Venice, St. Theodore and the winged lion of St. Mark, though the statue of Theodore is no earlier than 1329. The columns have carvings representing the occupations and trades of the Venetian citizens, and this emphasis on the city's crafts was in the course of the thirteenth century to become a feature also of the sculptures within St. Mark's.[6] By about 1200 the famous Rialto bridge had been built, though of timber – the present bridge is the sixth on the site. The city which today in its crumbling beauty captivates the traveller was in the Crusading age a home of practical men whose main concern was to balance their accounts. The streets were still unpaved, and the citizens threw their refuse and garbage into the open. The canals were lined with orchards and meadows in which cattle grazed. The citizens, however, had a sense of beauty inherited from Byzantium, and a feeling of responsibility for the safety and prosperity of their Republic. The campanile, first built in the orchard of St. Mark as a defence tower, was often altered from the twelfth century onwards, and received the addition of a belfry. Close to the campanile was a hospice for pilgrims bound for the Holy Land. The piazza was enlarged in 1172 by Doge Sebastiano Ziani, and it was soon afterwards paved with brick and given loggias, though it still had a popular and utilitarian rather than an aristocratic character.

Commercially, Venice was early in the twelfth century building up a strong position also in the Crusading states of Syria, a development which made the Empire uneasy. The establishment of Venetian and other Italian trading colonies in the Levant in the years after the First Crusade caused a serious fall in the volume of the Empire's transit trade, and as a result the feelings of Byzantium towards Venice became embittered. In 1124 the emperor John II went to the point of expelling the Venetians from Constantinople, and they fought back with naval attacks on the Greek islands, led by Doge Domenico Michiel, later to be remembered as the 'Terror of the Greeks'. In 1126 John was compelled to restore and ratify Venice's trading privileges, originally gained from Alexius I in 1082.

In 1146 there was still more serious trouble between Venice and Byzantium. In that year the Normans, led by Roger II of Sicily, invaded Greece, and the emperor Manuel called for Venetian help. A fleet from Venice duly defeated the Normans off Cape Malea, but there was a quarrel between the victors which became ugly when the Venetians dressed a Byzantine ship overall as the emperor's vessel, and put on it a black slave arrayed in imperial robes. The point of this curious exercise was that the emperor was a man of dark skin, and was known to be mocked about it behind his back. The incident itself might not have been important but Manuel at this early stage in his reign did in fact conceive a dislike for the Venetians, despite his generally pro-Western outlook. Although the Venetian quarter in Constantinople was enlarged in 1148, in a chrysobull establishing and defining it as it was to remain until the end of the century, difficulties arose when Manuel tried to cultivate good relations with Venice's rivals the Genoese and Pisans. The Venetians were intensely annoyed that other Italian merchants were gaining a footing in Constantinople, the emperor for his part taking a poor view of the Venetians for their presumption in entertaining opinions as to whom he should favour in his own city. In 1151 the Venetians withdrew from their alliance with Byzantium against the Sicilian Normans, and in 1167 they even took the side of Hungary against the emperor.

The crisis came on 11 March 1171, when good relations between the Empire and Venice were finally shattered. On that day Manuel ordered the arrest of all Venetians within the Empire and confiscated their property, in an attempt to assuage the rising anti-Latin feelings of the people of Constantinople. About 10,000 Venetians were arrested in the capital alone – so packed were the prisons that some of the men seized had to be interned in monasteries instead – and owing to the impossibility of holding so many prisoners, large numbers had soon to be released on bail. In response to this hostility Venice sent a powerful fleet to the East, under the command of the doge himself, Vitale Michiel II. Some Dalmatian coastal towns were taken and the islands of Lesbos and Chios were pillaged, but plague broke out on the ships at anchor off Euboea, where the emperor had persuaded the doge to stop and confer with his ambassadors in an attempt to negotiate a peace settlement. The Byzantines eked out the conference for as long as possible, thus testing the patience of the Venetian sailors and troops. The steady spread of the plague forced the fleet to return to Venice, where popular fury at Doge Vitale Michiel for his failure and mismanagement led to his lynching by the mob, in May 1172. One result of this disaster was to quicken a movement aimed at limiting the doge's powers. From now on there was an annually elected Great Council, and an Inner Council to advise the doge – the bodies which were consulted by Doge Enrico Dandolo before arranging the Frankish-Venetian treaty.

Manuel was successful in driving the Venetian galleys from the Aegean, but the Venetians reacted with yet another campaign of attacks on Byzantine commerce. Strong feelings were meanwhile rising in Constantinople over the virtual monopoly of the wharves along the southern shores of the Golden Horn by Latin traders, native merchants being almost deprived of their use. Manuel's policy against the Republic was applauded by his subjects; he had acted boldly and decisively, though in fact the mass arrest of the Venetians was a fatal mistake, for which Byzantium would pay dearly.

Soon afterwards, in 1176, there came the disastrous defeat of Myriokephalon, when the Seljuks overwhelmed Manuel and the Byzantine army. There were now moves to placate the Venetian Republic, and by 1179 many of the imprisoned Venetians had been released. But there could be no restoration of the old and reasonably cordial relationship, and in so far as the Venetians did continue to trade in Constantinople it was in modest numbers, which explains why there were so few Venetian casualties in the great Latin Massacre of 1182. Whereas to Italian merchants in general the events of 1182, with their horror and unbridled savagery, marked the turning-point in relationships with the Empire, to the Venetians the true divorce, as it were, had come in 1171. From that year the basic trust had gone.

The Venetians, however, were above all realists, anxious that trade should continue with Byzantium, and after the troubles of 1171 they sent a mission to Constantinople which included Enrico Dandolo, with the aim of restoring normal commerce. Later, when an opportunity for reconciliation was offered by the emperor Andronicus, the Venetians took it, and in 1182 the remaining Venetians still in custody were released. In the spring of 1184 another mission from Venice arrived in Constantinople. The doge at this time was Orio Malipiero, who in his anxiety to restore good formal relations sent three outstanding citizens, Peter Ziani, Domenico Sanudo, and, again, Enrico Dandolo. By now the Venetian merchants were back in their Constantinople quarter, and it would appear that the principal subject of discussion between the three ambassadors and Andronicus was the question of compensation for the seizure of the Venetians' property in 1171. This was conceded in principle by the emperor. Andronicus was at that moment awaiting the expected onslaught on the Empire by William II of Sicily (to culminate the following year in the sack of Thessalonica), and he doubtless tried hard to obtain the promise of Venetian naval support. But the old palmy days of co-operation were past and no such promise was given; when the Sicilian Normans attacked in 1185, the Venetians did not lift a finger nor raise an oar to help the emperor.

There was now a new factor in the general situation. Byzantium was becoming very weak at sea. The tendency to rely on the Venetians for ships had lessened the Empire's own naval consciousness, and neither Manuel nor any of his successors ever grasped the supreme importance of sea-power. The Empire had been at fault during the second half of the twelfth century in neglecting the fleet, and the point had now been reached where the passage through the Dardanelles was wide open.[7] Andronicus's successor Isaac II did manage to arrange a treaty of naval assistance from Venice in specific terms, as a defence against the Normans, in return for the restoration of the old trading privileges and a promise that the Venetians would soon be compensated in full for their losses of 1171. Nevertheless, when Isaac was overthrown in April 1195 the agreed compensation had still not been fully paid. Byzantium simply could not find the money.

Meanwhile, Enrico Dandolo was elected Doge of Venice early in 1193. Apart from serving as a member of the missions to Constantinople, Dandolo had not hitherto played any dramatic or outstanding role in Venetian affairs, but his appointment to the highest office, though seemingly near the close of his life, was to be followed by several years of vigorous and intelligent leadership. Dandolo was faced with a combination of problems. Interested above all in commerce, he quickly settled some trading difficulties between Venice and Verona. Of greater urgency was Dalmatia, which had been lost to Hungary, and there was also the need to strengthen the Republic's weakened trading position in Constantinople. The failure of the Venetians to obtain full compensation for the confiscations of 1171, negotiated by the very embassy in which Dandolo himself had participated, must have been an issue particularly close to his heart.

Under Alexius III, who became emperor in 1195, relations between Byzantium and Venice again worsened. Alexius called a halt to any further payments of compensation. Reversing his predecessor's policy, he started to harass the Venetian merchants in the city, imposing customs dues on them, and also favouring their rivals the Pisans and Genoese. One outcome of this development was outright fighting between the Venetians and Pisans, and in the spring of 1196 a Venetian fleet, fully equipped for war, prepared for hostile action and even appeared in the Dardanelles. Its specific aim was to threaten the Pisans in Constantinople, but it doubtless crossed the minds of more than one Venetian that they were in an excellent position to attack the capital itself if they had wished to do so and if they had had a strong military force to operate in conjunction with their fleet. The Byzantine navy at this time was approaching its nadir.

Dandolo decided that an agreement with the emperor was essential to Venice's prosperity, and embassies passed to and from Venice and Constantinople. By the end of 1198 a formal treaty was concluded by which, in return for maritime assistance should she be attacked, Byzantium guaranteed to Venice unimpeded commercial movement within the Empire. The Venetian community in Constantinople was declared virtually free of the imperial law, and it was to have its own courts and judges except where serious crimes such as murder were concerned. Unfortunately the agreement failed to produce the harmony for which the doge had hoped, and in effect harassment of Venetian merchants continued. The failure of Alexius III and his officials to implement the agreement fully, and to act in its spirit of conciliation, was to prove expensive for Byzantium.

Early in 1200 there was angry quarrelling in Constantinople between the Venetians and the Pisans who were trying to oust them. Dandolo sent embassies to the emperor demanding a restoration of Venice's former position, besides final payment of all outstanding compensation for the events of 1171. And then, in the spring of 1201, news reached Dandolo that the emperor was in official touch with a mission from Genoa, led by Ottobono della Croce, aiming to secure concessions at Venice's expense. This was probably the point when Enrico Dandolo decided that the Eastern Empire would have to be dealt with drastically, even to the point of being brought under renewed control in which Venice would play a dominant role.

That Dandolo had a personal animosity towards Byzantium is clear. The Byzantine historian Nicetas calls him an enemy of the Empire.[8] Dandolo was well experienced in Byzantine affairs, and, though we do not know his exact age, an old man: according to a sixteenth-century Venetian source, Marino Sanudo the younger, he was eighty-five when elected doge in 1193.[9] If this is correct, Dandolo would have been about ninety-five years old in 1203 and 1204, which is hard to believe. Neither can we accept it as likely that he was completely blind, as often stated. Villehardouin says that his blindness was caused by a brawl in which he had become involved. But the explanation of Dandolo's blindness (or defective sight) given in the *Novgorod Chronicle*, is different.[10] Manuel had been discreetly warned by his advisers (presumably during the 1171 mission) that Enrico Dandolo was a dangerous person who one day was likely to cause the Empire grave harm. The emperor did not dare to go as far as to assassinate him, but had him seized and blinded by the use of glass. The full strength of the sun was brought to bear on his eyes, destroying or, more probably, seriously impairing them without changing their outward appearance. If the story is true, it would certainly account for Dandolo's personal venom towards the Empire. The blind old doge has become one of the legends of Italian history. But the tale of a totally blind man of almost a hundred years old standing on the poop of his galley at the first siege of Constantinople, in 1203, directing the battle and landing on the beach with the army passes the bounds of credibility.[11]

Constantinople was by far the largest of the numerous Venetian trading-stations in the Empire.[12] The Venetian quarter was on the southern shore on the Golden Horn, immediately opposite the Galata district and covering the area between the sea and the hill on which now stands the mosque of Suleiman. Large as the quarter was, conditions were crowded, and the Venetians found it necessary also to rent houses elsewhere in the city. The quarter itself consisted of a narrow strip a third of a mile long, through the middle of which ran a section of the city's sea-wall, with several openings, the best-known of which was the Drungarion Gate. Along the Golden Horn stretched the wharves, three of these being reserved for the Venetians, who also controlled a thoroughfare called Drungarios Street. This, and another street proceeding parallel to the inside of the wall, were tightly packed with two- or three-storey buildings, with shops and working rooms below and living apartments above. The principal warehouse was known as the Embolo, where the merchants transacted business and discussed their affairs, probably a building surrounded by a large courtyard with roofed arcades, like a cloister.

The organization of the colony which was causing Dandolo so much concern was relatively loose and undefined. Besides the governing council there were judges and finance officers; but when missions from Venice visited Constantinople to negotiate with the emperor, the envoys took over the leadership of the community, at least formally, for the duration of their stay. At no time before 1204 was there a *podestà*, in the usual Italian style, as the effective head of the community. The truth is that the trading colony of Venetians was too preoccupied with its business affairs to make any close control of it really necessary. But this total concern with commerce demanded the assurance of complete security from any threats or interference by the native people or their government.

The merchants were well served spiritually, and the existence of the Venetian colony, as indeed of the other Italian enclaves, meant that the Latin Church was present in strength in Constantinople. The Church was closely linked with the life of the Venetian community, the clergy serving the merchants not only in such obvious capacities as confessors and mass-priests, but as clerks, secretaries and executors of wills. The principal Venetian church was St. Akindynos, in the centre of the quarter, handed over to the Venetians in the early concessions by Alexius I. Its clerics, besides attending to their spiritual functions, were the official overseers of weights and measures; and attached to this church was a bakery. Amongst other churches was St. Mark's, the property of a monastery, St. George's, whose own buildings were incorporated into the sea-wall. There was also St. Mary de Carpiani and St. John de Cornibus; and we know of a Venetian monastic house in the city itself, St. Nicholas. All the churches in the Venetian quarter came under the ecclesiastical jurisdiction of the Church of Venice and we do not know of a bishop of the Venetian Church in Constantinople, though such would have been the normal Italian practice in arranging its ecclesiastical administration in small, numerous sees. Adjoining the Venetian quarter on its eastern side was that of the Amalfitans, who had been amongst the earliest Italians to maintain merchants in Constantinople but who by the late twelfth century had declined in importance. Further eastwards was the Pisan quarter, which in addition to its wharves, warehouses, and shops, had two churches and a hospital; and at the mouth of the Golden Horn was the quarter of the Genoese.

In the history of the relationship between the Italian merchants and Byzantium, the two significant dates are undoubtedly 1171 and 1182, the years respectively of the mass arrest of Venetians by Manuel and the massacre of the Latins under Andronicus. It is certain that these two events, the one a calculated but clumsily executed piece of policy on the part of a ruler, the other an outbreak of savagery by a brainless rabble, were contributory causes of the forthcoming diversion of the Fourth Crusade to Constantinople. By the closing years of the twelfth century Venice, the Queen of the Sea, was in a confident and expansive mood, and determined to assert herself in the pursuit of prosperity and power. She knew the Empire and its capital city well and exactly where the imperial weaknesses lay. She herself had a will of steel, and from her long association with Byzantium she had acquired an acuteness of mind which was to enable her to exploit the martial prowess of feudal Europe for her own ends.

Chapter 7

The Affair goes Awry

When in 1195 Isaac II was deposed and blinded by his brother, who became Byzantine emperor as Alexius III, he and his twelve-year-old son Alexius were both taken into custody – shortly after the marriage of Isaac's daughter Irene to Philip, the powerful king of Swabia. It would not be quite true to say that Isaac and the young Alexius were imprisoned, as they were allowed some personal freedom and even the opportunity to meet foreigners, but the new emperor kept a very close eye on their movements.[1] In 1201 Alexius III decided that it was safe to release the youth, on the strength of a promise that he would not plot against him; but the *Novgorod Chronicle* says that the prince, having been set at liberty, wondered how 'he might get away from the city to far-off lands and there seek to obtain his throne'. Alexius III himself was preoccupied in 1201 with a rebellion in the Balkans, and he took the prince with him on the necessary campaign. But the young Alexius, encouraged by his father, managed to escape, and slipping away on a small boat boarded a Pisan ship lying off the port of Athyra (the modern Turkish Büyük Chekmeje) on the Marmora. Though he was pursued, and the ship was even overtaken and searched, Alexius avoided capture. One story says that he eluded his pursuers by changing into Italian clothes and cutting his hair in Western style.[2] According to another account he squeezed himself into an ingeniously constructed barrel with just enough room for himself at one end, the other containing water and fitted with a plug. When the ship was searched, all the water-barrels were tested, the plugs being removed to see if water came out.[3]

What is certain is that the ship sailed away with Alexius aboard and arrived at the town of Ancona on the Italian Adriatic coast. The time was probably the late summer or early autumn of 1201, as the voyage would be unlikely to begin once the winter had set in.[4] Alexius made straight for the Swabian court, at that time established in Hagenau, and there he was affectionately greeted by his sister Irene, glad to see him after his misfortunes in Constantinople and anxious for news of her father. He was also hospitably received by her husband Philip of Swabia, son of the great Frederick Barbarossa. Here at the court in Alsace the prince was to stay for some months.

Philip was an ambitious man, aiming to achieve the dominant position which his brother Henry VI might well have attained had he lived. Despite his marriage connections, Philip disliked Byzantium; and he was also inclined to feel sympathetically towards the victims of Alexius III. There is no evidence that he had a grand design for conquering the Eastern Empire, though he may not have been averse to listening to any proposals which might lead to the undoing of Alexius III, the persecutor of his wife's father. Moreover, Philip was out of favour with Innocent III, who had excommunicated him earlier in 1201, and if only for that reason was perhaps ill-disposed to the pope's near ally Alexius III. Philip himself, however, had far too much engaging his attention in Germany, especially problems with his rival Otto of Brunswick, to allow himself to be diverted into adventures further east.

Also at Philip's court, and arriving at about the same time as Prince Alexius, was Boniface of Montferrat, the recently elected leader of the Crusade. As we know, Boniface was at the court or in close touch with it for most of the winter of 1201–2, and he was certainly with Philip for the Christmas feast of 1201, as was Alexius.[5] It was the convergence of these three men at the Swabian court which seems in the first place to have produced the idea of the Crusading army being diverted temporarily to Constantinople to unseat Alexius III, and indeed an anonymous biographer of Innocent III says that it was reported that Boniface discussed with Philip the possibility of using the Crusading army to put young Prince Alexius on the throne.[6] There would have been nothing remarkable or revolutionary in such proposals, as preceding Crusades had passed through the Byzantine capital on their way to Palestine.

In Hagenau Prince Alexius was now in the company, perhaps almost daily, of the man soon to sail from Venice in command of a powerful force of Western soldiers, a man who had already shown his will to make decisions and accept responsibility. Boniface was not moved by the same Crusading zeal which fired many of the lesser barons and knights who had heard the preaching of Fulk of Neuilly, and we know that many Crusaders were uneasy at his election. Boniface's two brothers Rainier and Conrad having earlier been in close contact through marriage with the Byzantine court, he might have felt entitled, as it were, to be concerned with affairs in Constantinople. Moreover, Boniface's father William of Montferrat was the husband of Sophia, daughter of Frederick Barbarossa and sister (or half-sister) of Philip. The meeting of the three men therefore, Philip of Swabia, Boniface, and Prince Alexius, particularly during the Christmas festivities, had something of the air of a family party. But Alexius was a very young man, hardly out of his teens, and almost everything that we know of him suggests that he had little ability. He was being used, but by whom? By Philip, who had quite enough to occupy his mind at home, or Boniface, with his family interests in the Byzantine Empire and especially in Thessalonica?

The idea of the diversionary move to Constantinople may indeed have been initially voiced by Irene, championing the cause of her wronged father and brother. She was after all a queen, her brother only a teenage refugee. Her deposed father Isaac had actually written asking her to use her influence on his behalf. Though not wishing to be heavily involved personally, Philip would be agreeable to any scheme which offered the chance of weakening Byzantine power. Here was a golden opportunity. Boniface on the other hand saw chances for personal advancement, and it was unlikely that any serious fighting would be necessary to displace Alexius III in favour of the rightful heir. But knowing that papal support would be necessary, or at least highly desirable, for the diversion of a Crusade which was Innocent's brain-child, the two men agreed that an approach should be made to Rome.

Soon after Christmas, therefore, the young Alexius was sent to Rome to put the scheme for a Byzantine expedition before Innocent, who met the prince in February 1202.[7] The bait of a unification of the Catholic and Orthodox Churches was a strong and tempting one. But though the young man poured out his troubles and begged for papal help and sympathy, Innocent was not impressed by him.[8] In any case, Innocent was at this time on good terms with the reigning Byzantine emperor Alexius III, and the discomfited prince left the papal presence, his mission a failure, and for a period of about six months there is a gap in our knowledge of his activities or whereabouts.

Realizing the importance of obtaining the pope's goodwill for so daring a project, the main protagonists tried again. There was no question of Philip of Swabia, at present excommunicate, visiting the pope, so Boniface himself went to Rome, in March. His task was eased by a letter of support which he had obtained, when visiting Paris after his election as commander-in-chief, from his cousin Philip Augustus, the French king, who had been strongly in favour of his election. Innocent, by now alerted to the diversion idea, was prepared for the encounter. He bluntly warned Boniface to keep the army from attacking any Christian territories and to concentrate his attentions on Palestine. After this rebuff Boniface left Rome for northern Italy to proceed with preparations for the Crusade. In April he was in Lerici, and next in his own marquisate of Montferrat. On 9 August, in Pavia, his son was formally placed in control for such time as his father might be absent. A week later Boniface was in Venice.[9]

It is plain that Innocent III himself must be cleared of any connivance in the original plan for a diversion to Constantinople. The *Novgorod Chronicle*, in its account of these happenings, does indeed say that Philip of Swabia sent word to the pope advising him that it would not be necessary after all for him to make war on Constantinople as here was an excellent chance, by putting the prince on the throne, of helping forward the deliverance of Jerusalem. But the implication here that the pope was actually meditating a direct assault on the Byzantine capital is not to be taken seriously. The Chronicle reflects what came to be the standard Orthodox tradition, that Innocent III was the arch-villain in the conquest of Constantinople.

Villehardouin does not tell the whole story of the young Prince Alexius's travels in the West.[10] He says nothing of the visit to Rome for papal approval, and he seems in fact never to have had much personal contact with Alexius, despite his own prominence in the higher ranks of the Crusade. He mentions summarily the deposition of Isaac II Angelus and the usurpation of Alexius III. His chronological treatment in his Chronicle sometimes tends to be faulty – and an episode which he includes in his account of the prince's travels is especially difficult to place in the overall picture. He records that while journeying through Italy to visit Philip, Alexius stopped at Verona, and while staying there happened to meet some parties of Crusaders on their way to join the host at Venice. The idea was put into Alexius's head by members of his own entourage that he might well appeal for help directly to the powerful army now assembling. Attracted by the idea, Alexius sent messengers to Boniface, the commander-in-chief, and the barons. The latter were somewhat taken aback by the suggestion, and this was in fact the first they had heard of the diversion proposal. But in principle they saw nothing wrong or irregular in it, and told the prince's envoys that if he would consent to help them in their attempt to take Jerusalem, he could rely on their support in trying to recover the Empire. The episode would seem to have followed Alexius's rebuff by the pope, and to have taken place not during his initial journey to the Swabian court after landing in Italy, as Villehardouin's narrative suggests, but some time between 15 August 1202, when Boniface joined the army in Venice, and 1 October, when the army set out on its expedition to the Dalmatian port of Zara. Encouraged by the favourable response to his own overtures, says Villehardouin, Prince Alexius returned to the Swabian court, this time accompanied by representatives of the barons, who doubtless wanted confirmation of the scheme from Philip himself. Meanwhile they had the prudence to withhold knowledge of the matter from the rank and file of the assembling Crusading army.

Throughout the winter of 1201–2 the Crusaders in fairly substantial numbers remained resolute in their intentions, and when spring arrived began to leave their homes. 'Many was the tear that was shed as men bade farewell to their lands, their families and friends.'[11] Between Easter and Pentecost 1202 they were on their way southwards in baronial parties through Burgundy and into Lombardy, using the Mont Cenis pass, and so to Venice, where they were assigned the island known to the modern tourist as the Lido. Today the place is alive with entertainment; then it was noted for its monastery of St. Nicholas, with relics of that saint. The Venetians charged extortionate prices for food, as the Lombards had also done as the Crusaders made their journey to the point of assembly. Many men must by now have almost exhausted their money, but despite this the Franks were impressed with Venice, in process of becoming the beautiful city she has since remained; the Queen of the Sea was already casting her spell. The wealth of the city was steadily increasing; and because of its long contact with Byzantium, Venice's aura of wealth and sophistication exceeded anything known in the West, and the Crusaders, many of them from dreary villages or small market towns in north-western Europe, were astonished by the riches and evidence of material prosperity around them.

Some Crusaders had their reservations about the agreement with Dandolo, and were understandably suspicious of the motives leading the Venetians to cast in their lot so readily with the Crusade. Some did not like the idea of choosing to attack the enemy in Egypt, for though at first kept secret, knowledge of this plan had by now become widespread. To the leaders a landing in Egypt was the best policy, but the rank-and-file Crusader wanted to strike a blow for Christ on the soil of Palestine itself, the recovery of the Sepulchre remaining central to the popular conception of a Crusade. In addition, many Frenchmen who had taken the Cross probably resented having Boniface of Montferrat as their leader, and hesitant members of the expedition now began to slip away. The worst defection from the main host was that of a fleet from Flanders under Jean de Nesles, castellan of Bruges. He had given his word to Count Baldwin, who himself left Flanders in April 1202, that after negotiating the straits of Gibraltar he would sail to join the army at Venice or wherever according to his information it might happen to be. On the strength of this solemn oath, sworn on the gospels, Baldwin and his brother Henry had actually entrusted some of their own vessels, loaded with vital provisions, to Jean. Great hopes had been placed in this fleet, not least because it carried a high proportion of the reliable Flemish sergeants. But Jean disregarded his oath, and rather than make for Venice chose to sail by way of Marseilles to Acre, arriving there at the end of 1202.

A force of French knights and sergeants, led by Gautier, bishop of Autun, and including Guigues count of Forez and several other men of good standing, also decided to give Venice a wide berth. Leaving Marseilles, they sailed direct to Acre, arriving there shortly after the Flemings. Their action was much resented by those who had assembled at Venice, and with some justification, as it was felt that men with adequate maritime transport of their own, in thus taking advantage of their position, were dividing what had promised to be a formidable army. On the other hand, those who now sailed straight to the Holy Land on their own account must have seen no reason why they should contribute to the provision of a Venetian fleet, and fight in the knowledge that half their conquests would go to Venice, when they had good ships of their own. And they were under no canonical obligation as individually sworn Crusader-pilgrims to make their sacred journey to Jerusalem by the route laid down by Villehardouin and his fellow delegates.

Yet another group of Frenchmen went to Palestine, directly from Venice, in vessels of their own. We do not know the total number of men actually involved in these defections, though later in his Chronicle Villehardouin does say that the Crusaders who sailed direct to Syria exceeded in numbers those besieging Constantinople.[12] Even if this is an exaggeration, it does at least imply a very large number of defectors. At Venice confidence was badly shaken. The leaders of the Crusade were relying on as full a muster as possible to enable them to settle the agreed payment of 85,000 marks. Some men who were encamped on the Lido decided to withdraw, and made for home or sailed over to Italy to look for an alternative port. Clearly all was not well on the island of San Niccolò. The heat, constant thirst, and enforced idleness in a confined space played havoc with the tempers of the individual soldiers, and to make matters worse there was an outbreak of plague.

Baldwin was already in Venice, the first of the principals to arrive. He was a worried man, having been let down by some of his own subordinates, and much disturbed by the news of those making their way independently to Syria. The chivalrous and devout Baldwin was evidently a trusting as well as a trusted man. He sent messengers to Louis, count of Blois, who was slow in arriving, and to other Crusaders who seemed to be hesitating. The messengers, Geoffrey de Villehardouin and Hugh, count of St. Pol, were under instructions to emphasize that the Venice route was the only feasible one. Making their way westwards to Lombardy, the two men found that matters were indeed not satisfactory. They met Count Louis in Pavia, but though he had a large force, many of its members were doubtful about the wisdom of proceeding to Venice. Geoffrey and Hugh were able to persuade at least some of these to follow the Venetian plan. But the two men found to their dismay that a large force of knights and sergeants had broken away to march south into Apulia. The force included some fine soldiers, amongst whom were a highly regarded knight, Vilain de Neuilly, and Gilles de Trasignies, a vassal of Baldwin, who had thought so well of him and so implicitly trusted him that he had given him money to defray his travelling expenses to Venice. The aim of these men, amongst whom was also an excellent soldier, Renaud de Dampierre, was to make their voyage straight to Acre. The leaders had a gloomy foreboding that something might go wrong. As Villehardouin put it, 'there was a grave decrease in numbers of those who were expected to join the army in Venice, which was consequently in a difficult position.'[13]

In the meantime, the Venetians were fully aware of the reluctance of many Crusaders to become involved in an assault on Egypt, and they themselves could hardly afford to jeopardize their trading connections. Although there is no documentary evidence of a formal treaty, it is possible that an understanding of some kind or other was reached between Egypt and the doge at this time; it is in any case difficult to believe that Dandolo could have had any real intention of transporting the Franks directly to Egypt, no matter what the barons might have been planning. If he was going to land them anywhere on Muslim territory it would be Syria.

The dilatory Count Louis and his force duly arrived in Venice and joined the Crusaders on the Lido. The muster was now virtually complete, but its numbers were much smaller than those calculated when the six envoys had made their agreement with Dandolo a year before. Certainly there were in Venice nothing like the 33,500 men originally anticipated, and Villehardouin bitterly reproaches the defectors who had avoided coming to Venice: 'Ah, what incalculable damage was caused by those men who went to other ports!'[14] The real culprits in the looming débâcle were of course the six envoys themselves, including Villehardouin, who in their dealings with Dandolo had grossly overestimated the size of the potential army. They had naïvely negotiated with the doge to build a huge transport fleet, simply on the basis of chivalrous enthusiasm in Champagne and in seeming ignorance of the fact that the age of fiery Crusading zeal was in decline. And now in the summer of 1202 the lagoon at Venice contained a fleet of transports and warships far larger than the Crusade could possibly need. Villehardouin in fact says that the splendid Venetian fleet now awaiting them 'could easily have carried three times as many men as there were in the whole army put together'.[15] This suggests a total muster in Venice of about 11,000 men, and with their customary efficiency in shipbuilding and in the transacting of business, the fleet which the Venetians produced would be capable of transporting just the contracted number. It might be objected that no reliance can be placed on Villehardouin's estimates of troop numbers, and that he should be expected to show the common propensity of medieval chroniclers towards numerical exaggeration. But as marshal of Champagne he would have included amongst his official duties the organization and assembling of troops, and have a keen sense of the actual size of an army.

The Venetians, like good businessmen, had fulfilled their part of the bargain. The ships were ready, and they asked for the money.

A contract had been made, and it would not have been in the Crusaders' minds to do other than meet their obligations. To keep a pact was part of the medieval soldiering code, and the sanctity of oaths and contracts was instinctively felt by men reared in a feudal society. At no stage in the course of the Fourth Crusade did the Franks swerve from their intention to pay the Venetians their money. This was a precise obligation, taking precedence over more general notions such as that of desisting from attacking other Christians. In any case, the ships were needed. The army just could not move without them.

Each member of the army was ordered to hand over the 'fare' for his passage. As many of the troops did not have enough, they paid what they could. When the total sum was collected it amounted to less than half of what was required, and the Crusading leaders met to discuss the crisis. 'The Venetians have faithfully and very generously fulfilled their part of the agreement,' they said, 'but there are too few of us here to fulfil our part. The blame lies on the men who have gone to other ports. For God's sake let us each hand over as much of our money as we possibly can – better to lose all of it rather than default on the agreement. For if the expedition has to be abandoned, the chance of our delivering Outremer will be lost.'[16] Some were in favour of abandoning the enterprise altogether and letting the army break up, each party being freed to make its way home or wherever else it wanted to go. This course would clearly have entailed repudiating the Venetian contract. It met with strenuous opposition, and the next move was for the principal leaders, resolved on keeping the army intact, to hand over their personal money and valuables, such as gold and silver dinner-services. Those who did so included Boniface, Baldwin, Louis, and Hugh de St. Pol. They also had resort to borrowing. Venice, as a merchant city, had ample facilities available in this respect, though interest rates could be as high as 20 per cent or more. It was a standard practice in Venice for sea-voyages to be financed by loans, the ecclesiastical prohibition of usury being simply ignored. Baldwin, as a loyal churchman, had in his Flemish dominions during 1199 actually tried to prohibit the lending of money at interest; but what his personal attitude was in Venice, on finding himself acutely short of money, we do not know.

After these expedients the leaders found that they were still 34,000 marks short of the 85,000 required. Those barons who had argued for the dismantling of the expedition (and refused to contribute to the special collection) were now confident that the whole affair could speedily be wound up. Clearly the Crusade was in danger of collapse. No money could be expected from Innocent III's income tax on the clergy, as this was intended for the Crusade's expenses when it actually reached the Holy Land.

Dandolo consulted his own advisers, and after pointing out to them that the Westerners had paid all they could and had clearly arrived at the limit of their financial resources, maintained that the Republic would be justified in keeping what had been paid even if the enterprise was to be now abandoned. Such an insistence, however, might create a bad impression abroad and bring reproach on the Venetians. Businessmen always try to keep the goodwill of their customers. The doge therefore now suggested a radical course of action which it is difficult not to suspect that he had been harbouring in his mind for some time.

Since about the year 1000 much of Dalmatia had been under Venetian control, though the pivot of the coastline, the port of Zara, had rebelled against Venice in 1111, to be regained only after years of fighting, in which Doge Ordelafo Faliero was killed. The control of the Dalmatian coast was important to Venice for several reasons. It made possible the prevention of piracy in the Adriatic waters, and it ensured a series of harbours for Venetian merchant ships. Moreover, during the twelfth century Dalmatia was a prolific source of oak, much in demand in Western Europe and not least in Venice and the other merchant cities of Italy for their shipbuilding. Towards the close of the century Hungary was casting covetous eyes on Dalmatia, and when in 1186 Zara, resentful of Venetian taxes, again rebelled, the Hungarian king Bela III seized his opportunity and moved in. Venice made several efforts to retake the port, all without success.

Dandolo now reassured the Crusaders that if they would promise faithfully to settle the outstanding debt from the proceeds of their first conquests, he would provide the contracted transport. When news of this came through there was jubilation in the camp. The men lit torches in exhilaration, so that it seemed that the whole camp was ablaze.[17] But to the barons Dandolo made it clear that postponement of payment of the debt of 34,000 marks was not unconditional. He would expect them to help him in a further attempt to recover Zara. He sugared the pill for the ordinary soldiery by declaring that the great campaign against the Muslims was soon to begin, though as winter was drawing near Zara might well be dealt with first. It was in fact July. Winter, he said, could be spent at Zara, and the expedition for the relief of Outremer set out on Lady Day (25 March 1203).

Those barons disillusioned with the Crusade and in favour of its abandonment were much opposed to the Zara proposal, though it was accepted by the leaders. Some barons regarded the plan as iniquitous because Zara was a Catholic city. The Hungarian king, Emeric, was himself one of the pope's formally sworn Crusaders. It would be quite wrong for Cross-soldiers to attack Christians, with the slaughter, fire, and rapine which were the normal accompaniment of sieges. On the other hand, minor diversions were not unknown in Crusading warfare. For example, many of the Crusaders must have been aware that in 1147 a fleet of Englishmen under Henry Glanville, with some men from Flanders and Frisia, bound for Syria to join the French and Germans in the Second Crusade, had been persuaded by Count Alfonso Henry of Portugal to break their voyage and help him to capture Lisbon from the Moors. This diversion had indeed involved fighting against Muslims, not fellow-Christians, but the English Crusaders had in fact been uneasy in their consciences over the abandonment of their vow to go to Syria; and the outcome of this diversion had been that Glanville's expedition had proceeded no further than Portugal.[18]

In Rome the pope was disturbed at the trend of events. On first hearing of the Frankish-Venetian arrangement for the provision of transport, he had instinctively suspected that the Venetians would turn it to their advantage by contriving some such scheme as that of the recapture of Zara, and though he had ratified the treaty he had also issued a warning to the Crusaders not to fight against Christians. On 22 July the papal legate, Cardinal Peter Capuano, arrived in Venice, his fellow Crusade legate Soffredo having already gone to the Holy Land in advance. Peter objected strongly to the Zara proposals and urged that the expedition should set out immediately for Egypt. The doge bluntly replied that the army was very pleased to have Peter with it, but only in the capacity of preacher and spiritual counsellor.[19] Otherwise Peter was virtually told to mind his own business. Rebuffed, he returned to Rome, told Innocent of the Zara plan in full, and also spoke with him about the scheme which was quietly brewing to put Prince Alexius on the throne at Constantinople. After the legate's departure, the pope wrote to the Crusaders, sending the letter by a Cistercian monk, the abbot of Lucedio (also named Peter), with a specific instruction that no Christian town was to be attacked. Innocent reminded the Franks that Zara now belonged to a sworn soldier of the Cross, Emeric King of Hungary.

In the army uneasiness increased. Still more men defected, some homewards, some for Rome in unsuccessful attempts to be officially released from their vows, some in search of another port from which to embark for Outremer. Moreover, many Crusaders making their way (particularly from Germany) to join the army at Venice, on hearing of what was happening, turned back; and Cardinal Peter Capuano, now in Venice again, maintained his protests. Then this man, the pope's legate, suddenly changed his mind completely, and accepted that it might, on balance, be better for the Zara attack to go ahead than for the whole Crusade to be abandoned. After all, the pope when ratifying the original Frankish-Venetian treaty had included a vital saving clause in his prohibition of war against Christians. If the papal legate accompanying the army was of the opinion that there existed a 'just or necessary' cause, he was empowered to grant permission for such warfare. Peter Capuano now convinced himself that the proposed Zara campaign would not preclude the ultimate object of the Crusade, the deliverance of the Sepulchre. On the contrary, a refusal to accept the Zara proposals would mean the withdrawal of the Venetian fleet, and consequently the total collapse of all the Crusade's objectives. The logic was inescapable. The Church therefore gave its official blessing to the Zara attack. Many Cistercians with the army were hesitant, Abbot Martin of Pairis asking the legate for a dispensation from his Crusading vows. Peter Capuano refused, and as if to clinch the matter made Martin the 'chaplain-general' of the German contingents.

Chapter 8

The Crusade at Zara

One Sunday in late August or early September 1202 a solemn mass was sung in St. Mark's, in the presence of a crowded congregation of Venetians and Franks.[1] Before the service the doge addressed those present, declaring his intention of accompanying the Crusade. He said, 'I am old and frail, and should now be taking my ease', but he himself was determined to lead the Venetian forces, his son Rainier staying behind as regent to look after State affairs at home. The doge said that the Venetians would be allies of 'the finest and most valiant men in the world', and, in an emotional scene, he knelt before the altar while a cross was sewn on his cap. He was followed by other Venetians. It would be naïve to dismiss these proceedings as insincere. Some of Dandolo's predecessors had ended their days as monks, and there is plenty of evidence throughout the twelfth century of genuine Catholic piety on the part of Venetians, who were eager builders of churches, of which Venice had large numbers besides St. Mark's. The Venetians' distinctive genius lay in an ability to keep religion and commerce in separate compartments. And now, the sacred service over, it was high time, with summer drawing to a close, for the Zara expedition to get under way, and the Venetians handed the promised transport ships over to the Franks.

Meanwhile there had arrived in Venice news of the death of Fulk, 'that good and holy man', the first to preach the Crusade. He died in May 1202, in his parish of Neuilly, still full of enthusiasm for the cause. He was buried in his own churchyard. At the time of his death there were available considerable sums of money which he had collected, and the French king, Philip Augustus, directed these to be entrusted to the safekeeping of Odo de Champlitte and Guy de Coucy. Most of the money collected by Fulk was in the end not to be used for the expenses of the Fourth Crusade at all but sent to Palestine for the repair of Crusader castles. The untimely death of Fulk must be borne in mind as we try to understand the change of character in the Crusade which was apparent from about this time. The barons and the army were saddened at the news, as they had great respect for the man who had so stirred their emotions. But an event which encouraged them during this troubled summer of 1202 was the arrival in Venice of a powerful group from Germany, including Conrad, bishop of Halberstadt, Count Berthold von Katzenellenbogen, Garnier von Borlande, Heinrich von Ülmen, and other men of noble rank, with their followers.[2]

The fleet set sail from Venice early in October, and the departure is described by Villehardouin and Robert de Clari. Each noble had a ship for himself and his own followers, with an accompanying transport vessel. Recalling the loading of the ships, Villehardouin many years afterwards could not help exclaiming, 'Heavens! what splendid war-horses!' The shields were hung along the sides, and banners were hoisted aloft. The doge had fifty galleys, he himself being sounded aboard his gaily painted ship by an ensemble of silver trumpets and drums. From the castles or wooden towers, of which there were two on each ship, fore and aft, rose the strains of the hymn *Veni Creator Spiritus*, 'Come Holy Ghost, our souls inspire', sung by the clergy. The actual sailing was heralded by a fanfare from a band of one hundred trumpets with drums and tabors.

The departure of this fleet was an imposing sight. There were more than two hundred major vessels in all, of which half were horse transports, known as 'huissiers' (from the 'huis' or door in the side). Some ships were very large, such as the *Paradise* of Névelon, bishop of Soissons, the *Pilgrim* of Garnier, bishop of Troyes, and the *Viola* of Stephen du Perche. There was one particularly big vessel, manned by Venetians, the *World*. In addition to the larger ships, some of which were oar-propelled galleys assisted by sails and some sailing-vessels pure and simple, were many smaller craft such as barges. Robert de Clari's heart swells with pride as he tells that 'when the sails were spread and the banners were hoisted high on the poops, it seemed as if the sea was trembling and on fire'. There was a feeling of elation amongst the pilgrims. At last something was being done, and the weary months of waiting on the Lido were over. But many of those aboard had sad forebodings and misgivings; not for this kind of warfare had they pledged themselves soldiers of the Cross.[3]

The fleet sailed near to the coast, and after calling at Trieste and Pola, where it reprovisioned, it arrived before Zara on 10 November. The harbour chain was broken and the knights, sergeants, and horses disembarked, to begin the siege of the port the next day. A few men had been left behind in Venice for sickness or other reasons, one of whom, Étienne du Perche, took the chance to defect when he recovered, making his way to Apulia with other knights – a party which was to sail direct for Syria in the spring of 1203. Amongst the Franks who stood before Zara there was also much uneasiness, as the city was Catholic and they themselves were Cross-soldiers armed with the papal blessing. Discontent had been growing as the project of the Fourth Crusade had unfolded itself in unexpected ways, resulting in several defections. Many men still with the army had wanted to return home, but this was not easy as it was regarded as a social disgrace for a Crusader to arrive home with his vow unfulfilled. After the special collection of money taken in Venice, few men would anyhow now have the resources for a return journey, and Innocent III, desperately anxious to keep his cherished Crusade intact, was not helpful in the matter of granting dispensations from Crusading vows. Nonetheless, dissatisfaction was increasing; and it was at Zara that the dissentients came for the first time to constitute a distinct and recognizable group.

Soon after the start of the siege there followed a diplomatic muddle. On 12 November representatives of Zara, having decided that defeat was inevitable at the hands of so powerful a force, emerged to parley with the doge. They were ready, they said, to surrender the city on condition that their lives were spared – a proposal which would achieve Dandolo's objective and restore Zara to the Venetian fold. Dandolo, however, replied, not unreasonably, that before concluding any terms he must first discuss the matter with his allies the barons,[4] and the Zara representatives were left waiting in the doge's pavilion. While Dandolo was absent consulting the leading Franks, the dissentients came forward to speak with the Zarans. They were led by Simon de Montfort and Robert de Boves, and in effect said to the Zarans, 'Why do you wish to surrender your city? The French certainly have no intention of fighting against you. It is only the Venetians you have to worry about.' The result of this intervention was that the Zaran deputation, much happier in mind, returned to the city. In the meantime the doge had spoken with the leading barons, who agreed that the surrender should be accepted, but when the doge and the barons accompanying him came back to the pavilion, they found the Zarans gone; they were furious at the meddling of Simon de Montfort and his friends.

With the Venetians, the barons, and the leading objectors gathered in the doge's pavilion, there was a bitter scene. To complicate matters the pope's letter of prohibition, delivered in Venice shortly after the expedition had set sail for Zara, had just arrived. It unequivocally forbade any attack on Christians. The Cistercian abbot of Lucedio, Peter, finding the Crusaders departed from Venice, had hastened to Zara with the letter and now handed it to Guy, Cistercian abbot of Vaux-de-Cernay, who triumphantly produced it in the pavilion and read it aloud, 'in the name of the pope of Rome', with its strict prohibition of the siege.[5] At this point Simon de Montfort and others had to intervene in person to protect Guy from the seething anger of the Venetians. The doge managed to calm the situation with his customary adroitness and appealed to the knightly instincts of French chivalry, reminding the Crusaders of their promise to help him to reconquer the port. The Crusaders were in a dilemma, and withdrew to consider the matter. Angry over the interference which had wrecked negotiations on the point of success, the majority now decided that it would indeed be dishonourable to break their word given to the doge. They agreed to join in the assault, though Simon de Montfort and others stood aside, refusing to have anything to do with it.

The siege lasted five days. The defenders hung crosses from the walls, to remind their assailants that they themselves were subjects of a Crusader king, but it was to no avail.[6] The besieging army was well equipped with catapults, some of these being mangonels, which bombarded the walls with heavy stones, others of a differently constructed type of machine known as petraries, which showered small stones over the walls. Scaling ladders were prepared on the ships lying in the harbour; and sappers started to dig a tunnel to undermine one of the towers. Realizing the futility of resistance since the Franks were after all joining in the assault, the city surrendered on 24 November. On Dandolo's suggestion, the conquerors now decided to settle down in the city for the winter, the Venetians and Franks dividing it between them, the former taking the half nearer the harbour. The best houses in the city were commandeered, and though there was no slaughter of the citizens there was a wholesale sack. The barons took the bulk of the spoils, the rank and file faring badly, and this perhaps helped to create the ill feeling which culminated in the determination of the lower ranks of the army to get everything they could out of the later stages of the Crusade.

There was soon more trouble between the allies. After only three days the Venetian and Frankish soldiers became involved in serious brawls and hand-to-hand street fighting in which many were killed or wounded. The casualties included a Flemish noble, Gilles de Landas, who died from a wound in the eye. Ironically enough, therefore, the first people against whom the Western Crusaders actually drew their swords were the Venetians.

On hearing of the sack of Zara, the pope's anger was evident. It was not the looting of a town as such, even a Christian and Catholic one, which aroused his wrath, but the fact that this had been done by men who had formally taken the Cross and were accordingly committed to fight only on behalf of Christ and his Church. Zara, moreover, was part of the kingdom of a sworn Crusader, Emeric. The attack of the army on the port was outrageous, and to Innocent's mind the unity of the enterprise must now have shown every sign of breaking. He felt a sense of personal betrayal in that a Crusade which was peculiarly his own had disgraced itself in this way. By virtue of previous papal warnings, the Franks by their attack on a Christian city were now in grave danger of excommunication.

When they heard of the pope's indignation the barons were genuinely alarmed and decided, towards the end of 1202, to send representatives to Rome. After all, the papal legate, Peter Capuano, had given his sanction to the assault. Pending Innocent's decision, the bishops serving with the army eased the consciences of the barons by assuring them that their sinful attack on Zara was provisionally forgiven.

In the embassy to the pope were two secular clergy, Névelon bishop of Soissons and Jean de Noyon, a clerk in Baldwin's entourage, and two knights, Jean de Friaize and Robert de Boves. The last had been a leading member of the party which had earlier upset the Zara operation by speaking soothing words to the citizens' deputation, and he now seized the chance to slip away and go to Syria. The delegation also included Abbot Martin of Pairis, who was probably sent to represent the German contingent but who, whilst in Rome, tried without success to obtain papal dispensation from his own Crusading vows. Thereupon he too left the army and went straight to Syria. The faithful three, Névelon, Jean de Noyon, and Jean de Friaize, met the pope and explained the difficult position in which the Crusaders had found themselves, blaming it on the numerous defections. They were humble and apologetic about it all, and found Innocent understanding and sympathetic. At the same time the deputation took the opportunity to obtain Innocent's views on the grand project shortly to be brought into the open – the placing of the young Alexius on the Byzantine throne. But the pope was already fully aware of this proposal; first Alexius himself, then Boniface, had been rebuffed, and the Crusaders' deputation now fared no better. Alexius III had already himself sent a deputation to the pope, asking him to prohibit the proposed expedition aimed at unseating him. The young prince, he said, had no legitimate claim to the throne, either by birth or election, and the pope had replied to the emperor on 16 November, not hiding his impatience with Constantinople over its tardiness in promoting the unity of the two great Churches, a project on which he had set his heart. Innocent was, nevertheless, still not in favour of the Crusaders' support for the prince,[7] and throughout 1202 he had remained constant in his dislike of the diversion plan, and kept alive his 'special relationship' with Alexius III.

During the course of his interviews with the envoys, however, Innocent realized the awkward predicament in which the Crusaders had been placed through their dealings with the Venetians. They had clearly acted under duress, and although he declared null and void the provisional absolution given by the bishops of the army, he promised his own absolution to the Crusaders on condition that they made vows of future obedience to Rome, and he gave a letter to a papal emissary to this effect. The delegation would therefore be able to return to Zara easier in their minds. But Innocent made it clear that the Crusaders must not again attack a Christian people. The only exceptions would be when their journey might happen to be obstructed, or there was 'other just or necessary cause'.[8] Whilst in Rome the three envoys pleaded also on behalf of the Venetians, but in their case the pope was inflexible, and the papal messenger who carried the letter of absolution for the Franks also took with him a specific sentence of excommunication for Dandolo and the entire Venetian expeditionary force. When the messenger arrived in Zara, Boniface was so alarmed that he flatly refused to allow him to deliver the excommunication to the Venetians. He wrote to the pope pointing out that it would mean the dissolution of the Crusade, and begging him to think again.[9] The papal legate, Peter Capuano, at this point came to the conclusion that the Crusade was doomed to disintegration, and sailed for Syria. He was not to return to the main Crusading army until after the conquest of Constantinople in 1204.

The insolent way in which the Venetians had earlier treated Peter Capuano probably rankled in the pope's mind. Moreover, why had they slighted him by not troubling to be represented in the delegation to Rome? Innocent was adamant, and refused to lift their excommunication. But he was fatally slow in informing Boniface of this decision; it was not until June 1203 that he replied to the marquis, ordering him to hand over to the Venetians their sentence of excommunication, at the same time categorically forbidding the proposed expedition to Constantinople. 'Go at once to the help of the Holy Land! Avenge the insult done to the Cross!'[10] But by this time the Crusade was in fact well on its way and almost within sight of the Byzantine capital. The truth is that for several months during 1202 and 1203 Innocent simply could not make up his mind, and although he himself doubted the wisdom of the diversion scheme, he dreaded the possibility of the Crusading army melting away.

A notable absentee from the assault on Zara was Boniface, even though he was the army's commander-in-chief. Where was he? Villehardouin says that 'some business detained him'. It has been suggested that he went to consult the pope,[11] but such a visit to Rome is most improbable and it is far more likely that Boniface's 'business' was in Germany. Ambitious thoughts, much further-reaching than the attack on a Dalmatian port, were brewing in his mind. The facts are that only a fortnight after the capture of Zara he duly arrived at the port, and shortly afterwards, on 1 January 1203, he was followed by envoys from the Swabian court with definite proposals from King Philip and Prince Alexius.[12] If the Crusading force would restore to Alexius his rightful inheritance (which would of course involve a detour to Constantinople), he in his turn would help it in the forthcoming campaign against Islam. He would pay the Crusaders 200,000 marks and also keep them supplied with provisions. This was not all. A contingent of 10,000 Byzantine troops would accompany the army, and if the Crusaders desired he himself would march with them, and for the rest of his life he would maintain a regular force of five hundred Byzantine knights in the Holy Land. He promised to place Byzantium under papal authority – and so heal the schism between East and West on the basis of the primacy of Rome. 'My lords,' declared the envoys from Hagenau, 'we have full authority to come to an agreement. . . . Terms like these are quite unprecedented, and we think that only a most unambitious man could reject them.'

Boniface clearly knew that this formal offer was going to be made; and the prospects of most pleasant lands in Greece, or exalted honours, were perhaps already lurking in his mind. He made an approach to Dandolo, who liked the scheme; it would guarantee that Venice received the money owing to her, and there was above all the possibility of the establishment of political conditions in Constantinople which would make the Republic's commercial position there finally secure. We cannot claim that the doge foresaw by this plan the beginning of the long era of Venetian maritime and commercial imperialism which lay ahead. What must have weighed most heavily in his mind was the chance of ending the wretched uncertainties which had plagued Venetian merchants in the Byzantine Empire over the last few decades.

The plan was discussed by the army leaders on the day after it was received, but whatever their views might have been, there was much discord amongst the lower ranks when they heard of it. This was probably the first time they had heard of the proposed diversion to Constantinople. These men found their spokesman in Guy, Cistercian abbot of Vaux-de-Cernay, who had earlier opposed the attack on Zara. They were reminded by other Crusaders, however, that an immediate campaign in Syria was not necessarily the best way by which the ultimate objective might be attained, and convenient news was arriving that the earlier defectors who had made straight for Syria had fared badly. To go by way of Constantinople and Egypt seemed more sensible. The clergy accompanying the army were divided on the issue. Having in mind the principle that if gold rust, iron can hardly be expected to do otherwise (as Chaucer in a later age put it), Villehardouin wondered how laymen can avoid squabbling if even the Cistercians were at variance. Though the abbot of Vaux-de-Cernay and other clerics spoke to the troops urging them to proceed at once to Syria and at least make an honourable fight on true Crusading soil, another Cistercian, Simon, abbot of Loos, with other religious heads, appealed in their sermons for the army to hold together as a single fighting force. 'Surely this is the best way of trying to reconquer Outremer.' Their argument did not lack a certain realism and common sense.[13]

The argument was virtually a clash between the militants and the practical moderates of the army, and, as might be expected, the responsible leaders, when faced with the realities of the situation, saw the worldly logic of the 'moderates'. The debt to Venice had to be paid; it was as simple as that. It was all very well to talk about making straight for Syria or Egypt, but for the army as a whole this would be impossible without the Venetian ships. The capture of Zara had taken the edge off many consciences, and when it came to the point the pope had forgiven them. In their ignorance of the true facts, they did not realize that young Alexius, if placed on the imperial throne, would not have the financial resources necessary for the fulfilment of his lavish undertakings. Byzantium in Western eyes was still a fabled land, and it was not appreciated how comparatively impoverished it had become in recent years. Dandolo knew quite well that the prince would never be able to fulfil his promises, as Venice was still awaiting the full compensation for the confiscations of 1171. But he held his peace.

The Crusaders were restless and by now rather tired of the constant upsets and delays. Many had probably received help or promise of help towards the cost of their journey before they set out, from the general collection made in church chests. Such grants had been given or promised on condition that in due course they produced certificates stating that they had actually reached their destination.[14] The leaders decided that the situation was dangerous and must be settled without delay. Their own minds were made up. Boniface, Baldwin, Louis de Blois, and Hugh de St. Pol made it known that they supported the Constantinople scheme. With Dandolo they met the envoys from Alexius and accepted the proposals with a formally sealed agreement. Villehardouin says that eight others also took the necessary oaths. He does not name them, and clearly implies that many others refused publicly to associate themselves with the treaty. 'I feel bound to say that only twelve men took the oaths on behalf of the Franks; no more could be persuaded to come forward.'[15] The bishops, however, were generally agreed on the plan, and the clerical element was very important in helping to hold the army together for the forthcoming approach to Constantinople. Despite the widespread misgivings about the Byzantine adventure, the fateful decision had been made. Philip's envoys returned with the sealed charters to the Swabian court, taking with them two knights whose responsibility would be to escort the young prince to the Crusaders' camp. It was expected that he would arrive at Zara not later than Easter of 1203.[16]

After the agreement there was a spate of desertions. In their eagerness to get away five hundred men crowded on to one ship, which was so heavy-laden that it sank with all aboard. Another group of defectors tried to escape by land, northwards through Dalmatia and Croatia, meeting with such opposition from the native inhabitants that the survivors were forced to return to Zara. One serious defection was that of a high-ranking German, Garnier von Borlande, who boarded a merchantman and departed. 'His action was very strongly criticized,' says Villehardouin. The powerful French baron, Renaud de Montmirail, also withdrew. He persuaded Count Louis to send him on a mission to Syria, and for this he was provided with a ship and sailed away with several knights, including a certain William, in due course to become Grand Master of the Templars and to meet a hero's death in battle at Damietta in 1219 during the Fifth Crusade. The object of Renaud's mission was simply 'to deliver a message'. We are not told what this was, but we may presume it was to persuade the defectors now in Syria to rejoin the main army. Renaud's men swore solemnly on the gospels to return to Zara promptly after accomplishing their mission, but they failed to do so.

It was during the occupation of Zara that the news arrived of the defection of Jean de Nesles, castellan of Bruges, with his powerful Flemish fleet. First, a message came for Count Baldwin (some of whose ships, loaded with provisions, were with de Nesles's fleet), saying that Jean had put in at Marseilles intending to winter there whilst awaiting Baldwin's orders. Baldwin sent word that Jean should sail at the end of March, and join him at the port of Methone (Modon) in the Peloponnesus on the western side of the Messenian promontory. But Jean changed his mind in the meantime and decided to sail straight to Syria from Marseilles. By the time his message reached Baldwin at Zara, he was in fact already at Acre.

By now, the number of defectors assembled at Acre was growing, and Renaud de Montmirail on his arrival was able to give them the latest news of the main army. He made it clear to them that it was likely to be a long time before it arrived in Syria. The new arrivals were eager to start fighting, though the titular king of Jerusalem, Amalric, advised caution. An earlier defector, Renaud de Dampierre, departed in high dudgeon seeking action further north in the service of Bohemond, prince of Antioch and count of Tripoli, who at the time was at war with Leo, king of Armenia. He took eighty knights with him, but the force fell into a Saracen ambush and was virtually annihilated. Amongst those who were killed was Gilles de Trasignies, a disloyal vassal of Baldwin. Renaud de Dampierre was

5a. A military provision cart carrying helmets, cooking-pots, etc., from the early thirteenth-century Maciejowski Bible, which has Old Testament illustrations showing medieval armour. Odo de Deuil, in *De Profectione*, tells how the many horse carts slowed down the French army during the Second Crusade.

5b. Soldiers in battle, with early thirteenth-century armour and various types of weapons. From the Maciejowski Bible.

6. The frontispiece of *Li Livre du Grant Caam*, by an English artist of the late fourteenth century, depicting Venice. It shows St. Mark's (with the horses), the Doge's Palace, and the winged lion on a column.

7a. Pope Alexander III, in 1177, presents Doge Sebastiano Ziani with a ceremonial sword, investing the Venetian Republic with its prized lordship of the seas. This print is thought to be an early copy from a drawing by the fifteenth-century Venetian artist Gentile Bellini.

7b. A nineteenth-century impression of Acre, the gathering-place for many disaffected Crusaders.

8a. The five domes of St. Mark's, which were modelled on those of the Holy Apostles church, Constantinople.

8b. St. Mark's interior, where Doge Dandolo, in 1202, addressed the Crusaders and himself took the cross.

taken prisoner, to remain in Muslim hands for thirty years.

By Easter 1203 the Crusade was preparing to leave Zara, though it had just suffered one of the most serious defections so far. The redoubtable Baron Simon de Montfort (the same who within a few years' time would lead the Albigensian Crusade in Provence, and whose younger son Simon was to come to England in 1231 and become famous, as earl of Leicester, as the 'father' of the English parliamentary system) had been for some time secretly planning to extricate himself from the whole affair and depart independently for Syria. He now defected, first making his way to Hungary, taking with him his brother Guy and several other prominent Frenchmen. With them, probably to the relief of Boniface and the other leaders, also went the voluble Guy, abbot of Vaux-de-Cernay. Eventually they found themselves at the Apulian port of Barletta, whence they embarked for Syria. Two other nobles of high rank, Enguerrand and Hugh de Boves, deserted shortly afterwards, taking many men with them. They were the brothers of Robert de Boves, who had left for Syria earlier; the three men, who came from Boves just south of the Somme near Amiens, are a striking example of a Crusading family group.

During April the ships were loaded for the voyage to Constantinople, and while the Crusaders moved their camp near to the harbour the Venetians levelled most of Zara to the ground. The main fleet with the army aboard set sail on 20 April, with Corfu as its immediate destination. The doge and Boniface stayed behind, Prince Alexius not yet having arrived. The prince duly reached Zara on 25 April, and with Dandolo and Boniface he at once left the Dalmatian port and sailed down the Adriatic, putting in at Durazzo some three hundred miles to the south, his first port of call within the Empire. The citizens of Durazzo came forward with alacrity to swear loyalty to the young prince appearing amongst them backed by such imposing allies.

On 4 May Alexius, Dandolo, and Boniface reached Corfu, where they found the army encamped. Tents had been pitched and the horses brought out of the transports for exercise. Alexius took up his quarters in a tent close to Boniface, who had been appointed his guardian by Philip of Swabia; the young prince was now the justification of the entire expedition, and his safety was of the utmost importance. The natives of the island, who had at first welcomed the Crusaders, became violent when Alexius arrived and gave him a bad reception, bombarding the anchored fleet with stone-throwing machines. Their action was ineffective and short-lived, but it boded ill for the attempt to obtain a good reception for Alexius from the Byzantines of Constantinople.

On Corfu, in the presence of Dandolo and the assembled barons, Prince Alexius solemnly affirmed the agreement. He would pay the Crusaders 200,000 silver marks, maintain the fleet for a year, and provide food for the army when in due course it embarked on its great enterprise to deliver the Sepulchre, besides contributing a Byzantine force of 10,000 troops. This was the price for being put on the imperial throne. The leaders now made the terms of the agreement officially public, and what many knights and sergeants had increasingly suspected was confirmed. The rumours were after all true. To the Crusaders, many of whom had taken the Cross with genuine motives, the whole design now appeared clear. They could remember how Boniface, on his election as leader, had somewhat inexplicably departed and spent a whole winter with Philip of Swabia, who was on bad terms with Innocent III at whose bidding they had taken the Cross. They would realize that Dandolo, from being a mere provider of transport (as at first intended), had become directly involved in the high command – and he was well known to be a bitter enemy of Constantinople. It was such suspicions which had already led many Crusaders to hesitate over joining the army at Venice, preferring to sail directly from Marseilles. Many Germans had failed to join the army, some of these probably because Otto of Brunswick had drawn back from the Crusade when he heard of Boniface's visit to his enemy Philip.

Innocent III was still perturbed, and in a letter to Philip Augustus, king of France, in May 1203, complained that the leaders of the Crusade, Frenchmen, had not only turned their arms against fellow Christians, contrary to his prohibition, but according to his information were now planning even worse things.[17] He did not know, of course, that by this time the Crusade was actually on its way to Constantinople.

The army stayed for three weeks on the island of Corfu. It was springtime and probably exceedingly pleasant. There was an abundance of good food and wine. But there now broke out the most serious dissension so far. The hesitant members of the army decided that if they were to break away it was now or never. They longed, in the words of Walther von der Vogelweide, 'to arrive at the place where God walked'. It was now fully obvious to all, rank and file included, that the immediate aim of the expedition was to put Alexius on the throne at Constantinople, and there is no reason for suspecting Villehardouin of exaggeration when he says that more than half the army were inclined to defect.[18] It is clear that morale was low, and that there was widespread opposition to the diversion scheme. Villehardouin mentions Jacques d'Avesnes, Peter d'Amiens, and Richard de Dampierre as amongst those who took a leading part in the protests. The opposition did not consist merely of sullen mutterings but was sufficiently vocal and organized for the dissentients to contrive a plan that when the fleet sailed from Corfu they would simply refuse to move. As soon as the ships were out of sight they would send word to Count Gautier de Brienne, who was in Brindisi, asking him to despatch transports to enable them to join him. In this risky enterprise they would rely on some co-operation from the native people of Corfu. The army was now in a state of outright schism, to the point where the objectors were a recognizable body, clearly defined, meeting for its conferences in a valley apart from the main camp.

The leaders realized that the expedition was in danger of utter collapse, and Boniface, Baldwin, Louis, and Hugh count of St. Pol, with other nobles, took

Alexius with them to the valley to confront the doubters. They were also accompanied by the bishops and abbots, which reinforces the impression that the objectors comprised the more 'dedicated' elements, the men who still had in mind their solemn vow to fight for the Cross. An emotional appeal was made to the dissentients not to desert. 'The marquis [Boniface] and his companions fell at the feet of those men, weeping bitter tears and refusing to get up until they promised not to defect.' The feelings of all present were deeply stirred. The men talked the matter over and the chivalrous instinct, that true knights should never abandon their comrades in arms, prevailed.

The dissentients agreed to stay with the army until Michaelmas (29 September), another four months, on one condition: the leaders must promise unequivocally, by swearing on the gospels, that if at any time the doubters subsequently were to decide to go to Syria, they would be provided with the necessary ships within a fortnight. The leaders agreed, and the army set sail at once for Constantinople, since it was now even more clearly in the interests of Boniface and his colleagues to proceed with the newly declared business as quickly as possible.

Chapter 9

City of the World's Desire

The city for which the Crusaders now sailed was founded, under the name Byzantium, by Dorian Greeks in 657 BC, as a colony of the flourishing seaport-state of Megara. It was well placed for commerce, every vessel plying between Greece and Scythia being obliged to pass beneath its walls, the city itself lying on a pear-shaped promontory at the south-west end of the Bosphorus, projecting from the European shore of the straits. North of the promontory was the elongated bay known as the Golden Horn, reaching inland between steep banks for about seven miles – one of the world's great natural harbours. Though sometimes difficult to enter because of the prevailing north-easterly winds, it was calm and well sheltered, and so deep that large vessels could approach closely to the shore. It was out of reach of the fierce Bosphorus current and, not being a river, was free from the danger of silting. To the south was the Sea of Marmora which, like the Bosphorus, teemed with fish, and the Asian shore opposite was studded with venerable Greek cities, such as Chalcedon, like Byzantium founded as a Megarian colony. The Bosphorus, with a width of only a mile or less, had necessarily to be negotiated by any fleet approaching from the south, and resolute naval opposition would add to the difficulty of obtaining entry into the harbour. Land attack was impossible except on one side, and during the earlier centuries of its history Byzantium had in fact never been taken by storm, its few capitulations resulting from treachery.

After a strengthening of its defences, and vast improvements which included the embellishment of the public buildings with marbles and columns taken from pagan temples, the city had been formally dedicated, on 11 May AD 330 by the emperor Constantine, to the Holy Trinity and the Mother of God, and 'New Rome' had rapidly become the greatest city in the Christian world. With the passing of the centuries, its wealth became legendary, even in the farthest lands of the West. There is a story told of a late eleventh-century Canterbury monk Eadmer who broke off a fragment from a relic of St. Prisca and was about to take another piece when Archbishop Anselm stopped him, saying, 'You already have enough, and the lady to whom this relic belongs would not exchange it for all the gold in Byzantium.'[1] Benjamin of Tudela, a Spanish Jew who arrived in Constantinople about 1162, reported that 'from every part of the Empire of Greece tribute is brought here every year, and strongholds are filled with garments of silk, purple, and gold. Like unto these storehouses and this wealth, there is nothing in the whole world to be found. The Greek inhabitants are very rich in gold and precious stones, and they go clothed in garments of silk and gold embroidery and they ride horses, and look like princes.'[2] Other twelfth-century visitors to Constantinople included al-Harawy, an Arab, who was later to write of it enthusiastically, 'May God make this Islam's capital!'[3]

To get their hands on the city's riches had been the dream of adventurers since the time of the Vikings, for whom Mikligarth, as they called Constantinople, was the ultimate goal. Byzantine poets extolled the splendour of their capital, of which they were intensely proud. To Constantine of Rhodes, who wrote of the mosaics of the church of the Holy Apostles, Constantinople was 'the city of the world's desire'. Moreover, with the entry of the Seljuk Turks into Asia Minor, those hitherto rich lands had become very insecure, and wealthy men had consequently tended to bring their valuables for greater safety into the capital held by all to be impregnable. The wealthier inhabitants of the islands and coastal towns of the Aegean, much troubled in the later years of the twelfth century by piracy, had also migrated into Constantinople, and so by 1200 the city itself was in terms of tangible wealth richer than ever before, though the Empire as a whole was poorer and in a larger sense its economic position unsound because of the loss of trade to the Italian merchant cities.

Of outstanding importance amongst Constantinople's treasures were its sacred relics, whose profusion had struck Fulcher of Chartres a century before the Fourth Crusade, and there was a steady stream of pilgrims from the West who came just to see them. The Greek scholar Nicholas Mesarites proudly claimed that while Jerusalem retained Golgotha and the Holy Sepulchre, Constantinople possessed innumerable relics of the Nativity and Passion.[4] There might even be said to have been a surfeit of relics, and when early in the twelfth century an Englishman in the service of Byzantium, Ulfric, who was a native of the still largely Danish-speaking East Anglia, was sent by Alexius I on a mission to Henry I of England to recruit for the Varangian Guard, he took with him many relics for distribution as gifts.[5]

So large was the number of relics in the city in 1204 that Villehardouin said there must be as many there as in the rest of the world put together.[6] Constantinople was thought of as a 'safe' city, unlike Rome, which had been sacked on more than one occasion. Relics were regarded as inviolable there, and their number and variety made the city a thriving place of pilgrimage. Devotees came from as far afield as Scandinavia and the north, the last important Norseman known to have made the pilgrimage being Rognvald, jarl of Orkney, who came in the mid-twelfth century. Pilgrims came too from Russia, such including Dobrynia Iadreïkovitch, who arrived in Constantinople in 1200. He returned home with many relics, amongst which was a piece of the True Cross which he presented to the cathedral of Novgorod, whose archbishop he subsequently became – taking the 'religious' name of Anthony. Soon after his visit he made a list of Constantinople's relics, one of which was 'the linen on which is the likeness of Christ'; and he was much impressed by the ceremonial in St. Sophia, where 'the singing was beautiful and sweet, like that of angels'.[7]

Constantinople was the largest city of the medieval world, even though the frequently mentioned figure of about a million for its population by the close of the twelfth century must be an exaggeration. The population of the city was multi-racial, and though it is common to call them Greeks, not many of them were now actually Greeks in the classical and Hellenic sense. They themselves preferred to be known as 'Romans'. Over the centuries many immigrants had arrived – for example, after a serious revolt in 741 following the destruction of icons, Constantinople had been largely repeopled with settlers from Asia. In fact the Byzantines had very little consciousness of the idea of 'race', and a man was one of them, in their view, if he spoke Greek and was Orthodox in religion. Constantinople, despite its large population, was not unduly overcrowded, though it was only seven miles long and five miles wide (at its westernmost point). The population was dense on the northern shore, with its wharves, but on the southern side facing the Sea of Marmora and in the western districts there was ample space.

The main street, the Mesê, lined with arcades and shops, and crowded during daylight with lively and talkative people, ran through the centre of the city westwards from the Milion, the starting-point for all roads in the Empire. After a mile and a half it forked into two roads, the one turning left and leading to the Golden Gate at the southern extremity of the land-wall, the other continuing in a north-westerly direction towards the Blachernae palace. The city had street-lighting, an amenity unknown or at least extremely rare in Western Europe.

The land-wall still shielding the city in the twelfth century was the famous Theodosian Wall, built in 413, replacing the original wall of Constantine, which was shorter and enclosed a smaller city area. The earlier wall fell into disuse soon after its replacement, though some remains of walls, probably part of the Constantinian, were still to be seen in relatively modern times near Isa Kapoussi. The famous Golden Gate, with its two large bronze elephants, was the southernmost of several gates piercing the outer land-wall, and traditionally the state entrance to the capital. In 1200 the land-wall was for most of its length double, though some of it was triple, and at intervals were defensive towers, ninety-six in all. The walls were high, and constituted the most formidable system of fortification in Europe at the time. In addition to the land-wall there was a sea-wall along the Golden Horn, and another shielding the city on the Marmora shore. It was the centuries-old protection of the city from assault by these walls which had helped to encourage the decline of the navy during the late twelfth century. A long siege did not hold for Constantinople the terror which it had for most medieval cities, as there was a plentiful supply of water in the cisterns, the most impressive survival of these being the great underground cistern known as Yere Batan Serai, with its 336 columns adorned with Corinthian capitals. This vast cistern drew water from the aqueduct of the emperor Valens, completed in 378. In its entire history from 330 to our own times the city of Constantinople has been stormed only twice, by the Latins in 1204 and the Turks in 1453, on each occasion as a result of a combined land–sea operation.

The imperial palace covered a large area in the south-eastern corner of the city, on the sloping ground rising from the sea to the hill on which now stands the mosque of Sultan Ahmed I, the Blue Mosque. The way in from the Augusteum was by a sumptuous entrance known as the Brazen House. There was a view from the palace over the sea – and part of the façade, pierced with windows set in marble casements that once opened directly on to balconies, survives as a feature of the coastline. The palace complex, the work of successive emperors and known to the Latins as the Bucoleon from the statue of a bull and lion fighting each other which had previously stood in the palace harbour, consisted of residential buildings, baths, chapels, corridors, and halls. Until the twelfth century it was the emperor's normal residence, though the Blachernae had been restored and enlarged by Alexius I, who was actually residing in it at the time of the arrival of the First Crusade. Manuel I and his successors used both palaces, and Manuel carried out much building work in the Great Palace as well as the Blachernae.[8] It was the Great Palace which the first Latin emperor was to choose when he took possession in 1204. Though the Blachernae was richer in mosaics and ornamentation, the Bucoleon had about it an aura of imperial grandeur and tradition – here was the imperial treasure, and here were the official reception halls. On a promontory stood a lighthouse or pharos to guide sailors into the Bosphorus and towards the safety of the Golden Horn. Inside the Bucoleon was Constantinople's most important collection of relics, with many classical statues, and it was regarded by the 'Greek' population as the real heart of the city and Empire.

The city's inhabitants lived in houses of all grades from the mansions of the nobles to the slum-like dwellings of the very poor, but without much sense of segregation of classes along 'neighbourhood' lines. Sites by the sea were naturally favoured by the rich for their villas. The palaces and numerous mansions were of stone or even marble, though brick was a favourite building material throughout the city. The many fires in Constantinople's history also suggest an extensive use of timber. A rich man's house, usually of two storeys, would have few or no windows on the outside, the family life being conducted around the inside courtyard with its fountain of dancing water. The poorer houses, often balconied, lined the mazes of narrow alleys and passages. Two amenities which would appear strange to the approaching Latin Crusaders were the ample parks and gardens maintained for the citizens from public funds, and the drainage system which carried the effluent to the sea, the latter contrasting favourably with what is known of the crude Western sanitary arrangements.

Like all medieval cities, Constantinople was a forest of churches. The greatest of these was St. Sophia, the church of Holy Wisdom, close to the Bucoleon and like the palace itself a centre of city life. Though the actual foundation was Constantine's, the church as it stood in 1200 was the inspiration of the emperor Justinian, completed in 547, and the work not of professional architects but of a mathematician, Anthemius of Tralles, and an engineer, Isidore of Miletus. The distinguishing feature of the building was its shallow dome, whose outward thrust was met by a complex series of semi-domes and lesser domes, the whole giving an impression of effortless suspension from heaven. The orator Michael of Thessalonica, in a rhetorical description of St. Sophia in the mid-twelfth century, said that Man built it but God surely took part in its construction. He praised the mosaic ceilings, the sculptured columns, the walls completely covered, as it were, with 'stone cloaks'. Michael spoke of the floor as a sea in which lay the sanctuary, anchored by columns of silver. Except for a few patches, the paved floor existing today is much the same as that known to Michael, and its slabs of Proconnesian marble suggest the formation of waves.[9] Governed by its dome, St. Sophia is almost a square, and the prevailing idea is that of a central apse, unlike that of the corridor or avenue characteristic of basilical and Gothic architecture. St. Sophia was admirably suited for the gathering of crowds, and on occasions it echoed to the shouting of the citizens as well as to the unearthly music so admired by Anthony of Novgorod. South-west of St. Sophia and directly connected with it was the palace of the patriarch, including the offices of the central ecclesiastical bureaucracy, all this closely adjoining the Augusteum.

The basilical type of building, however, had been well known in Constantinople at earlier dates, and one such building was the venerable church of St. John of Studius, near the Golden Gate. An aisled structure with Corinthian pillars, it was to suffer badly at the hands of the Crusaders, and the present paving forms part of the restoration work undertaken after the departure of the Latins in 1261. There was a famous monastery attached to the church, founded by a consul named Studius in the 450s. Also basilical was the church of St. Polyeuktos, built in Justinian's reign. Close to the modern Town Hall its ruins have recently come to light, and there are several carved capitals identical with those to be seen outside the south-west angle of St. Mark's, Venice. Near the Bucoleon was a small domed church almost overlooking the Marmora, built by Justinian and dedicated to SS. Sergius and Bacchus; and in the centre of the city stood the illustrious church of the Holy Apostles, burying-place of Constantine the Great and, with its series of small domes, the prototype of St. Mark's, Venice. Other churches included those of Holy Peace and the Holy Resurrection, both of them foundations of Constantine, and the church of St. Mary at Blachernae, renowned for its precious relics of the Virgin.

The city had numerous monks and nuns. Although the Byzantines preferred to establish their monasteries on remote mountains (such as Mount Athos), as many as seventy-eight monasteries are identifiable in twelfth-century Constantinople. The monks moved freely from one house to another, there being no distinct religious Orders like those of the Latin West. In general the monks were respected, and they were popularly recruited, containing a higher proportion of the proletariat and peasantry than did the Catholic abbeys. The monks, said Michael Psellos, 'model their lives on the Divine', though there were, evidence confirms, some rogues and charlatans amongst them. Though many monasteries had libraries, there were few instances of Byzantine houses developing into great centres of education and learning, as so often in the West; but a notable exception was the Studius monastery, a centre of manuscript illumination, verse composition, and liberal scholarship. 'I pass my days in a cell that is like a palace,' wrote one monk of his life in Studius. Rather more important, however, were monastic good works, notably in medicine and nursing. The monastery of the Pantocrator ('ruler of all'), founded in Constantinople by the emperor John II and his empress Irene in 1136, included a hospital, with more than fifty beds as well as a psychiatric ward for dealing with cases of mental illness, and also an out-patient clinic. Besides nurses there was a staff of thirty-six physicians, some of whom were women. The greatest concentration of monasteries in Constantinople was in the north-westerly district known as the Petrion, along the shore of the Golden Horn.[10]

A traditional centre of the city's life was the Hippodrome, immediately adjoining the Great Palace, in earlier times famous for its amusements and as a gathering-place for the people. By the twelfth century the baiting of wild animals was prohibited, and chariot races had lost their old appeal. Moreover, the great annual festival commemorating the inauguration of the city on 11 May was less popular.[11] It was a sign of the times that the westernizing Manuel used the Hippodrome to familiarize his subjects with the idea of tournaments. The structure of the Hippodrome has now gone though on its site alongside the Blue Mosque remains a fragment of a bronze serpent originally from Apollo's temple at Delphi, and a granite obelisk made by the Pharaoahs and erected here by the emperor Theodosius about 390. In 1200 there was much monumental work of superlative quality in the Hippodrome, including the famous horses which later were to stand over the main portal of St. Mark's in Venice.

In addition to the Hippodrome there were the Forums of Constantine, of Theodosius, of Arcadius, and the Bovis Forum; and there was also the great square known as the Augusteum, between the Bucoleon and St. Sophia, surrounded by colonnades in which citizens could meet, loiter, talk and argue. On the site of Constantine's Forum there is still a battered porphyry column scorched by fire, which in 1200 was in sound condition and in fact had been restored by Manuel. A statue of Constantine, represented as Apollo, stood on top of it. In the Forum of Theodosius fragments of the great triumphal arch have in recent years been found. Constantinople had many ancient columns and statues, and the city must have had the aspect of a Hellenic museum, enshrining the memory of past glories.

The city for which the Crusading expedition was making had long been a centre of learning and culture. It would, of course, be wrong to assume that Constantinople, or indeed the Byzantine Empire in general, was uniquely eminent in the matter of scholarship, and there was no sharply defined contrast between a gentle and scholarly East and a rough and barbaric West. The Byzantines themselves at this time may well have been largely unaware of the high intellectual attainments of Western Europe.[12] Enormous strides had been made in the West during the twelfth century in several fields of scholarship, and the universities were beginning to take shape. Nonetheless, education was deeply respected in Byzantium, and was more firmly rooted, especially in the lay mind, than in most Western countries. An educated person would be expected to have a knowledge of the classics, Homer being held in particularly high regard. True, there had been bleak periods in the history of Byzantine education and learning: Justinian had in 529 stopped the teaching of law and philosophy at Athens by appropriating the professors' salaries, and Phocus in the following century had closed the university of Constantinople. But subsequently in the East there was a revival, and the expression 'twelfth-century renaissance' should be held to include wide areas of Europe within its scope and not only the Western countries, though it has come to be especially applicable to northern France with its great cathedral schools. In the decades preceding 1200 there was some increased enthusiasm for Greek and Latin scholarship in the Empire, if of a nostalgic character. At its base was a pride in the glories of Hellas. This revived interest in the classical authors, and the consciousness of being their heirs and successors, helped to make the Byzantines contemptuous of Westerners and quite unjustly regard them all as dolts and ignoramuses.

Prominent amongst late twelfth-century scholars was Eustathius. Educated in Constantinople, he became a member of the clerical establishment of St. Sophia and a highly regarded teacher with a flourishing school. Later he was archbishop of Thessalonica, where he remained until his death about 1192. A religious leader and monastic reformer, he also commented authoritatively on Pindar and Homer's Odyssey and Iliad. Amongst his pupils was Michael Choniates, who was born in 1140, a native of Chonae (the Colossae of St. Paul) in Phrygia. After many years in Constantinople Michael was for over thirty years archbishop of Athens, where he resided on the Acropolis, maintaining his cathedral inside the Parthenon itself. He regarded the spirit of Athens as part of ultimate being, and though he loved the old monuments, of which many survived, to him it was the wisdom and character of the ancient Greeks which had created Hellenism. Like Byron in a later age he thought that the people around him were scarcely Greeks in the original sense. He appealed to them to emulate their distant ancestors – an ambition far beyond them, though they loved and respected their learned archbishop nonetheless. Michael is one of the most attractive figures of the twelfth century.[13] Hardly less capable was his brother Nicetas, a civil servant who rose in the bureaucracy of the Angeli dynasty of emperors to the rank of Grand Logothete, and in due course was to write his *History* covering the period between 1118 and 1206. He was to write as one with a personal knowledge of the inner workings of imperial government and, though capable of prejudice, he enables us to see the Crusaders through Byzantine eyes.

It is impossible to calculate how many books and libraries existed in Constantinople at the close of the twelfth century. We must not assume too readily that vast stocks of ancient manuscripts perished in the fires which were to be a ruinous feature of the Crusaders' attack on the city. The real damage had been done centuries before, when the splendid library founded by the emperor Julian, with its 120,000 volumes, was destroyed by fire in 476. There was now no great library, though some monasteries and churches had good collections, mostly devotional and theological. But the revival of classical studies in the twelfth century, and the fact that education in Byzantium was less limited to the clergy than it was in the West, did mean that there would be copies of old Greek and Latin authors in the city, often in the mansions of the nobility. Some of these were undoubtedly to be lost in the coming fires. Classical Greek, as distinct from that of the markets and streets, was widely studied, and the masterpieces of ancient literature and philosophy correspondingly treasured.

Though one speaks of 'East' and 'West' as representing the two great branches of Christendom, the Byzantine Empire had in fact shrunk by the closing years of the twelfth century to a fraction of its former size, and on the map appears as a small area compared with Europe as a whole. From Constantinople were governed, besides the immediately surrounding regions, the whole of Greece proper, a country poor in natural resources, and the Aegean islands. The emperor's government was still maintaining a hold on about a third of Asia Minor, in the centre of which, however, the Seljuks were now firmly established in their Sultanate of Rum, with its capital at Iconium. Constantinople retained its authority around the southern coasts of the Black Sea, and this was so especially in the Trebizond region. In many areas the actual boundaries were ill defined and at some points liable to change almost overnight. In 1191 Cyprus had been taken by Richard of England and lost to Byzantium for ever. By this time, moreover, there was no longer any question of the Empire claiming territorial jurisdiction over Italy and Sicily. The great days of Byzantine imperialism were over.

After a period of financial stability whose length of about eight centuries is probably unique for any State in world history, the economic position of the Empire in the twelfth century had weakened. This was largely because the Crusaders had opened up a direct route from the West to the Levant, it now being possible to by-pass Constantinople. As a result the emperors made strenuous efforts to get the Italian merchants into the capital, offering many financial and trading concessions by way of inducement. Under Manuel there was much extravagance;[14] and there was a tendency to shift the burden of taxation away from the wealthy to the poorer classes. Andronicus had come to power largely as a champion of the latter, and not only as being an opponent of Manuel's policy of favouring Westerners.

Throughout his reign Manuel encouraged a move towards a form of feudalism, the landowners becoming increasingly independent of central government and emerging as local potentates in their own right. The grant to individuals of land or other endowments, known as *pronoia*, became common. Grants '*in pronoia*' were not hereditary, reverting to the State on the death of the recipient, and there was nothing in the Byzantine system which corresponded with the Western practices of homage and sub-infeudation. Nonetheless, the granting of *pronoia* was a development which would facilitate the breaking-up of the Empire on feudal lines by the Crusaders after 1204.

For administrative purposes the Empire was traditionally divided into provinces known as 'themes', each under a *strategos*. At one time there had been almost forty of these divisions, but with the contraction of the imperial frontiers due to Turkish and Bulgarian conquests they were reorganized in the twelfth century, the term *strategos*, which had a military significance, being replaced by that of *dux*, which implies mainly administrative functions. The subordinate officials of the governor or *dux* were known as *catepans*. The 'theme' system was less important by the closing years of the century, though the influence of the bureaucracy throughout the Empire remained constant, and there was a civil service tradition such as the West hardly knew. This tradition made for social stability, but the non-productive class was disproportionately large, and when this consideration is placed alongside the commercial decline resulting from the loss of the carrying trade to the enterprising Italian city-republics, the economic difficulties of the Byzantine Empire in the decades leading to 1200 are easy to understand.

The loss of the bulk of Anatolia to the Turks had been disastrous. The 'themes' of Asia Minor, with their ancient cities, had constituted the real strength of the Empire, and it was the villages and valleys of this region which had provided many of the army's finest recruits. Native imperial troops could still be raised, in such regions as Greece proper, but the Greeks of the eleventh and twelfth centuries were many generations removed from the men who had hurled back the Persians of classical times. Waves of Slavic immigrants had changed the character of the people, and it was only in the islands and coastal regions of the Aegean that Greeks of the original ethnic stock were now to be found in substantial numbers. Moreover, the hardy men of the Balkans were no longer so readily available for the Byzantine armies after the establishment of the second Bulgarian kingdom late in the twelfth century. But the Comneni emperors, from Alexius I onwards, did not neglect their army, and indeed spent on it greater sums of money than ever, enough to add to the financial embarrassment of the Empire. This was because the 'Greek' army was now largely composed of units, generously paid, drawn from men of many nationalities. The Byzantine army is consequently often referred to as a mercenary one, which is unfortunate in view of the derogatory sense which has come to be attached to the term 'mercenary' in our day. The foreign contingents of the Byzantine army might be compared rather with the famed and highly respected Gurkha battalions recruited for the British Army from the independent State of Nepal. The Byzantine foreign units were quite different in character from such troops as the 'free companies' under their contracting captains who did much of Western Europe's fighting in the later Middle Ages. The 'mercenaries' of Byzantium were actually regularized units of an imperial force.

However, before the defeat of Manzikert in 1071 the Byzantine army had been a more truly native force. In its discipline and sense of organization it had continued the tradition of the old Roman army. It was excellently equipped, well led according to the soundest principles of military doctrine, and there was a right emphasis on the use of tactics to suit particular occasions and adversaries. Thus it was standard policy that, if possible, pitched battles should always be avoided with the Franks, whose strength lay in a massed cavalry charge. Aggression was to be discouraged, greater reliance being placed on defensive measures. War was a science, to be waged intelligently, and the officers were better educated than the knights of Western armies and well read in military manuals and textbooks, such as the *Strategicon* of the emperor Maurice (582–602) and Leo VI's *Established Tactics* of three centuries later. Leo's treatise was essentially a description of the tactics of the various enemies of Byzantium, and the methods by which these should be met.

The organization of the old imperial army was based on the territorial 'themes', and many of the soldiers, particularly those of the cavalry, were maintained by the grant of small agricultural holdings, which they farmed while keeping themselves ready for military service as required. Foreigners had been enlisted early, especially for the emperor's own bodyguard, but on the whole in the three or four centuries preceding Manzikert the army was Byzantine and the troops would have had the consciousness of defending their homeland. After the crushing defeat of 1071, however, the principle of recruitment by way of the native 'themes' was lost, and not only was it difficult to enlist and sustain a regular native army but there was a growing practice of purchasing exemption from compulsory military service. There were some élite formations, like the Archontopuli, raised by Alexius I from the orphan sons of aristocrats, but by the closing decades of the eleventh century men from many countries outside the Empire were taking service in the Byzantine army – not only Russians and Western Europeans but also Turks and other Muslims. Under the Comneni dynasty foreign recruitment became a regularized practice, especially under Manuel, who even appointed Westerners to high commands.

Prominent among the foreign troops were the men of the Varangian Guard, which had its distant origins in the commercial activities of Swedes from the Baltic. It was perhaps about the year 1000 that they were first recruited for the emperor's bodyguard, taking the place of the old Immortals, a regiment of élite Byzantines raised by Michael II in the ninth century but which disappeared in the course of the eleventh. The new guards were known as the 'axe-bearers' from their favourite weapon, and they were seen as a peculiarly northern force, though in addition to Swedes and other Scandinavians they included some Slavs. Amongst high-ranking officers of the Guard was the brother of St. Olav, Harald Hardrade ('the ruthless'); and an apparent reference to a Swedish commander in the Varangian Guard occurs in a runic inscription carved on a rock at Edd in Uppland, in which it is said that Ragnvald was commander of the carls in Graekenland. Several other Swedish runes, mostly of the eleventh century, commemorate Vikings who died in the land of the Greeks.[15]

The term Varangians or 'vaerings' was strictly applicable to any group of men, whether merchants or warriors, who took oaths of loyalty to each other and their chief, and the term is cognate with 'vārar', oaths. The Varangian Guards were especially valued as men with a strong sense of loyalty to their leader, a quality in accord with Viking and also Anglo-Saxon tradition. The Anglo-Saxon word 'wāer' carries with it the idea of fidelity, and in Alfred's translation of Orosius the verb 'werian' means 'to defend'. The Byzantine emperors valued specific promises of loyalty, and the oaths which they sought were of a different type from those usually sworn in Western Europe in return for protection and endowment. The Varangian oath was not feudalistic but rooted rather in Nordic ideas. Anna Comnena, the historian daughter of Alexius I, thought well of the Varangians, saying that with them loyalty was a tradition and regarded as sacred.[16]

After the Norman Conquest of England there was a large emigration of Englishmen around the year 1075, in a fleet of over two hundred ships led by Sigurd, jarl of Gloucester, and including many men of high rank. Travelling by way of the Balearics and Sardinia to Byzantium, they helped to relieve Constantinople from a siege about 1081, and were well received by the emperor. Some of the English fretted at the prospect of a confined and subservient role in Constantinople, and persuaded the emperor to allow them to establish a colony for themselves in the Crimea, which they appropriately called New England (nova Anglia). But others enlisted in the imperial service, and fought for the emperor during the Norman invasion of the Greek mainland led by Robert Guiscard from southern Italy. They were much praised by Anna Comnena, who said that the English were as warlike as the Normans and even more courageous, though less professional in battle. During the reign of Alexius I (1081–1118) there was a considerable recruitment of Englishmen into the Varangians, by now regarded not only as the emperor's personal guard but as the élite force of the imperial army.[17] With the Anglo-Saxons were Danes from the English eastern counties, the Danelaw.

From now on, right through the twelfth century, the Varangians continued to include Anglo-Saxons, as the most substantial element in a generally Germanic and Scandinavian force, recruited partly from a constant flow of adventurers and emigrants, partly from the sons of veteran Varangians. The Varangians were called 'Germans' by Nicetas, though he referred to them also as 'English'.[18]

Villehardouin in his narrative consistently called them 'Englois et Danois'. The Varangians were well paid and fed, and splendidly accoutred; and they would be the 'show' troops on ceremonial occasions. They were also regarded as fine and dependable soldiers. They did sometimes get out of hand, particularly through their hard northern drinking habits, but they were generally well disciplined and were to play a prominent part in the forthcoming defence of the capital against the Franks and Venetians, who would find them tough adversaries.[19]

The Byzantines had carefully looked after their navy during the Arab aggressions of the seventh and eighth centuries, Constantinople in consequence remaining inviolate. There was, also, a period in the ninth century when Michael III and Basil I paid careful attention to the fleet, but this did not last long and by the eleventh century the navy was in such decay that when the Normans attacked in strength, help had to be sought from the Venetians. Alexius I tried to strengthen his fleet, levying a general tax for the construction of warships and the training of sailors in 1109. The navy was still effective under Manuel, being successful against Venice in 1171, but this emperor tended to treat it with comparative neglect, allowing the islands and coastal districts to purchase exemption from service in the navy, a folly deplored by Nicetas.[20] After Manuel's death the decline of the Byzantine fleet became serious. Michael Choniates, archbishop of Athens, says that in 1198 Alexius III ordered special taxes for the fleet but that this money did not invariably reach its proper destination. Whereas the Venetian Republic was accustomed to maintain its ships in constant readiness from the profits earned by overseas trade, Byzantine fleets were controlled by the bureaucracy and paid for out of taxes, which meant that whenever there was no immediately pressing danger the tendency was for the Empire to relax its naval guard.[21]

A thought which must have been uppermost in the mind of Dandolo was that Venice, as the supreme maritime power in the Mediterranean, now had the key to decisive success. There was little wrong with the quality of Byzantine seamanship, and the standard imperial warship, the dromond, was formidable in action. This vessel was a bireme, manned by a crew of about three hundred and armed with a ram which could be used with deadly effect against opposing vessels. Byzantine ships were well built and manœuvrable, and there was a large population familiar with the sea, on the coasts and in the Aegean islands, on which to draw for crews. It was actually easier to man the fleet than the army, and the Empire need never have turned for help to the Venetians. The rapid deterioration of the navy in the latter decades of the twelfth century is both inexcusable and inexplicable, and was undoubtedly a cause of the collapse of 1203–4.[22]

It is significant too that in the defence of the city against the Crusaders the famous Greek fire, which had saved Constantinople on so many occasions, was either not used or, if so, with little effect. Reputedly the invention of a seventh-century Syrian Greek, Callinicus, Greek fire could be used devastatingly

against ships. It was a mixture of crude oil and other materials, producing an
inflammable liquid, so that not only were enemy vessels set alight but also the
surrounding water. The mere knowledge of the existence of Greek fire tended to
keep potential aggressors away from Constantinople. The liquid was discharged
to the accompaniment of much smoke and noise from bronze tubes, normally
fitted into the sides of ships though capable of being used as land weapons. Greek
fire could also be used in the form of grenades. The mixture was so secret that it is
still not known with complete accuracy, and though it would be going too far to
say that the formula was never at any time in Byzantine history betrayed or
divulged, in general it was well guarded, possession of the knowledge being
considered a solemn trust. But the weapon was of no help to Constantinople in
the great crisis of 1204, the only apparent explanation being that the correct
materials for making it were temporarily unavailable.

The Byzantines were not on the whole a naturally bellicose people, and for this
reason were often despised by Westerners as effeminate. The emperors did not
use their armed forces unnecessarily, preferring when possible the arts of
diplomacy in attempting to achieve their political ends. Foreign ambassador-
ships in the modern style were not maintained, though the government did make
it its business to know what was happening in neighbouring countries, and
considerable skill was often shown in playing off one foreign people against
another, and letting other States or armies do the required fighting. It was in
accordance with this principle of Byzantine policy that Alexius I used his allies,
the warriors of the First Crusade, to fight his battles with the Turks. Part of the
reason for the 1204 débâcle is that the traditional Byzantine device of using one
opponent to confound another was either not employed or was unsuccessful.
Earlier Byzantine governments might well have tried to separate, or set at one
another's throats, the Venetians and Franks; and in view of what had happened
in the streets of Zara, where the two parties came to blows, this should not have
been impossible. The readiness with which the young Alexius made promises of
subsidies to the Crusaders was also fully in line with Byzantine tradition. The
payment of money to potential enemies or allies was a perfectly respectable
aspect of imperial policy.[23] It was a practice which over a long period helped to
drain the treasury, undermine the economy, and at the same time encourage
outside peoples to believe that Byzantium was fabulously rich. The freehanded-
ness of successive Byzantine governments had made possible a flexible and
adaptable diplomacy; but by 1204 the treasury had ceased to be inexhaustible.

Chapter 10

The First Siege

On the eve of Pentecost, 24 May 1203, the Crusading host sailed from Corfu, an occasion of which Villehardouin in later years would write with nostalgia: 'We had a beautiful, sunny day, with a gentle and light breeze . . . the sails were unfurled, and never was there so fair a sight, for as far as the eye could see there were only sails of the ships . . . the hearts of our men rejoiced'; the Crusade was at last on its way to high adventure. As it rounded Cape Malea the fleet chanced to meet two vessels filled with knights and sergeants returning from Syria, part of the detachment which had sailed direct from Marseilles. Count Baldwin sent a boat with messengers to ask who they were, upon which the men in the returning ships were so embarrassed that 'they did not dare even to show their faces'. But one of the sergeants suddenly decided to join the army, slipping over the side of his vessel and jumping into the boat. He called out to his fellows, 'You can help yourselves to my belongings . . . I'm going with these men, who obviously look as though they are on their way to win some land.'[1]

Sailing north through the archipelago the expedition reached the island of Euboea, where the leaders discussed the progress made so far. The fleet here divided. While a force of knights led by Boniface and Baldwin, and accompanied by Alexius, sailed to secure the submission of the island of Andros, the rest of the fleet crossed the Aegean and made straight for the Dardanelles, putting in at Abydos. Harvesting was under way, and the troops spent a week commandeering the corn as it was reaped. Meanwhile they were rejoined by the men who had gone south to Andros. The whole fleet then sailed up the Gallipoli strait and entered the Sea of Marmora. On 23 June the fleet cast anchor off the monastery of St. Stephen, a few miles west of Constantinople. The Crusaders were now within sight of the city, its vast and unexpected size filling them with alarm at the magnitude of the operation which they had undertaken. 'Men who had never seen Constantinople before gazed hard at it. They could not believe that anywhere in the world was there so splendid a city, with its lofty walls and strong towers encircling it, its rich palaces and tall churches so numerous as to be unbelievable had they not been before their eyes.' They noted the length and breadth of the city 'which was sovereign above all others'. A certain awe came over the Crusaders as they contemplated an enterprise 'greater than anything so far undertaken in the history of mankind'.[2] The doge and the principal barons landed for a conference in St. Stephen's abbey. Dandolo knew the vicinity well and the barons naturally leaned on him heavily for advice. His view was that as it was essential for the troops to be well fed, they might first thoroughly ransack the Princes' Islands, the archipelago of nine islands some ten miles from Constantinople and just off the Asian coast.

The fleet did not in fact make the proposed visit to the islands, but after sailing past the city-walls so closely that the citizens crowded on to the battlements in wonder at the sight, disembarked the entire army at Chalcedon, on the Asian side of the strait almost opposite the capital. On 26 June the ships sailed on and anchored at Scutari. Marching up, the troops pitched camp within sight of their ships, so that the army was now directly opposite the area on the north side of the Golden Horn known as Estanor, whose occupation would give them control of the great harbour. Only a mile of the Bosphorus waters separated them from their objective. Meanwhile the emperor Alexius III, whose defensive preparations had been lax, now brought a force out of the city and placed it in a position on the west side of the straits, facing the Crusaders, who during the next few days foraged in the surrounding countryside for food.

On 1 July there was a fight between a detachment of eighty knights of the Crusading army, which had been detailed to guard the camp and protect the foragers, and about five hundred Byzantine horsemen encamped on the east side of the strait. The skirmish took place at Damatrys, on the Marmora shore some miles south of Scutari,[3] and was the first clash between soldiers of the Fourth Crusade and those of the Empire. Forming into four companies, the Crusaders charged the Byzantines who, led by Michael Stryphnos, put up a half-hearted struggle and were quickly routed. The Franks overran their enemy's camp, captured some valuable horses, and (as Villehardouin casually remarks) 'such booty as is usual in an affair like this'.

On the next day a message was sent to the barons by Alexius III, conveyed by a Lombard in the imperial service, one Nicholas Rosso. The emperor expressed his concern that men pledged to deliver the Holy Cross and Sepulchre of Jerusalem had appeared in this provocative manner outside his capital, and warned them not to attempt anything foolhardy. 'Even if you were twenty times as numerous as you are, you would not be able to avoid defeat and heavy loss.' They were, however, offered supplies to help them on their way. For their spokesman the Franks chose Conon de Béthune, who replied, 'the lands which we have entered do not belong to your lord at all but to his nephew. Let your lord therefore agree to put himself at his nephew's mercy and restore to him his crown and empire. We will use our good offices with the prince to ensure that your lord has an income sufficient for him to live in comfort.' This was a virtual declaration of war against Alexius III.

The leaders, however, were under the impression that Prince Alexius was going to be welcomed with open arms by the people of Constantinople. In this they had doubtless been encouraged by the young man himself, and it is also

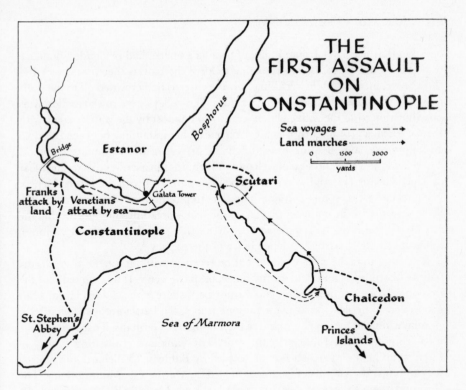

THE FIRST ASSAULT ON CONSTANTINOPLE

Sea voyages ─ ─ ─ ─ →
Land marches ·········· →

0   1500   3000
yards

Bosphorus

Estanor

Bridge

Scutari

Galata Tower

Franks attack by land

Venetians attack by sea

Constantinople

Chalcedon

St. Stephen's Abbey

Sea of Marmora

Princes' Islands

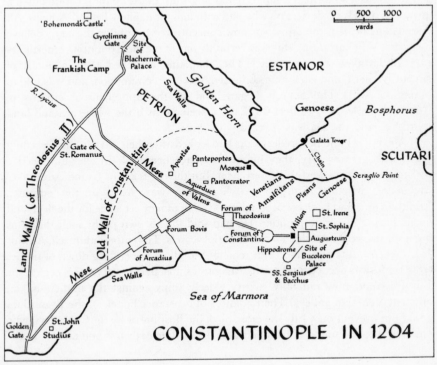

0   500   1000
yards

'Bohemond's Castle'

Gyrolimne Gate

Site of Blachernae Palace

ESTANOR

The Frankish Camp

Sea Walls

Golden Horn

PETRION

Genoese

Bosphorus

R. Lycus

Galata Tower

SCUTARI

Chain

Gate of St. Romanus

Apostles

Pantepoptes

Mosque

Seraglio Point

Venetians

Amalfitans

Pisans

Genoese

Aqueduct of Valens

Pantocrator

Mese

Forum of Theodosius

St. Irene

St. Sophia

Forum Bovis

Million

Augusteum

Forum of Constantine

Hippodrome

Site of Bucoleon Palace

Forum of Arcadius

SS. Sergius & Bacchus

Sea Walls

Land Walls (of Theodosius II)

Old Wall of Constantine

Mese

Sea of Marmora

Golden Gate

St. John Studius

CONSTANTINOPLE IN 1204

possible that his sister Irene, Philip of Swabia's queen, had persuaded Boniface that this would be so. Before resorting to force the barons therefore decided to show the prince in public, recalling how the citizens had crowded on to the walls to watch the ships sail by a few days before. Ten galleys were rowed as closely as possible alongside the walls, which were in fact almost by the water's edge, with Prince Alexius prominently displayed on one of them, standing between Dandolo and Boniface, and heralds proclaimed the arrival of the legitimate emperor. There was, however, no sign of welcome. Villehardouin ascribes this to sheer fear of what Alexius III might do to any open sympathizers with the prince.[4] There was nevertheless some genuine popular trepidation at the arrival of the Westerners, and the emperor played on this fear, spreading rumours around the city that the Latins had come to destroy all that was dear to the Byzantines, including their cherished independence of the papacy.[5]

Realizing that the prince would not be received without a fight after all, the barons heard mass and held a conference, or 'parlement'. It was agreed that the first objective must be a landing on the northern shore of the Golden Horn. They proceeded to deploy the army, arranging it in seven battle-groups ('batailles'), Boniface himself taking command of the Lombards, Germans, Tuscans, and the men from southern France, in the rear. The vanguard, consisting largely of Flemish archers and crossbowmen, was led by Baldwin.[6] Villehardouin himself was amongst the knights of Champagne, led by Matthew de Montmorency. The Burgundians also formed a separate battle-group. Louis de Blois commanded a group, as did Hugh de St. Pol, who had with him his nephew Peter d'Amiens. All dissensions healed, the army was now concentrated to subdue the city. 'Believe me,' says Villehardouin, 'this was certainly one of the most daunting enterprises ever undertaken by an army.' The chaplains preached their sermons of encouragement, and each man confessed, received communion, and was told to make his will. The assault began, and to the apprehensive citizens of Constantinople, says Robert de Clari, it seemed 'as if the whole sea and land trembled, and the sea was covered with ships'.

If Alexius III and his predecessors had looked after their navy in the preceding years with greater care, they might now have been able to offer an effective resistance to the powerful Western fleet. But the *megas dux* or Grand Admiral of the navy, Michael Stryphnos (whose wife was sister of the empress, Euphrosyne), had been corrupt, appropriating money set aside for the fleet, and even sharing in pirate plunder. He had sold for his own profit such things as anchors and sails intended for the imperial vessels. The emperor himself, Alexius III, a keen huntsman, had been reluctant to allow the cutting down of timber from the forests needed for the construction of ships. Because of years of neglect the Empire could now put only twenty elderly ships against the numerous and efficient Venetian galleys. Their chances of resistance hopeless, the Byzantines could not prevent on 5 July the crossing of the Bosphorus by the Crusaders, who embarked to the sound of trumpets and the rattling of drums and tabors. In the first ships were the archers and crossbowmen, whose task was to clear the beaches for a landing. Transports were towed by the galleys, and the army duly landed on the western shore, the horses being led or ridden down gangways on to the beach, while knights leapt into the sea to their waists.

Alexius III withdrew into Constantinople the troops which he had taken outside, in his haste leaving much equipment and supplies behind to be captured by the Franks. How large his army in Constantinople was it is impossible to determine, but it is likely that it outnumbered that of the Crusaders. The latter now pitched camp in Estanor, which contained the quarter occupied by the city's Jews and also many Genoese. This undoubtedly pleased the Franks as, in the chronicler's words, 'Estanor was a fine and rich district'.[7] Here was the Galata tower, a highly sensitive point in the Byzantine defensive system. Entry to the Golden Horn harbour was barred to ships by a chain on wooden floats, stretching from the tower to the city wall opposite in the area of Seraglio Point. This tower is not to be confused with the present Galata tower, built in 1348 and virtually all that survives of the elaborate fortifications protecting the later medieval Genoese colony. The original Galata tower, containing one end of the harbour chain, was directly on the waterfront, on the site now occupied by the underground mosque known as Yer Alti Camii.

The troops defending the tower, the capture of which was essential for an effective control of the northern banks of the Golden Horn, included detachments of Englishmen and Danes of the Varangian Guard. Realizing the danger, the emperor rushed reinforcements across the Horn in barges, and fighting for possession of the tower by the Latins began in earnest. There were brave deeds, like that of a Flemish knight, Nicholas de Jenlain, who at great danger to himself rescued his wounded lord, Jacques d'Avesnes. The Venetian warships joined in the siege with catapults, and the Galata garrison, with its reinforcements, tried to drive the Franks back with frequent sallies. One sallying party failed, however, to get back in time, and was hotly pursued by the Franks, who burst into the tower with the defenders. The tower fell, and so at the very outset the Byzantines had lost a vital position. Next, the chain was rammed and snapped by a large Venetian ship called the *Eagle*, and on the following day the entire Venetian fleet with its galleys and transports sailed into the Golden Horn, capturing a number of Byzantine ships.[8] The Empire had paid dearly for neglecting its fleet.

There followed a land-sea operation of the kind which the Franks could never have undertaken without their Venetian allies. In a conference of the leaders, the Venetians argued strongly for the entire assault to be made from the sea. But the French recoiled from the prospect of fighting on water, arguing that 'they would give a better account of themselves on land, with their horses and customary equipment'.[9] They were undoubtedly right in this view – horses were as natural to them as ships were to the Venetians. So it was agreed that the Franks should attack by land, the Venetians by sea. Rather less than a week after the capture of Galata, the army marched in full order along the north-eastern bank of the

Golden Horn to a position opposite the corner of the city occupied by the Blachernae palace. Just beyond this point was a narrow stone bridge which the Byzantines had tried to destroy. It was quickly repaired, and the whole army marched over the Horn and pitched camp between the abbey of SS. Cosmos and Damian (known as 'Bohemond's castle' because Bohemond had stayed there during the First Crusade) and the section of the city walls directly shielding the Blachernae in the north-west. By crossing the bridge the army had been able to avoid a lengthy land march around the head of the Horn. The Franks were greatly surprised that the imperial army had made little or no attempt to contest the crossing, which with a determined defence might have been held indefinitely.

Meanwhile, the Venetian galleys were moving into position for an assault on the sea-walls at the western end of the Horn, which would be co-ordinated with a Frankish attack on the adjacent land-walls. Scaling ladders were erected on the ships, with wooden ramps or platforms, each wide enough to take three men abreast, and with rope railings, specially constructed for boarding operations against the walls. The ships were hung on the sides with hides,[10] and each transport was fitted with a catapult. The plan was for the vessels to approach closely to the walls and swing the boarding ramps on to the parapets. On land, the army put its mangonels and petraries into position. Such machines, which hurled stones in catapult fashion, were, with movable wooden towers and battering rams, much used in medieval siege warfare. Armies of the period, usually quite small, seldom tried to invest a whole castle or city, aiming rather at concentrating the attack on selected points. In practice, medieval castles were not often taken by direct storm, the defending garrison normally trying to hold off its attackers until they lost heart and withdrew, the besiegers on their part hoping that starvation and disease would force a capitulation.

The land-walls of Constantinople, stretching for over four miles in a curve from Blachernae on the Golden Horn southwards to the Golden Gate on the Marmora, were of triple thickness at the point chosen for attack, with a moat protecting the outermost wall. They were strengthened by carefully sited towers, and to breach the defences would be a formidable task for even the largest and best-equipped of armies. There is no reliable way of arriving at the size of the Frankish forces now moving into position to attack the most strongly fortified city in the world. The failure of the initial enlistments to reach expectations, and the numerous defections, must have brought it far below the original estimated strength, and Villehardouin says that the whole army did not exceed 20,000.[11] As far as the non-Venetian elements of the army were concerned, it was almost certainly a great deal smaller.[12] Remarking on the length of the fortified city walls, Villehardouin says with some exaggeration that the entire army was only large enough to besiege a single gate.[13] As the Franks dug into their palisaded camp and prepared the siege engines, the Byzantines made several sallies from the land-wall gates, these being led by the emperor's son-in-law Theodore Lascaris, who showed far more enthusiasm in the capital's defence than did the emperor himself, and longed to get to grips with the besiegers.[14] Shortage of food was a problem for the Franks, who were even eating horses killed in the fighting. It was not easy to send out foraging parties from the camp, every man being needed for the assult, and supplies of flour and bacon were at this stage enough for about three weeks.

The sorties of the defenders continued for ten days, by which time the Latin army was ready for the direct assault on the walls. The plan was that three battle-groups, those of the Burgundians, the knights of Champagne, and the forces under the command of Boniface, should stay in reserve and watch for any possible Byzantine movements in the countryside around. The attack was to be made by the 'batailles' led by Baldwin, his brother Henry, Louis de Blois, and Hugh de St. Pol.

The first attempt to scale the walls, which at this vital point guarding the palace were manned by Varangians and some Pisans, was a failure. The Franks put up two ladders against a sea-wall barbican near Blachernae, and two knights and two sergeants, followed by fifteen men-at-arms, managed to get on top of the wall. They found themselves opposed by 'the English and Danes, and the fight which followed was hard and ferocious', says Villehardouin; and the courage of the Anglo-Danes put heart into the hesitant troops inside the barbican, who now threw themselves into the fray. This first wave of attackers was driven from the wall, and although the number of men involved was small, there was concern amongst the army leaders over the setback. Two Franks were taken prisoner, to be led before a much encouraged emperor.[15]

In the meantime the doge had arranged his warships in line of battle and, advancing as closely as possible to the shore, they hurled stones with their mangonels at the sea-walls while the archers and crossbowmen showered arrows and bolts on the defenders of the battlements. In some places the scaling ladders of the ships were almost near enough to make contact with the wall. Dandolo himself, despite his age and defective sight, was in his own galley, and proudly unfurled was the gonfalon, a banner suspended from a cross-yard on a pole, with streamers, the customary standard for an Italian city-republic. The gonfalon of Venice bore a winged lion, symbol of the evangelist St. Mark. Dandolo decided to land on the beach below the walls, and was actually the first to bring his galley aground. There followed a wholesale landing of Venetians, while soldiers on the boarding-ramps of other ships engaged the defenders of the walls. It is not clear how and where this was effected, but a vital breach was made in the walls by the Venetians, and there was a moment of elation when the attackers saw the Lion of St. Mark flying on top of a tower. Villehardouin tells his readers that more than forty eye-witnesses had assured him that they saw the gonfalon on the tower, though none of them knew who had actually hoisted it.[16]

The gates were thrown open, the Venetians surged in, and were quickly in occupation of twenty-five towers. They began to advance into the city, but a force of Varangians was rushed up and drove them back into the towers. When the barons, outside the land-wall which protected Blachernae and somewhat dispirited after their small but sharp reverse at the hands of the Anglo-Danes, heard of Dandolo's success they could hardly believe it. They were nevertheless delighted, not least with the gift of horses which the Venetians despatched to them by boat, as a share of the booty. The day was 17 July.

Meanwhile, to make safe their position in the captured towers, the Venetians had set fire to the buildings between themselves and the imperial troops advancing against them, so that the two sides were now separated by a wall of flame, 'which became so intense that the Greeks were unable to see their adversaries, who consequently could retreat to the security of the towers which they had captured'.[17] The blaze raged along the harbour from Blachernae to the church of Christ Euergetes, destroying a line of warehouses and docks. This was the first of a series of conflagrations which in the course of the conquest was to destroy much of Constantinople. It was not contrary to the rules of chivalry and medieval warfare for buildings to be set on fire if the commander thought this necessary to the action – as the Dominican canon lawyer Raymond Peñaforte was a few years later to point out.[18]

Baffled as to what to do next, Alexius III decided to engage the Franks in open battle. Marching his troops through the land-wall gates, he marshalled them in battle-order and advanced towards the Frankish camp outside Blachernae, three miles to the north. The barons saw that a pitched battle might be imminent. There was nothing the Franks liked better, and many a young knight was doubtless elated at the thought of the coming charge. To Villehardouin it seemed that the whole plain was a mass of troops, marching in disciplined formations, the 'Greeks' outnumbering the Franks more than tenfold.[19] The Frankish foot-soldiers formed into ranks outside the palisade surrounding the camp. In front were the archers and crossbowmen, behind them the foot-sergeants and knights who had lost their horses. Even the cooks, fitted with improvised weapons and armour, were brought into the defence.

Villehardouin gives the impression that the Byzantine and Frankish armies, having taken up their positions, simply stood still and waited for the other side to move. But Robert de Clari tells of an attempted charge by the Franks. The order was given that Baldwin, Henry, and Hugh de St. Pol should engage the emperor's troops. In their separate companies the mounted knights moved forward at the trot, followed by the marching foot-soldiers, and the Byzantines advanced to meet them. Robert de Clari, who was himself amongst the knights, says of them that they 'rode so well in line that not one was ahead of the others'. But Baldwin decided that a charge would be risky, and turned back, as did his brother Henry. Their caution was scorned by Hugh de St. Pol, amongst whose men was Peter d'Amiens (and Robert de Clari). Baldwin was shamed into reversing his decision, and he spurred his knights after Hugh to join him in the coming charge. But the advance suddenly had to be halted because the small river Lycus was discovered to be just ahead. Moreover, the Franks realized that they had ridden over a stretch of rising ground and were now hidden from sight of their main camp. The advance was abandoned.[20]

Dandolo, on hearing of the situation, had come up as quickly as possible to the aid of his allies with as many troops in ships and barges as he could spare, even evacuating the captured towers. By the time they arrived all danger to the Franks was gone. Alexius himself also had decided not to attack, and withdrew his troops into the city. The whole action was watched by the ladies of the imperial household from the palace windows. On the emperor's retreat, the Franks returned to their palisaded camp and, utterly tired by the day's fighting and manœuvring, took off their armour and rested.

But suddenly, after such an inconclusive day's fighting, the issue was resolved. During the night Alexius III ignominiously fled, leaving the city to its fate. Taking with him as much money and jewels as he could carry, and accompanied by Irene, one of his daughters, and some of his mistresses, he made his way to Develtos a hundred miles away on the Black Sea coast, near the Bulgarian border. Nicetas says that the craven-hearted man had already prepared a refuge there.[21] The empress Euphrosyne was simply left behind, and two other daughters, Eudocia and Anna (wife of Theodore Lascaris) also remained in the city.

Chapter 11

The Die is Cast

The aim of the diversion to Constantinople had now, it appeared, been attained, and all that remained for the Crusaders to do was to put the young prince on the throne and collect their reward. But there followed almost at once one of those subtle manœuvres at which the Byzantines were adept. The *Novgorod Chronicle* says that when Alexius III realized the situation to be hopeless, before fleeing he first restored his blinded and deposed brother Isaac to the throne, saying, 'I crave your forgiveness – the Empire after all does belong to you'. This is most unlikely, in view of the value of every minute of time during the night for Alexius. The truth would seem to be that on hearing of the emperor's flight, some senior officials led by the finance minister Constantine, and aided by loyal Varangian guardsmen, hastily restored Isaac to his throne.[1] This happened during the night, and at the break of day on 18 July the Crusaders were informed of the fact.

The Frankish leaders were caught unawares, as they had never given serious thought to the possibility of the deposed Isaac being restored. The young Alexius had acted throughout on the assumption that he would be emperor if the Franks were successful, and that his father need hardly be considered, as blindness was usually regarded as an automatic and permanent disqualification for the highest Byzantine office. Nevertheless, the accomplished fact could not now be set aside, and the Franco-Venetian allies agreed that the best course was for them to recognize the emperor Isaac II on condition that his son reigned with him jointly as Alexius IV. But it was essential that Isaac should first ratify and confirm the arrangements made with them by his son. This is fairly clear evidence that the Franks still had in mind the original idea of proceeding to the Levant, which remained their professed objective. Meanwhile, until Isaac had formally ratified his son's promises to the barons, Alexius would not be allowed to make his entry into the city.

Four envoys were chosen to call on Isaac, two as representatives of the doge, and Matthew de Montmorency and Geoffrey de Villehardouin to speak for the Franks. The mission is recorded by Villehardouin in his Chronicle.[2] Entering by the Gyrolimne Gate, the four men arrived at the Blachernae palace and, dismounting, strode to the main entrance through a guard of Anglo-Saxons and Danes, paraded in full accoutrements with their battle-axes. Entering the imperial palace, the envoys found Isaac in robes so sumptuous 'that it would be impossible to find anywhere a better dressed man'. He was seated beside his wife Margaret, 'a very lovely woman'. It is not known where the empress (a Hungarian) had been during her husband's period of restriction or imprisonment, but the presumption is that her refuge was a convent. Members of the court were in attendance, Villehardouin being especially impressed by the attire of the ladies. The envoys were graciously received, but they asked if they might have their audience with the emperor in private, a request which suggests that the formal Byzantine manner for receiving foreign ambassadors was being observed; that is, with the emperor sitting statue-like on his throne, saying nothing, and letting his minister speak for him. The request being granted, the envoys went into a room with none present except the emperor and empress, the chancellor and an interpreter.

Villehardouin was the envoys' spokesman. He reminded the emperor that the Crusaders had loyally fulfilled their part of the bargain, and now asked him to confirm his son's undertaking to place the Byzantine Empire under Rome's spiritual jurisdiction, to pay 200,000 silver marks and a full year's provisions to the army, to send 10,000 men with them to Egypt and provide transport for them, and maintain a force of five hundred knights in the Holy Land. 'This is the covenant which your son made with us, and it was not only confirmed by oath and sealed documents, but underwritten by your son-in-law, King Philip of Germany' – the last phrase plainly revealing the complicity of the Swabian court. Isaac demurred, protesting that he did not see how such conditions could possibly be met. The actual terms had after all been none of his making, and as a previously reigning emperor he knew well that his son had made promises impossible to fulfil. But after some argument he confirmed the agreement with golden sealed charters.

Alexius was welcomed into Constantinople in scenes of popular enthusiasm, and father and son were openly delighted at the dramatic reversal of their fortunes. Court officials and nobles paid formal homage to the young man. Both Isaac and Alexius were alarmed at the prospect, however, of Frankish soldiers being quartered in the city, foreseeing inevitable trouble between them and the citizens. They therefore prevailed on them to make their quarters at Estanor, on the opposite side of the Horn. The troops were happy with this arrangement, as there was an abundance of provisions for them in the prosperous Estanor district, and it would be a simple matter for them to cross the harbour in individual groups as they wished, to tour the city and see the sights. During the time ahead many of them were to make the crossing by barge, or go round on horseback to cross the bridge at the west end of the Horn. They were to be impressed by all that they saw, by the fine houses and churches, by the evidence of wealth on every side, by the vast profusion of sacred relics. They also took the precaution of pulling down some of the city's fortifications, sensing that the present arrangements were temporary and that there could be further fighting to come.

On the feast of St. Peter's Chains, 1 August 1203, Alexius was solemnly crowned in St. Sophia according to customary Greek rites.[3] With music and ceremonial, anointings and censings, the young man was dedicated to the role of God's regent on earth. As Alexius IV he was now co-emperor with his father Isaac, though not as yet the effective ruler. He was disliked by the courtiers for his addiction to barbarian Western ways, among them riotous drinking bouts. He was suspected of preferring the Latin to the Greek Church. 'He often arrived in the camp to visit the barons,' says Villehardouin, 'and was very deferential to them.' Gradually Alexius gained the upper hand over his father, largely allying himself with those nobles who had originally blinded Isaac and were now terrified of his anger. As time went on Isaac tended to lose his mental grasp, and was drawn to astrology and the company of seers.

The barons meanwhile wrote a general letter to the pope and the crowned heads of Western Europe, justifying the diversion to Constantinople and assuring them that the assault on Egypt would be under way by the following spring. They appealed for further support from the West for this forthcoming venture.[4] They seem to have thought that this would satisfy Innocent, but Alexius made no serious attempt to convert his bishops and their flocks to the idea of subjection to the papacy. This, as he undoubtedly realized, would be utterly impossible. Innocent was subsequently to write to the Crusaders, in February 1204, reminding them that a true reunion would require more effort on their part. He also ordered the patriarch to come and collect his pallium in Rome, after the Catholic fashion, and so obtain formal authorization for the exercise of his pontifical office in Constantinople.[5] All this was quite unrealistic, though Innocent, as a conscientious pope, could hardly have taken any other course, as by this time the universality of papal jurisdiction was a firmly established doctrine in the West.[6]

But Alexius IV's most pressing problem was that of trying to fulfil his financial promises to the Franks. He had guaranteed 200,000 marks, and immediately after his coronation was able to pay something more than half of this sum. The Venetians were now paid the 34,000 marks still due to them from the Franks, and they also claimed and received 50,000 marks, as being half of the gains of conquest – this was according to the terms of the original agreement. Out of the money that remained it was also possible for the barons to refund to each man what he had been obliged to pay for his voyage from Venice.[7] The main beneficiaries of Alexius's initial payment were therefore the Venetians, and obviously the barons were going to be insistent on the balance of the 200,000 marks being paid in due course, so that they might secure their share of the fruits of the diversion.

But Alexius soon realized that he did not have the resources with which to meet his obligations. Palace treasuries were first drawn upon, then money was forced from the pockets of wealthy noblemen. Alexius III's empress Euphrosyne, and the Grand Admiral Michael Stryphnos, were amongst those whose property was seized. The Frankish army was due to leave Constantinople within a few weeks' time, at Michaelmas 1203, and Alexius was fearful of what might happen to him when his protectors were gone. In the influential circles of the city he and his father had few supporters. Going to see the army leaders and the doge in their quarters, he explained his shaky position: 'Most of the Greeks greatly resent the fact that it was with your help that I recovered my Empire.'[8] He appealed to them to defer their departure until March in the following year, by which time he was confident he would have established his position in the Empire. This would give him more time in which to collect revenues from his estates and to assemble the ships promised for the Egyptian expedition. Meanwhile he would keep the Franks and Venetians supplied with provisions. As he pointed out, there would lie before them the whole summer of 1204 in which they could proceed with their campaign against the Saracens.

The barons called a 'parlement' of the army's leading men, with most of the knights, and put the emperor's proposals before them. There was furious argument, and the large numbers of men who had almost refused to move at Corfu and represented about half the army were again incensed, complaining that their patience was running out. 'Give us the ships which you promised! We want to go to Syria.' But they were reminded by the leaders that winter was drawing near and the conditions for an immediate campaign in Syria were unpropitious. It would be far more sensible to get Alexius well established, thus making sure of the promised money and provisions, and in the spring of 1204 start the campaign in earnest. These were indeed persuasive arguments.

Again the opposition was quietened, largely because Dandolo said he would keep his fleet at the service of the Crusade for yet another year, that is from Michaelmas 1203 until Michaelmas 1204,[9] and Alexius agreed to pay for this extension. The doge doubtless guessed that the Franks would never obtain their promised money from Alexius. After all, the Venetians themselves had been trying for over thirty years to secure the compensation due to them for the 1171 confiscation. Clearly he foresaw the likelihood of the Crusaders becoming increasingly bogged down in Constantinople. This would suit him very well, as his ultimate objective was the creation of the best political conditions to promote Venetian commercial activity in the Mediterranean, and the Franks might be able to help.

In an effort to establish his authority in the Empire, Alexius set out during mid-August on an extensive progress, in which he was accompanied by some of the barons, including Boniface, Henry of Flanders, and the count of St. Pol.[10] Alexius knew that this expedition would be quite useless without Western troops, but Boniface and the other leaders on their part made it clear that they expected special payment for these services. Henry soon withdrew, when he realized that little extra money would in fact be forthcoming. The expedition convinced Alexius and his advisers that nothing could shake the position which the Vlach-Bulgarian king Kalojan had established in the Balkans during wars with the Empire. One of the emperor's specific objectives was to collect the desperately needed money, another to hunt down Alexius III, who had come out of his hiding-place in Develtos and announced himself as emperor at Adrianople. Neither of these aims was achieved. The fugitive ex-emperor eluded capture; and little revenue was raised, though many towns and castles were taken and duly milched.

During the emperor's absence there was another fire in Constantinople, started in a squabble between Latin merchants and native Byzantines. In August a party of Venetians, Pisans, and Flemings sailed over the harbour from Estanor with the intention of causing trouble and especially of destroying the mosque serving Muslim traders in the city. The mosque was on the shore close to the Pisan quarter, and it is possible that the Pisans resented its presence. For their part, the Crusaders would need no urging to harass any Muslims within their reach, and they burst into the mosque and laid hands on all whom they could find. The native Byzantines rushed to the aid of the Muslims, and to cover their withdrawal the Latins set fire to several buildings. Aided by a breeze blowing in from the sea, the fire was disastrous and swept the city. There was a wide area of devastation from the Horn southward to the Marmora Sea. The Forum of Constantine, with its fine houses, arcades, and shops, was destroyed, many churches went up in flames, and some parts of St. Sophia were damaged, including the patriarchal palace and the administrative sections of the great ecclesiastical complex. Numerous private houses were destroyed, and several lives were lost in the conflagration, which raged beyond control. The disaster genuinely saddened the barons, who, as they watched the blazing city from their camp on the other side of the Horn, 'furent mult dolent et mult en orent grant pitié'. They saw splendid churches, mansions, and merchants' buildings collapsing, but there was nothing they could do to save them. The fire lasted a week or more before it burnt itself out.

Until now, relations between the Crusader soldiers and the citizens had been reasonably good, but after this episode the native inhabitants were understandably incensed, and there followed a general exodus of Western traders and their families from the city (15,000 people in all, according to Villehardouin), who crossed the harbour to find safety in the Crusaders' camp at Estanor. This accession of numerical strength proved useful for recruitment purposes, Villehardouin saying of the city's resident Latins that 'their arrival was subsequently to be of great benefit to us'.[11]

It was to an embittered and half ruined city that Alexius returned on 11 November, his tour having accomplished little save to convince him that he was indeed now an emperor, with broad regions under his sway. The Western barons noticed a change in his manner towards themselves. 'His attitude to them became haughty, and he ceased to visit them in their camp as previously.'[12] But despite this new accession of imperial pride, there remained the pressing problem of his promises to the Franks. During his absence his father and co-emperor Isaac had not maintained the money payments satisfactorily, and several reminders were now received by Alexius; but he did no more than hand over small occasional sums of money. Although he had settled more than half his debt, the outstanding money was simply not available, as Dandolo knew all along would be the case. After having themselves experienced the unpleasantness of being in the hands of a creditor, the Crusaders now on their part brought pressure to bear on a hapless debtor. Alexius IV levied fresh taxes, and church plate and sacred objects such as silver lamps and icons were melted down. This enraged the clergy, already much perturbed by the attempt to bring the Orthodox Church under the explicitly acknowledged supremacy of the papal see.

Alexius IV became increasingly reluctant to pay anything more to the Franks, and in this attitude he was probably encouraged by his courtiers, many of whom were former supporters of Alexius III and who according to Nicetas dominated the young emperor after his return from his Thracian expedition.[13] Their views are reflected in a surviving oration, composed for intended delivery in Alexius IV's presence on the feast of the Epiphany, 6 January 1204, and until recent years little known by students of the Fourth Crusade. It is not clear whether it was ever actually delivered in the emperor's presence but it was certainly written, probably some time in December 1203, by an official orator Nicephorus Chrysoberges who had been in the service of Alexius III and had survived his fall. In the oration the young Alexius IV is addressed in flattering language. Like Caesar, 'he came, saw, and conquered'. He is urged to stand firm against the Latins, and is spoken of as the sole ruler, his father Isaac being virtually ignored. So flowery is the language that it is difficult to penetrate to any hard facts or clear intentions behind it, though Nicephorus does give an impression of lauding the young emperor for dealing cleverly with the Franks.[14]

By the time of Alexius IV's return from Thrace in November, relations between the Franks and Byzantines had deteriorated badly. The Western soldiers were again becoming restless through enforced inactivity, and groups had pillaged the city suburbs and the houses of wealthy inhabitants along the shores of the Bosphorus. They were also helping themselves to treasures from the churches. By December 1203 the individual Crusaders, at first quietly received, were beginning to excite bitter hostility, and their overbearing attitude in the streets was resented. Some of them were attacked and murdered. Anger was rapidly rising over the taxes levied to meet the Crusaders' demands, and at last the city crowd turned to open violence, venting its anger on such unarmed Latin residents as still remained in the city and butchering men and women alike. The barons, in their camp over the water, held back for the sake of the general peace, but their forbearance encouraged the mob to think that it could do as it pleased, and some rioters even rowed over the harbour in small boats to shout defiance at the allies. The Franks and Venetians were forced to retaliate, and used the disturbances as a pretext for seizing Byzantine grain ships in the harbour. These December disturbances appear to have been the result of spontaneous popular indignation, but the trouble-makers may also have received encouragement from certain members of the court, prominent amongst whom was Alexius Ducas Mourtzouphlos, a pronounced anti-Latin close to the emperor, and a great-great-grandson of Alexius I Comnenus. Ducas was his own family name, Mourtzouphlos simply a nickname given to him because of his bushy eyebrows.

To the barons these troubles in the city were disturbing. They had still not received all their money, and now here was the possibility of a revolution which might bring in a new emperor with no obligations to the Crusaders, supplanting the two present ineffective joint rulers. The disorder in the city became so bad that towards the end of the year 1203 the allies decided to send an official deputation to Alexius IV with an ultimatum. The mission was composed of three Venetians and three Franks, the latter including the ever-present Villehardouin as well as the eloquent and persuasive Conon de Béthune. The six men (taking care to carry their swords with them) called on the Blachernae palace, where they conveyed their message to Alexius and his father Isaac. What Conon the spokesman had to say was straight to the point. 'We have come from the barons and the doge, who wish you to be reminded of the service they have rendered you. . . . On their behalf, and in the presence of your nobles, we demand that you fulfil the contract which you made with them.' Otherwise, it was implied, forcible measures would be taken.

Only one concession, if such it can be called, was made. Alexius was assured that no fighting would start without a formal declaration of war. The young man protested that he had already given the Crusaders large amounts of money and implored them now to leave the Empire and cease troubling him. There was angry shouting from the Byzantines in the audience-hall against the envoys, who departed, and we can believe Villehardouin when he remarks that they breathed sighs of relief on getting away from the palace safely.[15]

The two sides were now almost totally estranged, and Alexius decided on bold measures to foil his tormentors: he would rob the Westerners of the sea-power on which their effectiveness depended. In the middle of December he launched a number of blazing fire-ships in the direction of the Venetian fleet at anchor. The attempt failed, and on 1 January 1204 Alexius tried again. Seventeen large vessels were tightly packed with wood, pitch, and all kinds of combustible materials, and at midnight, the wind being favourable, were set alight and allowed to drift towards the Latin ships. The Venetians at once realized what was at stake, and acted with extraordinary energy to save their fleet. 'The trumpets sounded the alert, and throughout the camp men sprang to arms.' Leaping into boats, the Venetians dragged the blazing Greek ships with grappling irons out of the harbour into the central current, whence they were carried out to sea. They fought off the Byzantines who came out in boats to rain missiles on them.

Alexius's scheme might have changed the whole course of the Fourth Crusade, and was thwarted only by the sheer courage of the Venetians and by their maritime skill. Villehardouin, who actually witnessed the incident, goes out of his way to praise the Venetians: 'No men ever put up a braver defence on the sea than

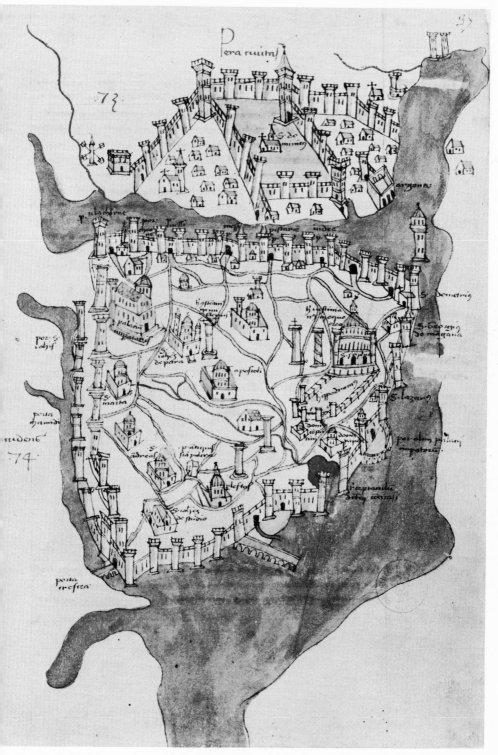

9. One of the oldest surviving views of Constantinople, from the *Liber Insularum Archipelagi, c.* 1420.

10. A tower in the walls of Constantinople, with an inscription of the emperor Theophilus (829-42) recording its restoration by him. On the Sea of Marmora, this tower would not have been engaged in any of the siege fighting, but the arriving Venetian fleet sailed closely by it, watched from the parapets by the citizens and defenders.

11. The tetrarchs Diocletian, Maximinian, Constantius, and Galerius, in porphyry, set into the south side of St. Mark's, Venice; a group brought from Constantinople after the sack. Constantius was father of Constantine the Great, whose mother Helena 'found' the True Cross.

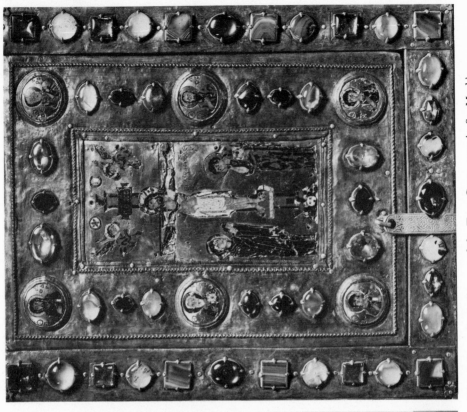

12b. A Byzantine reliquary of the True Cross, now in St. Mark's.

12a. Precious glass-ware from Byzantium, in St. Mark's.

did the Venetians that night.' Only one Western vessel was lost, a merchantman from Pisa, which caught fire.[16]

The next important event was a large gathering in St. Sophia on 25 January, attended by both people and nobles, to discuss what might now be done. Nicetas was himself present and spoke on behalf of Alexius IV, without whom the Empire would be deprived of its tangible link with the Crusaders. But dissatisfaction with the young emperor was widespread, and three or four days later the crowd surged into St. Sophia and proclaimed the deposition of Alexius and Isaac. An unfortunate young nobleman named Canabus happened to be at his devotions in the basilica at the time, though he does not seem to have been involved in the riots nor to have had any personal ambitions save that of being allowed to lead a quiet life. Despite his protests, the crowd seized him and declared him emperor. In his alarm Alexius appealed to Boniface to send Frankish troops into the Blachernae to protect him; but Mourtzouphlos forestalled any such move by enticing the Varangian bodyguards out of the palace and then occupying it, in the middle of the night. The date is not clear, but it was late in January. Alexius was taken away and imprisoned, and after several attempts to poison him had failed, he was strangled, though his death was announced as having taken place through natural causes. It was an inglorious end to a life which fails to elicit admiration. During his final crisis he had neither sympathizers nor defenders, even the Varangian guardsmen clearly finding it hard to recognize in him an emperor to whom they owed loyalty. He was, however, accorded a full State funeral.[17] Canabus was likewise imprisoned, as was his wife, and he must almost certainly have shared the fate of Alexius IV. Mourtzouphlos, helped by some of the nobles, became emperor as Alexius V and was duly crowned in St. Sophia. The blind old Isaac had been so stunned by these tortuous events that he had fallen ill, and in fact died shortly before his son, apparently of a stroke. The *Novgorod Chronicle* (a work of clerical or monastic authorship) says that he became a monk, which probably means that he died in a monastery.

About this time there occurred an incident which revealed the anger of the inhabitants at the growth of Latin influences in the city. Soon after the 'election' of Canabus the mob overturned and smashed to fragments a bronze statue of Athena, formerly on the Acropolis in Athens and at the time in the Augusteum; Athena's offence was that she was alleged to be facing west and beckoning the Latins to Constantinople. This statue was possibly the work of Phidias, the master of the Parthenon friezes.

Meanwhile, before news of the young emperor's death reached the Crusaders, Mourtzouphlos sent a message to them in Alexius IV's name, inviting their leaders into the city for peace talks. The shrewd Dandolo at once suspected a trap and persuaded the barons to hold back. The death of the young Alexius, when known, clearly posed a problem for the Crusaders and placed them in an entirely new situation. As the specific purpose of the diversion to Constantinople had been to place the prince on the throne, the legal and formal justification for their enterprise was now gone. They had no longer any right to be in Constantinople, other than that of military adventurers. But their problem now was that by the emperor's death they owed the Venetians a considerable amount of money (over and above the original 85,000 marks, which had by this time been repaid) for additional services rendered. Dandolo had extended the use of his fleet for a second year, as from September 1203, Alexius IV agreeing to pay for it. If this extra payment was not made, the ships might no longer be available, and the whole Crusade would collapse.

The idea was now mooted that no man who had committed such an act as that of Mourtzouphlos, the murder of his lord, was worthy of the ownership of lands. Treachery to one's lord was in Western chivalry's code of conduct an odious crime. The *Novgorod Chronicle* says that the Franks felt that if they left the scene without avenging Alexius IV it would be 'in shame'. Nonetheless, many of the Crusaders still hesitated before they could bring themselves to the point of again attacking a great patriarchal Christian city. Meanwhile a deputation, including Abbot Martin of Pairis, arrived from Syria, appealing to the Crusaders to hasten to the help of their brethren fighting the Saracens. They told how the Flemish force which had sailed direct from Marseilles had come to grief in Syria, many dying of disease and some going home.

In a final meeting with Alexius V Mourtzouphlos, the barons demanded as the price of their leaving the Empire the balance of the 200,000 silver marks still owing, a sum it was quite impossible for the new emperor to pay. Besides, unlike his predecessor, he had no moral obligations to the Franks. He did not owe his throne to them, they had rendered him no services, he had made them no promises. The talks ended in angry exchanges, and there were no further peaceful contacts. According to Villehardouin the clergy played a vital role in easing guilty consciences.[18] They assured the Crusaders that the forthcoming war would be a just one, as the intention was right, namely that of bringing the schismatic Greeks into the papal fold. 'The Crusaders were much comforted and heartened by this assurance.' The whole problem was debated at a 'parlement', held soon after the murder of Alexius IV, at which the bishops and other clergy were present, with the leaders of the army and the doge. This conference marks the point at which all pretences were cast off and the army frankly saw the conquest and occupation of Byzantium as its immediate objective. The recovery of Jerusalem was not forgotten, but it could wait awhile. When the men of the Cross in due course marched to the Sepulchre, it would be with the resources of a great Empire behind them.

Mourtzouphlos was a more energetic ruler than his predecessor. He was not universally liked, and amongst the ministers whom he dismissed was Nicetas Choniates, who had raised his voice on behalf of Alexius IV. But he was popular with the many Byzantines who resented the Crusaders' presence and the never-ending growth of Latin influences in the Empire. He worked hard to prepare the city defences for the coming assault, strengthening or repairing the walls and heightening them with wooden storeys to offset the Venetian boarding-ramps. Several wall-gates were bricked up, and extra troops were brought into the city. Mourtzouphlos tried to restore some sense of patriotic pride to citizens by now accustomed to the protection of foreign troops, and ordered them to take up arms and prepare themselves to defend the walls. The summons was received with bad grace, and much grumbling to the effect that by paying taxes for the maintenance of an army citizens were absolved from the duty of serving in it. Such native levies as were raised were almost useless as a fighting force, and the entire defence situation remained unsatisfactory. The various changes and uncertainties in the imperial court had lowered the morale of the army, even that of the Varangian Guard, despite its traditions of loyalty and discipline. A serious matter too was the work of Venetian spies, who were working like moles and using their money to weaken the will of the people to defend their city.

During the first few weeks of 1204 fighting accompanied the preparations for the grand assault. Catapults from the ships and near the land-wall bombarded the city defences. The Venetians heightened the boarding-ramps on their vessels, in readiness for the approaching attack. The Crusaders foraged the countryside around the city in search of food. Hunger and thirst were always amongst their most pressing problems, and the winter weather made it difficult for supply ships to get through. The most ambitious military effort during this period was late in January, when Henry of Flanders raided a town, Phileas, on the Black Sea coast. Much food was taken, including cattle; and Mourtzouphlos, receiving news of the raid, at once went with a strong force to waylay the Crusaders returning with their booty. The latter were surprised in a wood, but fought with such vigour that the emperor called off the attack and hurried back to the capital. He left behind him the imperial standards, and an icon of the Mother of God which previous emperors had carried with them into battle. Such a loss was seen as an ill omen by many citizens, and the Crusaders were delighted with the capture of the icon, which they entrusted for the time being to the bishop of Troyes, intending to present it later to the abbey of Citeaux.[19]

After a winter spent largely in random fights and skirmishes, all was now set for the second siege of Constantinople. The die was cast, and the Franks and Venetians had resolved to take the city and make it their own. The first siege had already provided a dress rehearsal, in which they had gained valuable experience. They now vigorously prepared their stone-throwing catapults, and equipped the ships with scaling ladders taller than those used in the earlier assault. Wooden machines on wheels, for the protection of troops approaching the walls, were also made ready.

Whilst these military preparations continued throughout March, discussions were also held by the Venetians and barons as to what to do if and when the city was taken. They agreed that all booty should be gathered together for a fair distribution. Every man was now required to swear on sacred relics that he would hand in all valuables which he might capture, and that he would not attack any church or monastery. He also had to promise not to molest any woman.[20] The Venetians were guaranteed three-quarters of the booty should it be apparent that their debt was not going to be cleared – otherwise they would receive one half as accepted in the original agreement. The most pressing matter, of course, would be the choosing of a new emperor, and the Crusaders were determined that he should be a Latin. A committee of six Franks and six Venetians would elect him; and whichever party (Franks or Venetians) failed to secure the election would fill the cathedral chapter of St. Sophia with its nominees, and these would choose a Latin patriarch. The emperor would take possession of the imperial palaces of Blachernae and Bucoleon as well as a quarter of the Empire, the remaining three-quarters being equally divided between Venetians and Franks. Another committee, consisting of twelve Venetians and as many Franks, would be responsible for the allocation of fiefs throughout the Empire to the lords and knights, who would all pay homage to the emperor. The new feudal State would have a trial period of one year, after which anyone dissatisfied with it might be free to go. Henceforth the sovereignty of the emperor was to be unquestioned.

In this agreement two factors stand out. First, the Crusade was effectively dead, the participants having no longer any immediate thoughts of Syria or Egypt. Even the dissentients, the men of conscience, had been won over. Secondly, the plan included the complete ransacking of the capital and the acquisition of the Byzantine Empire. It is difficult to know exactly how the Conquest of the Empire became the accepted plan. A plausible explanation is that the clergy at this stage made much of the fact that Constantinople was a vast repository of relics, and in respect of these priceless treasures made impassioned appeals to the simple piety of the Crusaders. Did they, perhaps, point out in their sermons that the city contained the largest number of fragments of the True Cross existing anywhere in the world? Did they assure the soldiers of the Cross that they would be justified in entering the city to take these fragments, with other relics of Christ's Passion, on behalf of the Catholic Church? We have no documentary evidence to this effect. It is more likely that the cupidity of the Franks had been aggravated beyond control during the months when they had been crossing the Golden Horn from Estanor as tourists, and had examined at leisure the richest city in the world. The first siege had been the result of an attempt to place a Byzantine prince on the throne, in return for badly needed money. But now the enterprise was openly aimed at a military and political takeover by the West. Over the past few decades many influences had been steadily and inexorably leading to this end, and now the decision had been made.

Chapter 12

The Storming of Constantinople

For the second siege of Constantinople a force of at least 20,000 men was now under arms, comprising the original Crusading Franks, the Venetians, and new recruits from amongst the resident Latins who had recently crossed the Golden Horn to escape from the city mob. The leaders (no longer including Count Louis de Blois, who had been ill for some time) discussed the tactics to be adopted.[1] In view of the success of the Venetians in breaching the sea-walls during the first siege, it was agreed that the main attack should now come from the harbour, rather than against the land-walls. This was probably to the chagrin of some Franks, but even Villehardouin appears to have been converted and he writes that the fleet was now ready, 'well equipped and prepared for battle, with all necessary provisions aboard'.

On Friday morning, 9 April 1204, the assault began. The fleet, drawn up in line of battle in the Golden Horn, was to Villehardouin 'a marvel to behold', the galleys, transports, and warships alternating with each other in perfect formation.[2] The ships approached the city and troops landed, in some places getting right to the base of the walls, though attempts to undermine the latter were foiled as the wheeled siege-engines were crushed beneath the weight of stones hurled by the defenders. Along the sea-walls the ships' ladders came so close to the battlements that the opponents were able to exchange blows. The battle raged for several hours; 'the attack was pressed home, fiercely and without respite, in over a hundred places, until about the middle of the afternoon'. But by that time victory lay with the Byzantines, who had fought with great confidence, heartened by the decisive leadership and the defensive preparations of the emperor. They were also helped by a southerly breeze which had slowed down the approach of the ships to the walls. Not a single ship had managed to swing its boarding-ramp actually on to the battlements.

Throughout the fighting Alexius V himself had his headquarters in the Petrion district, in the church of Christ Pantepoptes ('the all-seeing'). This church, founded about 1090 by Anna Delassena, mother of Alexius I Comnenus, and surviving today as a Turkish school, stood on high ground, allowing Alexius V a panoramic view of what was happening. The attackers landing from the transports were forced by the strong resistance to return aboard, and in their retreat they left behind much equipment.[3] They suffered casualties heavier than those of the Byzantines, who were elated by their success and jeered in derision at the retreating Crusaders. Many ships retired from the fray, though some remained at anchor near the walls to continue the bombardment of the city.

During the evening Dandolo and the barons met to discuss the situation in a church close to the encampment, in Estanor. There was some concern about the setback and the old qualms of conscience returned, many feeling that the reverse was God's punishment for men who had betrayed their Crusading vows. Some Franks were in favour of switching the attack to the comparatively weakly held southern sea-wall, facing the Marmora. But the Venetians, always alive to the danger of losing their fleet and the utter disaster which this would involve, argued that the ships might get caught in the currents of the straits and be borne away. Villehardouin says that there were those in the army who would have been only too glad of such an opportunity for escaping altogether from the scene. 'They did not care where they went, provided they could turn their backs on that land and proceed on their way; nor can one wonder at it, for certainly at the time we were in a very dangerous position.'⁴ But the leaders now decided on a new plan. First the men were given a complete rest for two or three days while the damaged ships and equipment were repaired. Attacks from the landward side would be abandoned altogether, and the entire effort concentrated on the northern sea-wall. While the men were resting, the forty largest ships, carrying the scaling ladders, were tied together in pairs, as it had become apparent during the assault that a single vessel with its ladder and boarding-ramp could not carry enough men to cope with the garrison of a tower.

On the Sunday, during these preparations, the clergy exhorted and preached earnestly, and masses were sung. Throughout the camp the summons was sent for attendance at these compulsory 'church parades', and the Venetians, though excommunicate *en masse*, were included in the summons. The troops were again assured, by the bishops of Troyes, Soissons, Halberstadt, and other preachers, that the war was a just one, as Mourtzouphlos had shown himself a traitor to his lord, and the Byzantines were schismatics. The recent reverse suffered by the men of the Cross was simply God's punishment for their moral failings. One consequence of this spiritual broadside was that the prostitutes and other loose women with the army were expelled from the camp, and put on a ship to take them well out of the way.⁵ This was a repetition of what had happened during the First Crusade at the siege of Antioch where, when things were going badly, the lechery of the Franks had been blamed and the camp followers banished in order to concentrate the troops' attention.

Early on Monday morning, 12 April, the assault was renewed, the ships advancing to the sea-wall. The battlements were crowded with eager defenders, now much more confident than before, and the din from the shouting was so deafening that it seemed to Villehardouin 'as if the whole earth was falling to pieces'. The attack was concentrated on the stretch of wall between Blachernae and the Euergetes monastery. Large stones were hurled at the ships, each of which, however, had been skilfully shielded by the Venetians with a network of cabling. Anchoring within range of the walls, they themselves bombarded the battlements. The battle raged until midday, when a providentially strong wind started to blow from the north, and the paired ships moved in to engage the towers. Two such bound ships, the *Paradise* and *Pilgrim*, which had on board respectively Névelon, bishop of Soissons, and Garnier, bishop of Troyes, came so close to one tower that a Venetian and a French knight, André d'Ureboise, were able to scramble on to it. The Venetian was killed, but André fought off the Varangian defenders so furiously that other French and Venetians quickly followed, and the tower was occupied, to triumphant Crusading shouts of 'Holy Sepulchre!' Another tower was almost immediately taken by a French knight, Peter de Bracieux, and Alexius V rushed up reinforcements to hem in the towers and prevent anyone leaving them.

There followed a brilliant exploit led by Peter d'Amiens. With ten knights (who included Robert de Clari, his vassal) and sixty sergeants, he landed on a stretch of beach between two towers. They started to hack out the filling of a bricked-up doorway, a *testudo* of shields protecting them from a storm of arrows, stones, and boiling pitch. They made a hole just wide enough for a man to get through. They knew the defenders would be waiting inside. No volunteer was forthcoming, and then a priest, Aleaumes de Clari (Robert's brother), who in the previous year had distinguished himself in the attack on the Galata tower, shamed them all and started to crawl through. His brother tried to pull him back by the ankles, but he jerked himself free. On getting inside Aleaumes rushed with berserk courage on the defenders, and managed to hold them off while the knights and sergeants crawled through with their lord Peter d'Amiens. When the emperor saw from his vantage-point what was happening, he galloped to the relief of the defenders, but then decided that this was risky and rode back to headquarters. A large gate was now broken open by the Franks inside the walls, the transports beached, and the mounted Franks rode in. Other gates were opened, and soon the attackers were pouring into the city.

The Franks made for the hill-top headquarters in the Petrion district, where Alexius V tried to arrange some order of battle, but the sight of the armoured and mounted knights charging towards them, lances at the ready, unnerved the Byzantines. The historian Nicetas, though he had no personal love for an emperor who had dismissed him from office, does not minimize Alexius's energetic attempts to keept the army together. But the defenders were losing heart for further resistance. The breaching of the walls had shattered their morale. Mourtzouphlos realized that the end was near, and after some futile efforts to rally his troops slipped away from the scene in the middle of the night, not wishing to fall 'into the jaws of the Latins as a piece of daintily prepared meat', as Nicetas puts it.[6] He escaped through the Golden Gate, with a small party which included his mistress Eudocia, the daughter of Alexius III, and her mother Euphrosyne, and eventually made his way to Thrace.[7] The imperial camp was overrun, Peter d'Amiens helping himself to the pick of the spoils. The soldiers rode round in an orgy of triumph, slaughtering all they met, both men and women, and seizing whatever valuables they could find. Villehardouin does not suppress the scene, which was one of 'massacre and looting, the Greeks being cut down on all sides, their horses, mules, and other possessions being taken as booty'.[8]

That night the Crusaders' army camped in a large open space within the walls, fully expecting some weeks of fighting before Byzantine resistance ended. Baldwin took up his quarters in the emperor's pavilion on Pantepoptes hill, while his brother Henry encamped close to the Blachernae palace. Boniface and his men (who included the Germans) settled down in the most 'densely populated parts of the city'. But during the night a fire was started by an unknown Western leader, according to Gunther of Pairis 'a certain German count'.[9] The aim of the fire was to hold off an expected attack on a group of Crusaders. This was the third conflagration to ravage Constantinople since the arrival of the Franks and Venetians. It raged out of control, burning through the entire night and the next day, devastating the area along the Golden Horn from the Euergetes monastery to the Drungarion district. Between them the three fires had caused enormous damage, destroying perhaps half the city, the harbour districts suffering especially. One can recognize a note of awe in Villehardouin's words when he says that 'more houses had been burnt in the city than are contained in any three of the largest French cities'.[10] Fortunately, Justinian's great church of St. Sophia escaped this disaster, though it would seem certain that some books and manuscripts must have been lost in these conflagrations. Books are inevitable casualties in a fire, and it is conceivable that our repertory of plays by Sophocles and Euripides might have been larger today but for the flames of 1204.

In the course of the night hours of 12/13 April there was an exodus of Byzantine nobles and their families through the city gates. Some refugees took themselves to the imperial palaces, Blachernae and Bucoleon, while the populace crowded into the churches, where they assumed that they would be safe. Meanwhile, a few Byzantine nobles kept their heads and, as soon as it became known that Mourtzouphlos had fled, met in St. Sophia to elect a new emperor. After all, there were still numerous imperial troops in the city, though the vital Varangian Guard was fast losing heart. The frequent and erratic changes of ruler (with six emperors during the last twenty years) must by now have been playing havoc with their traditional sense of personal loyalty to the head of the Empire. Two young men were brought forward, neither of whom had so far played any important role in public affairs. These were Constantine Ducas and Constantine Lascaris. On the advice of the patriarch, John Camaterus, the nobles chose Constantine Lascaris, and took him to the Milion, near the Hippodrome. A desperate appeal was there made to the Anglo-Saxons of the Guard to carry on the fight. The pride of the Byzantine army, they were now the Empire's only hope. It was pointed out to them that if the Latins succeeded in taking over the government, the Varangians as a special force could hardly be expected to survive. But they refused to fight unless their pay was improved. Nicetas writes bitterly of the Varangians, 'who scarcely troubled to disguise their greed, and saw the acute danger as an opportunity to drive a hard bargain'.[11]

Constantine Lascaris realized that with the arrival of daybreak, the morning of 13 April, the Crusaders would be on the move again, and he decided there was no time to lose. He made the crossing to Asia by boat, accompanied by his brother Theodore Lascaris, who in the event was to become the next Byzantine emperor (at Nicaea). Constantine Lascaris, despite his election, was never crowned. The patriarch John Camaterus did not cross to Asia but made his way to Selymbria in Thrace and thence to exile in Didymoteichon.

'And so perished the God-preserved city of Constantine and its Empire . . . it now belongs to the Franks.' The closing words of the account of the Conquest of Constantinople in the *Novgorod Chronicle* have an unintentional sarcasm. In four days of direct assault a Crusading army of probably little more than 20,000 Franks and Venetians and other Italians had defeated a defending force which, if we are to believe Villehardouin, was substantially larger. The ease of the victory is seemingly inexplicable, and some may be tempted to ascribe it to a dissatisfaction of the vast city mob with their rulers and their rebellious refusal to help in the city's defence.[12] In 1453 an enormous army of Ottoman Turks, equipped with cannon, was to take the city (with a fraction of the population which it had in 1204) after a siege lasting several weeks. But the fact is that though in 1204 Byzantium did have reserves of manpower, these were almost totally untrained for war. The city had become accustomed to leaving the fighting to professionals, whose morale at this time was low owing to arrears of pay by a government short of money. And in an operation which included fighting by sea, Byzantium suffered from the fatal disadvantage of being virtually without a navy.

Chapter 13

The Great Sack

The Crusaders were unaware of the crowded and frenzied happenings of the night of 12/13 April, during which all that was left of Byzantine authority in Constantinople disintegrated. With the coming of daylight on 13 April they expected a renewal of the fighting; the greater part of the city was still to be won, and there could well be prolonged hand-to-hand fighting in the maze of streets and amongst the charred ruins of the numerous houses destroyed by fire. There were many buildings still intact, and with determined defenders these might have to be taken one by one. There would be no further scope for the sea-craft of the Venetians, which had been so important a factor in the taking of the city, and little opportunity for massed cavalry charges, in which the heavily-armoured Frankish knights excelled. Moreover, there were large numbers of imperial troops in the capital, and the Crusaders themselves believed these to outnumber their own forces.

But it was no stubborn defending army which met the Crusaders in the morning. Instead, a deputation of clergy in full canonicals, with Varangian guardsmen in attendance, came to report that with the flight of Alexius V Mourtzouphlos all was over.[1]

The first action of the Crusaders was to take possession of the two imperial palaces. Boniface, who as official leader of the expedition assumed that he would become emperor, rode with his troops to occupy the Bucoleon on the Sea of Marmora. In the streets he was greeted with acclamations by the people. He found several high-ranking ladies sheltering in the palace, including Agnes, a Frenchwoman (sister of the king of France) who had been wife first to Alexius II, then to Andronicus I, and thirdly to a Byzantine nobleman Theodore Vranas. Robert de Clari says that the barons had already called on Agnes after the first siege to pay her their respects. Artless as ever, the Crusaders had apparently expected a warm welcome from her, but she had refused to speak with them except in Greek, and in any case was now more Byzantine than French.[2] Also in the Bucoleon was Margaret (daughter of the Hungarian king Bela III), widow of Isaac II. The other palace, at Blachernae, was taken by Henry of Flanders, who did not harm the refugees sheltering there. Both palaces were found to contain great stores of treasures, over which guards were set. The doge also found a suitable residence for himself, called by Villehardouin 'one of the fairest palaces in the world'.

The leaders safely ensconced in their palaces and headquarters, the turn came of the knights and the soldiering rank and file. They had realized the ultimate dream of north European soldiery, the capture of Constantinople, and there was no restraining them. They had survived much hunger and frustration, and after a long winter's wait and hard fighting the richest city in the world lay at their feet. The fact that the Byzantines had so lamely given up the fight on the breaching of the walls probably instilled contempt into the minds of the leaders, who gave leave for a general sack of the city. It lasted for three days, 13–15 April, and though it is not possible to construct a systematic narrative of what actually happened, the outrage itself is clear enough from contemporary sources. The irony is that the men who perpetrated this act were of the time, and came from the heartlands, of the famous 'twelfth-century renaissance', a movement which gave to Europe the first Gothic cathedrals, the music of Perotinus, and scholastic philosophy. The Crusaders cast aside all sense of restraint and combed the city for everything they could find, be it treasure, trinket, or money. The Normans had indeed in similar fashion sacked Thessalonica in 1185, but they had not been sworn Crusaders. Here in Constantinople was an opportunity for easy plunder which could never come again.

Villehardouin in his account understandably does not dwell at length on the scene, but he states as a factual matter that there was pillage and booty the like of which 'had never been obtained in any city since the world began'. The discovery of the wine-cellars and the orgies of drunkenness removed all restraint; and men who during the last year or two had often been forced to endure the agonies of thirst in a Mediterranean climate, now became completely out of control. But in all Crusading armies there was a high proportion of adventurers who did not fit easily into the orderly routine of feudal society; and the presence of many criminal types would moreover virtually be ensured by the various Crusading privileges, such as immunity from the secular courts and the right to 'essoin'. In 1216 Pope Honorius III, Innocent's successor, was in fact to deprive of their privileges men who had taken Crusading vows while in prison awaiting charges.

That there was some slaughter is certain, though we must not assume that it was all the work of Crusaders. Gunther of Pairis puts the number of slain at about 2,000, though adds that most of the killings were the work of former Latin residents of the city who had fled and who had returned with the Crusaders, with some old scores to settle.[3] It was plunder in which the Crusaders were above all interested, for whatever might have been their original motives in taking the Cross, they were now venal self-seekers. Such houses as had survived the fires were systematically ransacked, especially the mansions of the nobility, many of whom had fled the city. Individual citizens were searched, or tortured to make them say where their money or valuables were hidden. The sheer callousness of the sack by these men impelled Nicetas to write that even the Saracens had behaved better when they took Jerusalem in 1187.[4] The Muslims had at least respected the sanctity of the church of the Holy Sepulchre.

Some of the finest and easily the most accessible of the city's treasures were those in the churches, and far from these being spared by Christ's champions, they were the object of their most odious greed. The oath taken on the sacred relics before the assault – that churches should not be robbed – was totally ignored. It took hours to ransack the great church of the Holy Apostles, burial-place of Constantine and many emperors. The imperial tombs, it is fair to say, had already been tampered with by Alexius III in his search for valuables, but they were now desecrated and completely denuded of the precious stones and other ornaments with which the emperors had been buried. The body of Justinian, discovered undecayed, was stripped of its funeral jewellery; sacrilege could hardly go further. In the entire history of either barbarian or civilized countries it would perhaps be hard to find a more deliberately calculated piece of rapacity than the pillage of the imperial tombs. The soldiers descended on church after church, maltreating the refugees whom they found there and carrying away anything of value. Liturgical vessels and reliquaries were broken up, and Nicetas alleges that consecrated elements of the Eucharist were poured on the ground or thrown into privies.[5] The victors robbed the Mother of God church at Blachernae where, as the *Novgorod Chronicle* says, 'the Holy Spirit was accustomed to descend every Friday'. They knew exactly where to go, as for months they had been visiting these places as tourists, in which role they had been astounded at the wealth of precious goods on open display in the churches. In the Virgin's church of the Pharos, which was part of the Bucoleon complex, the very door-hinges were of silver. The monasteries were ransacked, and the monks and nuns subjected to every indignity.

The worst profanities were reserved for Justinian's church of St. Sophia, the pride and glory of Byzantium, which to Nicetas was a 'heaven upon earth, a throne of the divine splendour'. The richly ornamented doors were hacked down with axes and broken into fragments for their silver and gold. The silver pillars of the great screen were similarly treated, as was the silver altar rail. A special prize was the collection of silver lamps hanging from the ceilings, which when lit had given to the church a numinous and unearthly glow. These were taken down and tossed into a heap. The many thuribles were collected together. Twelve large crosses over the high altar were torn down, and the altar itself, made of precious metal, was smashed into fragments. Underneath the altar the spoilers found forty barrels full of gold, and a search of the treasuries and chapels brought to light the rich pieces of gold and silver plate acquired by St. Sophia over its long history. Liturgical books were mutilated by the removal of their precious stones and sumptuous bindings. Silken hangings were ripped down. The icons, symbol of all that was holiest in the Orthodox faith, were used as pieces of furniture as the soldiers caroused and drank from the altar chalices, 'and mules and saddled horses were led to the sanctuary to be loaded with the booty'. Having thoroughly ransacked the greatest church in Christendom, the soldiers showed their contempt of Orthodoxy by seating one of their camp-followers on the patriarch's throne to entertain them with bawdy songs. In describing this incident Nicetas does not conceal his loathing for the young woman, 'a priestess of devils'.[6] Remorselessly the pillage of the churches went on, and the author of the passages in the *Novgorod Chronicle* relating to the Fourth Crusade and the sack, who may well have been a Russian present in Constantinople at the time, says that the Franks 'plundered all, monasteries and churches, both inside and outside the city'.

The best booty apart from that of the churches was found in the two imperial palaces, Bucoleon with its five hundred mosaic-decorated rooms and thirty chapels, and Blachernae with its two hundred rooms and twenty chapels. In both palaces there was a rich haul of gold and silver plate, and of jewels, the treasures of Blachernae also including the crowns and ceremonial robes of the emperors.

A captured city had been looted. In broad terms the morality of this would not have been questioned by canon lawyers, let alone laymen, of the time or indeed for long afterwards. The spoils of war were rightful and honourable property. In early Western medieval Europe they represented a soldier's 'pay'. As for the confiscation of ecclesiastical treasures, this was something which had happened under the city's own imperial rulers. Churches were considered legitimate spoil by the Byzantines themselves, and there is even a case on record of a certain governor of the Praetorian Prison, during Alexius III's reign, who sent out inmates at night to rob churches for his benefit.[7] Though the minds of the Crusaders had been frequently troubled over the question of the diversion of their pilgrimage from the Holy Land to Constantinople, there was no twinge of conscience over the looting of the city once a military victory had been secured. The historians on the Latin side are enthusiastic about the immensity and variety of the plunder. Villehardouin says that it was impossible to estimate its value, with its gold, silver, and precious stones, its dinner-services, its satins and silks and ermined robes.[8] To Robert de Clari the spoils exceeded anything taken even by Alexander or Charlemagne, and the wealth of Constantinople was greater than that of the forty next most important cities in the world combined.[9]

Three churches were now chosen as reception-centres to which all plunder was to be taken for the agreed division, and a guard of ten French knights and ten Venetians, all of them known for their strict honesty, was put in charge. But it is clear that despite the injunction regarding a common pool, there was much private plundering. Money, for example, and gems, could easily be concealed and held back. Byzantine precision in craftsmanship entailed expertise in the making of easily portable objects such as enamels or ivories. Villehardouin complains that though some soldiers were scrupulously honest in handing over all they found, others were less so. Many looters in consequence were executed, these including one of the knights of the count of St. Pol, who was hanged with his shield about his neck. There can be no doubt, however, that others managed to get away with their deception, and amongst these were some of the trusted guards. There was resentment, expressed very strongly by Robert de Clari, amongst the knights at the undue share of the booty earmarked for the most powerful Crusaders and the unscrupulous manner in which they seized the best for themselves. Meanwhile many of the Venetians made the most of the opportunity, and under cover of darkness loaded much treasure on to their ships instead of handing it into the pool.

Despite the considerable amount that must have been concealed or spirited away, there was still at the end of the sack a huge sum in the common pool. There was paid over to the Doge of Venice 50,000 silver marks, which settled what might be owing to him once and for all; now as men of honour the Franks had fulfilled their obligation, at the cost of rivers of blood and the destruction of the world's greatest city virtually beyond repair. After finally paying off the Venetian debt, and allowing for what had been stolen, the Crusading leaders had spoils to the value of about 400,000 silver marks available for a general distribution. There were also some 10,000 horses of one breed or another, and as many suits of armour. The latter detail is of interest as indicating that the city's defending army was perhaps not so large as has sometimes been supposed.

The general terms of the agreement made before the storming of the city were now acted upon. After a quarter of the booty had been set aside for the emperor shortly to be elected, the remainder was equally divided between Venetians and Franks. Altogether something like 100,000 marks were paid out to the rank and file of the army. This worked out individually at twenty marks per knight, ten to each mounted sergeant and cleric, and five to each foot sergeant. The ordinary soldier who had borne the burden and heat of the hand-to-hand fighting scarcely became a rich man as a result of the great plunder. Amongst those who objected to this treatment was the priest Aleaumes de Clari, who stoutly claimed that he was as good as any knight.[10] The count of St. Pol upheld his claim, in view of his valiant deeds. The allotment, except in such, very rare, cases, was adhered to strictly and it was probably the certain knowledge that this would be so which had led to the large amount of private pilfering and concealment. Only the leading members of the Crusade could have made their fortunes out of the great adventure.

The clergy had played an invaluable part in sustaining the general morale of the Crusaders and in easing troubled consciences, and they were not backward in the hunt for treasure. Prominent amongst them was that same Martin, Cistercian abbot of the Alsatian house of Pairis, who had been one of the original preachers of the Crusade. Having some qualms about the diversion, he had made an unsuccessful attempt to obtain papal dispensation from his Crusading vows and had then gone to Syria, but, changing his mind, was back with the army early in January 1204, intent on joining in the second siege of Constantinople. During the sack he was determined to secure his share of the spoils, but out of respect for his religious office thought it more seemly that he should make his selection only from churches. His particular interest was relics, and he helped himself to many of these from the great store at the Pantocrator monastery in the centre of the city. While leaving the monastery he was met by other Crusaders, who asked him 'with what he was so loaded down, and with a beaming face he said, "we have done well", to which they replied, "thanks be to God".' When eventually he returned to his native Alsace in June 1205 (after refusing the offer of a bishopric in Thessalonica from Boniface), it was with an impressive collection of over fifty relics, acquired both in Constantinople and the Holy Land. These included such items as an arm of St. James, part of the head of St. Cyprian, the stone on which Jacob rested, a portion of the True Cross, and some drops of the Precious Blood. Gunther of Pairis says that Martin went into the pillage 'with both hands'.[11] Martin was also interested in more earthly treasures, and on his return home was to make a present of a fine jewel to Philip of Swabia, doubtless an act of prudence taken with an eye to the privileges of his abbey.

The main interest of the Crusaders generally was riveted on objects which would bring them material profit. After the hoards of money and the treasuries had been ransacked, there still remained Constantinople's profusion of bronze statues, which could be melted down and turned into small coin. As with the treasures of the churches and monasteries, spoliation of these works of art was not without precedent in Byzantium, but now, with the Latin capture of the city, there was an orgy of destruction. Statues from the ancient world, adorning the gateways and open spaces, were pulled down to be taken to the melting furnace. Amongst works of art which vanished in what must rank as one of the most wanton destructions in history were statues of Helen of Troy, the wolf of Romulus and Remus, and a large statue of Juno, originally from Samos and at the time in Constantine's Forum. A Hercules perished, brought long ago from Rome to Constantinople and the work of Lysippus (fourth century BC), master in the carving of athletic figures, who had made this piece in the first place for the people of Taras. A bronze statuary arrangement of an ass-driver with his animal, made by order of Augustus to celebrate his reception of the news of the victory of Actium, was destroyed. Of special interest was a tall obelisk known as the Servant of the Winds, with a figure on top which turned with the breeze. Its sides were decorated with basreliefs depicting the seasons with rural scenes, which were now wrenched off and taken away to be melted down.[12] The bronze plates recording the deeds of Basil I (867–86) and adorning an obelisk in the Hippodrome also perished, though a bronze equestrian statue of Justinian in the Augusteum, which Robert de Clari admired, managed to survive the spoliation.

The Venetians, who had an eye for beautiful things, were less destructive if even more rapacious, and they carried much loot back with them to Venice. They took a liking to a set of copper, mercury-gilded horses, in due course to be sent to Venice by the *podestà* Marino Zeno, for whom the trouble of transporting these figures to Venice must have been immense. The exact origin of these horses is not known, but they are certainly widely travelled. Of Greek or more probably Roman making, they were taken by Constantine to his new capital, where they were set in the Hippodrome. Besides the horses, there were also in the Hippodrome rows of other copper or bronze animals, such as camels and bears, 'all so well made and formed so naturally that there is no master workman in heathendom or in Christendom so skilful as to be able to make figures as good as these'.[13] Modern travellers who have seen the four horses will not be disposed to believe that Robert de Clari was exaggerating. When brought to Venice the horses were first put over the Arsenal, and by the middle of the thirteenth century in their present (or recent) place over the portal of St. Mark's. Napoleon Buonaparte removed them to Paris, whence they were restored to Venice after his final defeat.

Although their city was ruined, the great mass of Constantinople's citizens did at least preserve their lives. But they were subject to intolerable harassment, and this was so especially of the women, about which Nicetas bitterly complained.[14] Men died trying to protect the persons of their wives; nuns were raped, even in their own convents; girls were dragged away to become the enforced mistresses of soldiers who had for long lived almost exclusively in male company. The best that the women could do was to keep out of sight, or make themselves look as ugly and shabby as possible. There were exceptions in this matter and many instances of more restrained conduct by the Crusaders, and of official orders (at least towards the end of the three days) to leave the city's women alone. Baldwin himself we know to have been a genuinely devout man, who held fornication and marital infidelity in extreme distaste. Later, in 1207, the rhetorician Nicholas Mesarites, archbishop of Ephesus, condemned the physical indignities which the women had suffered during the sack, when the Crusaders systematically searched everybody's person for hidden ornaments and pieces of jewellery. Nicetas Choniates, in his *History*, could not contain his emotions as he lamented the ravaging of Constantinople and its inhabitants: 'O city, city, eye of all cities, known throughout the world and a sight for all, mother of churches, leader of religion, guide in true faith, guardian of letters and all that is lovely, bitterly have you drunk from the cup of the Lord's anger.'[15] Nicetas himself was amongst those who managed to escape from the city, he and his household first avoiding molestation by means of the good offices of a friend, a Venetian merchant, and then leaving through the Golden Gate.

When the rapacity of the victors was satisfied, after three appalling days, such houses or quarters as they needed were requisitioned. God was thanked that His warriors, after long tribulation, hardship, and poverty, could now enjoy wealth and finery, and with pride in their achievements the soldiers of the Cross celebrated Easter, welcoming the festal day on which God had triumphed over the powers of darkness. What nameless priest or deacon was it who sang the melody for the blessing of the Paschal candle, the *Exultet*, which Mozart centuries later was to say that he would rather have composed than all his other work? 'Let our Mother the Church rejoice . . . and this court resound with the mighty voices of the people!' It is quite possible that, instead of the customary Byzantine troparion or joyful proclamation of Christ's resurrection, there was also heard for the first time on Easter Day in St. Sophia, mutilated and despoiled but still standing with the assurance of perfect architecture, the great hymn of the Western Church, *Victimae Paschali*, composed a century and a half before by Wipo, chaplain to the German emperor Conrad II.

'Christians, to the Paschal Victim offer now your praises. Death and life have met together in a combat extraordinary. The Lord of life is dead – yet lives and reigns.'

The great Crusade initiated by Innocent III was over, without a single blow having been struck against an armed Muslim.

Chapter 14

A New Empire

The flight of Alexius V Mourtzouphlos had made the election of a new ruler necessary and a 'parlement' was therefore held to discuss the matter, Ville-hardouin remarking that 'for such a high honour as the imperial throne there was no shortage of aspirants', though the Crusaders thought it should go either to Baldwin or to Boniface.[1] It was felt that, of these two, the unsuccessful candidate should in compensation be given the mainland of Asia Minor and the Peloponnesus, which would ensure that he remained in the Empire and that Frankish strength as a whole was maintained. On Dandolo's suggestion, the two imperial palaces were temporarily occupied by the army. Boniface had already taken the Bucoleon, and he vacated it with an ill grace. Dandolo himself had no wish to be emperor; but equally he had no intention of taking an oath of fealty to the man elected. To some, the obvious choice must have been Boniface, the commander-in-chief of the expedition. On entering the capital he had been hailed by the citizens, and he was already indirectly a member of the imperial family. But Baldwin had behind him the Flemings and the French, who together constituted the bulk of the army, and as a less whole-hearted supporter of the diversion project he was probably favoured by the more 'idealistic' elements amongst the Crusaders.

As agreed earlier, a committee of six Franks and six Venetians was set up to elect the new emperor. The Venetian electors were Vitale Dandolo, Querini, Contarini, Navagiero, Pantaleon Barbo, and John Basegio. The leading Franks argued bitterly over their representatives, and resolved the matter by deciding that they should all be clerics – Jean de Noyon, Peter Capuano (papal legate), Névelon bishop of Soissons, Garnier bishop of Troyes, Conrad bishop of Halberstadt, and Peter abbot of Lucedio. The election itself was held on 9 May, in the doge's residence. After mass, and a solemn swearing on the gospels, the electors were confined in a chapel, the barons and knights awaiting their decision outside. There was some support amongst the electors for Dandolo, but the Venetians made it clear that he would decline; they feared too that if one of their own number were to be elected there might be a general exodus of Frankish knights from the Empire, which would be disastrous. Eventually the committee's spokesman, Bishop Névelon, emerged with his colleagues from the chapel and, going to the chamber where the Franks and the doge were waiting, announced their choice, Baldwin, count of Flanders and Hainault. 'We name him at the same hour in which God was born.' This suggests that the announcement was made at midnight, regarded in the Middle Ages as the moment of the Nativity. The proclamation was greeted with enthusiasm, cheers echoing through the building, and Boniface was the first to congratulate the new emperor, although without doubt he was deeply disappointed.

On 16 May, three weeks after Easter, Baldwin was crowned in St. Sophia, in a splendid ceremony for whose enrichment plenty of money was readily available, as the days of scrimping and begging were over for the Crusaders. Robert de Clari describes the coronation with a minuteness of detail which indicates that he was in the congregation.[2] Baldwin wore 'chauses' or hose of vermilion samite, and bejewelled shoes. Over a gold-buttoned tunic he was arrayed in a long cloak encrusted with precious stones, and above this was a mantle ornamented with eagles made of jewels. His attendants were Hugh, count of St. Pol, who carried the sword, Louis de Blois with the imperial standards, and Boniface bearing the crown, which was so heavy that two bishops had to support his arms. Baldwin, with a bishop on either side, was anointed, and then the bishops jointly placed the crown on his head. During the service Boniface and Louis de Blois did homage to their emperor, who afterwards, with a bodyguard of Varangians, went in procession to the Bucoleon, where general homage was received.

An important person was missing from these rejoicings. When Baldwin had left Flanders on 14 April 1202 he had not been accompanied by his devoted wife Mary, who had taken the Cross but was pregnant at the time of his departure. Her two young daughters having passed the cradle stage, Mary left Flanders early in 1204 but, quite unaware of the Crusade's diversion, sailed from Marseilles straight to Acre, arriving there in the summer of 1204, expecting to find her husband in the Holy Land. This is strong evidence that Baldwin was neither one of the authors of the diversion scheme nor an enthusiastic supporter of it, as one presumes that he had written to his wife during their separation with news of his movements and intentions. Arriving in Acre, Mary heard of Baldwin's recent coronation, though what her feelings were, as a devout Crusader, we do not know. She did receive, however, as the emperor's wife, the homage of Bohemond V, prince of Antioch – a fief of the Empire. Hearing of her arrival Baldwin sent envoys to escort her to Constantinople that she might join him as empress, but she fell victim, in August 1204, to an outbreak of plague, and it was Mary's corpse which the envoys took back with them to Constantinople. Of the deep affection which Baldwin and Mary had for each other there is no doubt – it was well known at the time, even to the prejudiced witness Nicetas, who also acknowledged Baldwin's piety. Mary's death caused much sadness, as the Franks had been looking forward to welcoming her as their empress.[3]

There had been fears that if Boniface was not elected emperor he might leave the new Empire in dudgeon, thus gravely weakening the Latin forces in Byzantium, the precedent troubling men's minds being that of Godfrey's election in Jerusalem following the First Crusade, and the subsequent bitterness of Raymond of Toulouse who had persuaded many barons to withdraw with him from the army.[4] But Boniface certainly had no intention of defecting, and was determined to establish a powerful position for himself inside the new Latin Empire. His ambitions were helped by his marriage, on the very day before the imperial coronation, to Margaret, widow of the late emperor Isaac II and mother of Alexius IV. As a daughter of Bela III of Hungary she had been baptized and reared a Catholic, though became Orthodox on her marriage, as a child, to Isaac. She was now married to Boniface with Latin ceremonies but remained deeply attached to the Orthodox Church, and though the papal legate persuaded her to return to her earlier faith,[5] she was always to be an Orthodox at heart. Some years later (when again a widow) she was openly to support the Byzantine clergy in their defiance of the new Latin hierarchy.[6] Boniface was duly given formal possession of Anatolia, but though this was historically part of the Empire it was now, with the exception of the coastal regions, occupied by the Seljuks, and of greater consequence was the central area of Greece, the Peloponnesus, which Boniface also secured. Instead of Anatolia he demanded that he should have Thessalonica, in which he had a family interest, and Macedonia. These demands were conceded, and as king of Thessalonica Boniface paid homage to Baldwin. On 12 August 1204 he sold Crete, which was his by virtue of a promise made to him earlier by Alexius IV, to the Venetians for 1,000 marks.

As a Frank had been elected emperor the Venetians had the right, in accordance with their agreement with the Crusaders, to appoint a totally new chapter of canons to the basilica of St. Sophia. The Byzantine clergy were ejected and the new Latin chapter proceeded to elect as patriarch a member of a patrician family of Venice, Thomas Morosini. Innocent III heard of this election early in 1205 and, though annoyed at not having been consulted, he confirmed the appointment.[7] In course of time Morosini was to prove tactless, unnecessarily upsetting the Byzantine clergy in Constantinople, who refused to recite his name in the liturgical prayers. Besides St. Sophia the Venetians also took control of other religious establishments, notably the great Pantocrator monastery and the church of Christ Pantepoptes, and they were naturally much interested in the church of the Holy Apostles, prototype of their own St. Mark's. They did not neglect their newly acquired architectural responsibilities, and indeed there is some evidence that they improved and restored the main fabric of St. Sophia, at the time in danger of collapse through a weakening of the structure caused by eleventh-century earthquakes. During the earlier decades of the thirteenth century the basilica's new Latin custodians were to strengthen it with flying buttresses of Western type, and they also erected a belfry.[8]

As emperor, Baldwin now was lord over most of Constantinople itself as well as Thrace, north-west Asia Minor, the Bosphorus and Hellespont shores, and some Aegean islands. The doge was excused the obligation of homage, and this was a great gain in that Venice's commercial position would no longer be dependent on the emperor's will but on the absolute lordship of the Republic. The general division of the Empire, according to the terms made before the second siege, was decided by a committee of twelve Franks and twelve Venetians which met in October. A quarter of the Empire was allocated to the emperor himself, three-eighths to the Franks and the same to the Venetians. In the arrangements which were eventually to emerge a Council was set up, including both Venetians and Franks, to ensure that the emperor did not play the part of autocrat, and the Western lawyers produced a constitution, the *Assizes of Romania*. But though intending to do for Constantinople what the collection of usages called the *Assizes of Jerusalem* had accomplished with some success after the First Crusade, the Latin lawyers in Byzantium in the event were to fail dismally in their attempt to draw up a blueprint for an eastern feudal State.

Meanwhile, the ex-emperor Alexius V Mourtzouphlos was still at large. Fleeing the capital, he had taken up residence at Mosynopolis in Thrace, and in the spring of 1204, shortly after the coronation festivities, it was heard that he had sacked the town of Tzurulum, only fifty miles west of Constantinople. This was serious news, and Baldwin marched from the capital with all the men he could muster.

There were now two former Byzantine emperors in Thrace. Besides Mourtzouphlos (Alexius V) there was Alexius III, who had escaped from Constantinople after the first siege. The two men, both with their headquarters in Mosynopolis, decided to arrange a pact against the common foe, and this was sealed by the marriage of Mourtzouphlos to Alexius III's daughter Eudocia. With some relish, Villehardouin narrates the sequel. Alexius III invited Mourtzouphlos to dinner and, having him safely inside his house, overpowered him and had his eyes torn out. 'I ask you to judge whether such cruel savages should be entrusted with the ownership of lands.'[9] On hearing of their lord's fate, Mourtzouphlos's followers scattered, some joining Alexius III. The incident came as a convenient conscience-salver to the Franks, at a time when some were having uneasy thoughts over the disruption which they had brought to the Empire. The emperor Baldwin duly arrived at Adrianople, left a small garrison to keep guard against possible trouble from the Bulgarians, and rode to Mosynopolis, but found that Alexius III was gone. While there Baldwin was joined by Boniface, who asked leave to go and take formal possession of his kingdom of Thessalonica. Although Boniface was quite capable of doing this unaided, the emperor insisted on marching to Thessalonica with him. Baldwin's decision puzzled Villehardouin, who says that he does not know 'by whose advice the emperor made up his mind to march to Thessalonica'. The result was a split between the two leading men. Boniface was still smarting over his non-election as emperor, and in a fit of temper he marched eastwards instead, to Demotica on the river Maritsa, where he was well received by the native Byzantines. He was accompanied by many Crusaders eager for fiefs, these including Berthold von Katzenellenbogen and other Germans, besides the Frenchman William de

Champlitte and the Fleming Jacques d'Avesnes.

While Boniface marched to Demotica and laid siege to Adrianople, which was defended by Baldwin's garrison, Baldwin went in the opposite direction westwards to the city of Thessalonica, whose people submitted. There was great concern in Constantinople when the quarrel between Boniface and Baldwin became known, and Villehardouin himself was sent to Adrianople to reason with Boniface, whom he persuaded to put the whole dispute in the hands of the doge and the barons, who at the same time wrote to Baldwin and asked him also to submit to their arbitration, making it clear that they would not tolerate internecine warfare of this sort.

Hearing of Boniface's siege of Adrianople, the angry Baldwin decided to humble his subordinate. He had other troubles also. In Thessalonica plague had weakened his army and many men had died, amongst them the emperor's chancellor, Jean de Noyon, a highly respected priest who had been a potent force in sustaining the spirit of the troops throughout the Crusade, and the redoubtable soldier Peter d'Amiens. While on his way to Demotica Baldwin received the message from Constantinople and, though he thought it impertinent, he agreed to return to the capital and leave Boniface unmolested. Boniface also came to Constantinople, and a settlement was made confirming Macedonia, and the Greek eastern region of Thessaly, as his kingdom, centred on the city of Thessalonica. By September the prospects for the Latin Empire of the East were beginning to brighten and Villehardouin, optimistically, could write, 'the emperor reigned in Constantinople, and the land was at peace and subject to his will'.[10]

In the autumn of 1204 the two ousted Byzantine emperors were both captured. Alexius III was caught by Boniface and taken to be imprisoned in far-off Montferrat. The blinded Mourtzouphlos with a few faithful followers was caught after escaping over the Dardanelles and handed over to Baldwin, who tried him on the charge of treachery to his lord. This was the man who had murdered the prince whom the Crusaders had championed and put on the throne. The sentence was death, and in full view of the populace Mourtzouphlos was taken to the top of one of Constantinople's columns and made to jump off.

By the close of 1204 news of the conquest of Constantinople had reached Syria, where many Crusaders quickly realized that there were easier winnings to be found in Greece. Men who had defected from the army and sailed direct to Syria now came to Constantinople, these including two cousins of Count Louis, Étienne du Perche and Renaud de Montmirail. Despite their earlier disloyalty, these two men were now well received; after all, as men of noble rank they brought many followers with them, and the Franks were deeply worried over their shortage of soldiers, faced as they were with the daunting prospect of holding down their newly acquired Empire. There also arrived several leading men, not defectors from the Fourth Crusade but established Crusaders in Syria, and with these veterans there came to Constantinople companies of Turcoples, Christianized semi-Orientals who were usually the sons of Turks married to

THE EASTERN EMPIRE
AFTER 1204

HUNGARY

VLACHS

R. Danube

GEORGIA

SERBIA

BULGARIA

Black Sea

Trebizond

EMPIRE OF TREBIZOND

Constantinople

PAPHLAGONIA

PONTUS

PRINCIPALITY OF EPIROS

KINGDOM OF THESSALONICA

LATIN

EMPIRE

Nicaea

EMPIRE OF NICAEA

SULTANATE OF RUM

Arta

LORDSHIP OF ATHENS

Philadelphia

Iconium

ARMENIA

PRINCIPALITY OF ACHAIA

Nymphaion

CRETE

CYPRUS

0   miles   200

0   kilometres   300

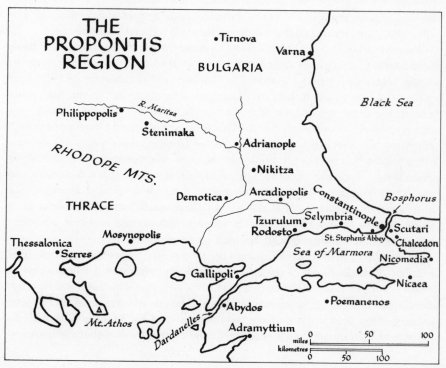

THE
PROPONTIS
REGION

Tirnova

Varna

BULGARIA

Black Sea

Philippopolis

R. Maritsa

Stenimaka

Adrianople

RHODOPE MTS.

Nikitza

THRACE

Demotica

Arcadiopolis

Constantinople

Bosphorus

Tzurulum
Rodosto

Selymbria

Scutari

Thessalonica

Mosynopolis

St. Stephen's Abbey

Chalcedon

Serres

Sea of Marmora

Nicomedia

Gallipoli

Nicaea

Mt. Athos

Abydos

Poemanenos

Dardanelles

Adramyttium

0   miles   50   100

kilometres

0   50   100

Byzantine women.[11] One of these contingents brought the young Geoffrey de Villehardouin, the marshal's nephew, who was campaigning in the Levant but does not seem at any time to have been a member of the Fourth Crusade.

Individual Franks were now seeking lands, though well aware that any fiefs which they obtained might involve hard fighting, and it was this realization that finally destroyed any lingering ideas of Crusading in the Holy Land. Of the principal leaders, Louis de Blois was granted Nicaea, on the Asian side of the straits, and he sent a force of knights to take it. To Hugh de St. Pol went Demotica in Thrace. The emperor's brother Henry gained Adramyttium in Asia Minor, and crossed the straits to secure it, though in the whole of this region a strong Byzantine resistance was mounting, under Theodore Lascaris. Lesser nobles included such as Renier de Trit, whose portion was Philippopolis. Guido Pallavicini, an adherent of Boniface, was enfeoffed with Boudonitza, which commanded the pass of Thermopylae; and two Flemish brothers, Jacques and Nicholas St. Omer, were entrusted with another strategic area, containing the pass of Gravia. Thomas d'Autremencourt obtained the barony of Salona, and the ruins of his castle survive above Amphissa.

By 1205 it was clear to the Byzantines that not only had they lost their capital but might well be deprived of the whole Empire. Dispossession was the prospect facing many Byzantine landowners, some of whom decided that their only course was to ally themselves with their inveterate enemies, the Vlach-Bulgarians. Envoys were therefore sent to King Kalojan, offering him the imperial throne if he would help them to get rid of the obnoxious Franks and Venetians. This alliance led to a serious crisis, centring around the city of Adrianople.

Early in 1204, before the capture of Constantinople, Kalojan had offered his help to the Crusaders in their forthcoming attack on the city if they in return would acknowledge his royal title. The Crusading leaders had refused his offer – 'a bad decision', said Robert de Clari, the ordinary soldier in the field, when recounting these events long afterwards.[12] Nicetas recorded the embassy and overtures of Kalojan, saying that the Western leaders replied to him arrogantly,[13] and thus the Vlach-Bulgarians and native Byzantines were driven into each other's arms.[14] Innocent III, however, had been in correspondence with Kalojan as early as 1199, congratulating him on his transfer of the spiritual allegiance of the Vlach-Bulgarians from the Orthodox Church to Rome. Innocent was moreover not unmindful that the Vlachs (Romanians) were a people of Latin stock, and the upshot of the contacts between Kalojan and Innocent was that a papal legate officially crowned Kalojan in November 1204.

About the time of the conclusion of the Greek-Bulgarian alliance Hugh de St. Pol, one of the stalwarts of the Crusade, died. He was lord of Demotica and his death encouraged the Byzantines to attack the city, garrisoned as it was by only a small detachment of knights and sergeants. The city fell, the Frankish survivors making their way to Adrianople, which was held by Venetians, though the citizens of Adrianople then rose in revolt and ejected the Venetians. All around, the Byzantines were restive, the Latin newcomers finding their fiefs difficult to hold, and the situation was viewed with concern by Baldwin and Count Louis in the capital. To meet the mounting crisis knights were recalled from their scattered fiefs, and there was also some panic amongst the Frankish rank and file. The baron Renier de Trit was deserted by so many of his men that he found himself defending his fief Philippopolis, and the neighbouring stronghold of Stenimaka, with only fifteen knights.

Baldwin decided to march. First he sent Villehardouin ahead towards Adrianople, strongly occupied by Byzantines. But instead of biding his time while the recalled knights hastened to Constantinople, Baldwin became impatient and made the fatal decision to follow Villehardouin's advance force with such troops as he could immediately gather together. Shortly before Easter 1205 he launched, with Louis, an attack on the gates of Adrianople. Dandolo also arrived with all his available troops, though by now he must have been feeling the strain of his age and the enormous pressures of the last three or four years. Meanwhile, Kalojan was hurrying to the relief of Adrianople with an army of Vlachs, Bulgarians, and Cuman horsemen.

The city held fast; and Baldwin realized that a pitched battle between his small army and the advancing Kalojan was imminent. The opening attack was made by the Cumans, but the Franks fell into a trap often set by horse-warriors of the steppes. After their charge the Cumans retreated and, when pursued by the Franks, turned round and showered them with arrows. Baldwin gave strict orders that ranks were not to be broken in future. Next day the Cumans charged again, and once more the Franks chased the apparently fleeing Cumans. Again the Cumans turned and discharged their arrows. Battle was joined in earnest, and Louis mortally wounded. When his men wanted to carry him back to the camp, he refused. 'God forbid that it should ever be said of me that I fled the field and deserted my emperor.' Although many Franks fought bravely, some panicked and fled from the field, and the outcome was utter defeat for the Latins. Baldwin was captured, and taken away to be imprisoned in chains in a stronghold, known to this day as 'Baldwin's tower', in Kalojan's highland capital Tirnovo, in Bulgaria. The dead included Étienne du Perche and Renaud de Montmirail, the defectors recently returned from Syria.

For the new Latin Empire, the battle of Adrianople was a disaster. It is illustrative of the fickleness of warfare that the army which had only a year before achieved the seemingly impossible, the capture of Constantinople, was now destroyed in pitched battle, the form of fighting in which the Franks themselves were held to be pre-eminent. Later, Kalojan was to remonstrate with the pope that he had tried hard but in vain to cultivate good relations with the Latins, protesting to them that he was crowned by papal authority, and that he had actually fought under a standard or *vexillum* presented by Innocent. The failure of the Crusaders to come to some arrangement with Kalojan is an indication of their lack of political prudence and their inability to guide the fortunes of a great empire. As for Kalojan himself, it is certain that as a result of his victory he now had definite designs on the imperial crown: the road to Constantinople lay straight ahead.

The demoralized survivors from the Latin army were kept in some sort of order by Villehardouin and Dandolo, and brought safely to Rodosto on the Marmora, but when news of the defeat arrived in Constantinople there was consternation. Baldwin had made his mistake by going to meet Kalojan without waiting for his scattered troops to muster, and in fact at the time when news of the calamity was received there were no fewer than 7,000 fighting men assembled in the capital.[15] When they heard of Adrianople and the emperor's fate, they decided that the whole venture of the Crusade was clearly a failure. The men crowded on to a squadron of Venetian transports in the harbour, and though Cardinal Peter Capuano and Conon de Béthune, with some barons, went down to the harbour and with tears in their eyes implored the men to stay, the defectors were adamant. They sailed to Rodosto, where Villehardouin met them and made the same plea, which they promised to consider, but at dawn on the following day they set sail without even waiting to say farewell.

This mass defection marked the virtual end of the army of the Fourth Crusade, and in effect decided, after hardly a year of existence, the fate of the Latin Empire, the forces remaining being too few and thinly scattered to be effective. Nevertheless, the survivors did not lose hope. Henry, Baldwin's brother, had returned from Adramyttium in Asia Minor on receiving the summons, and it was while on his way to Adrianople that he heard of the disaster. He joined Dandolo and Villehardouin at Rodosto, and those present accepted him provisionally as regent of the Empire. But Kalojan was in control of the countryside, and it seemed likely to many that he would be the next emperor. The despondent barons in Constantinople sent Bishop Névelon with an urgent message for help to France and Flanders, and to the pope.

To complete the picture of gloom, the Doge of Venice, exhausted by his recent exertions and the seeming collapse of his schemes, died on 1 June 1205. He was buried in St. Sophia.

Undoubtedly the directing intelligence behind the Fourth Crusade and the conquest of Constantinople, Enrico Dandolo had conducted his dogeship almost as a personal monarchy. He had often taken important decisions without reference to Venice itself: after his death care was taken that such a dogeship should not be possible again, and that the incumbent should act simply as the chief magistrate of the Republic. The Venetian community in Constantinople did not await instructions from Venice but immediately elected as their leader Marino Zeno, who took the title of *podestà* and proceeded to surround himself with the trappings of authority.[16] But this alarmed the Venetians at home, where Enrico's deputy had been his son Rainier. Peter Ziani was elected doge in August 1205 and took steps to ensure that the Republic's colonies, of which Constantinople was the greatest, were kept in subordination. Marino Zeno was soon replaced as *podestà*, and all future *podestàs* were to be sent from Venice and required to swear loyalty to the doge.

The winter of 1205–6 was a bad one for the Franks. News of one particularly serious reverse was brought to the regent Henry while he was taking part in a Candlemas procession (on 2 February) to the Virgin's shrine at Blachernae. The Bulgarian king took town after town, enslaving the people, while the depleted Latin imperial forces were virtually powerless to defend their new subjects. Kalojan was clearly aiming at the imperial throne and using terror as a weapon. His savagery so appalled the Byzantines that under the leadership of a certain Alexius Aspietes they repudiated their alliance with him and came to terms with the Franks. The Byzantines of Adrianople and Demotica prepared to defend themselves against what they realized would be the fury of the Bulgarian king. As he laid siege to Demotica both cities sent urgent appeals for help to Constantinople, and Henry decided to march. On 29 June he reached Demotica, and Kalojan prudently withdrew. A force including Villehardouin and Conon de Béthune amongst its leaders now rode to relieve Renier de Trit, who had been besieged for over a year in the exposed castle of Stenimaka in Bulgaria. Renier was able to confirm to his rescuers a report circulating in the Empire that Baldwin was dead. What apparently happened is that Kalojan murdered the emperor in a fit of rage on the return of the Byzantines to the Latin allegiance. According to the account of Nicetas, which though lurid is quite believable in view of what we know of Kalojan's character, the unhappy Baldwin was dragged from prison and thrown to the vultures, after having his legs chopped off at the knees and his arms at the elbows.[17] Whatever the actual manner of his death, it is certain that the emperor did indeed die in captivity. Baldwin, a man of chivalry and probity, deserved a better end, and long afterwards, during the Romantic Revival of the nineteenth century, he was to be to the Belgians a great national hero, surrounded by legend and commemorated in song.

Now that the Franks were convinced of Baldwin's death, Henry was duly crowned, on 20 August 1206, and he at once showed his confidence by marching far to the north on hearing of a long column of Byzantine men and women taken in a raid, and rescuing the captives after routing the Bulgarian king in a fierce engagement. There were strong hopes that the Latin Empire was over its crisis and at last had a chance of peace.

But during the spring and summer of 1207 Henry was again troubled by the irrepressible Kalojan, and also by the Byzantine, Theodore Lascaris of Asia Minor. These two men formed an alliance, and through the difficulty of fighting a war on two fronts Henry was forced to come to an agreement with Lascaris in order to give fuller attention to the Bulgarian king, the more dangerous threat to Constantinople.

Like his emperor, Boniface was much engaged in fighting, and in a minor skirmish with the Bulgarians in the Rhodope highlands he was fatally wounded, in September 1207. It was with his death that Villehardouin actually concluded his Chronicle, telling how Boniface was caught unawares in a surprise attack before he had time to put on his armour. He bled to death on the field from severe wounds in his arm. 'Ah, what a disaster for the emperor Henry, and all the Empire, whether Franks or Venetians, to suffer the loss of such a man in this accidental way – a man who was amongst the most noble and magnanimous of barons, and one of the world's finest knights.' About the same time, after a reign of ten years (1197–1207), Kalojan died, and it is possible indeed that Villehardouin also died at the time, and that this accounts for the somewhat abrupt ending of his Chronicle.

The emperor Henry found it difficult dealing with the Latin Crusaders and adventurers who had settled in Greece and Thessalonica, some of whom tried to rid themselves of their feudal obligations; these attempts came to nothing, but he paid close attention also to the affairs of the Church in Greece, where the barons were told to keep their hands off ecclesiastical property. In the spring of 1210 Henry convened a Council at Ravenica, and by the resulting agreement, subsequently confirmed by Innocent III, all churches and monasteries were declared free of feudal obligations and placed directly under the patriarch of Constantinople. In 1211 the patriarch Morosini himself died, to be succeeded by another Venetian, Gervase, a papal choice.

Henry, a patient ruler and a fine soldier, died on 11 June 1216, at the age of forty. His ten years of rule had helped to save the new Latin Empire from immediate disintegration, his success being partly due to his conciliatory attitude to the native Byzantines and his resistance to papal pressure that they should adopt the Roman liturgy. He was succeeded by Peter de Courtenay, who in 1217 was defeated and captured by Theodore, ruler of Epiros. Peter's wife Yolande (sister of Baldwin and Henry) became regent until her death two years later. During this chaotic period Conon de Béthune, now about seventy years old, played a leading part in helping to hold the Empire together. Veteran of the Third and Fourth Crusades, skilful negotiator, poet and trouvère, after Yolande's death he was virtually regent until he himself died in 1220. The new emperor, Robert de Courtenay, spoke of Conon as a man held in 'good memory'.[18] The line of Latin emperors was maintained, but the Empire, now an institution scarcely worthy of the name, was in irretrievable decline.

The new Latin order, however, did include two of the most interesting minor political creations of the Middle Ages, the principality of Achaia and the lordship of Athens, which were to leave a lasting imprint on the Greek-speaking world.

The former, whose first prince was William de Champlitte and which included much of the Achaian peninsula, is the post-Fourth Crusade State about which we actually know most. With its capital at Andravida, Achaia had twelve baronies, whose incumbents, with seven Latin bishops, constituted a High Council. Feudal castles were built, of which some ruins survive, as at Mistra, near Sparta, and there were fiefs not only for a hundred and thirty knights but also for mounted sergeants, who were thus rewarded for the valiant part which they had played in the conquest. Besides the High Council there was a court of burgesses, which dealt with everyday business. In the entourage of the prince himself were officials such as the marshal, chancellor, and chamberlain, and strict adherence to feudal law left no scope to the prince for playing the autocrat. A striking feature of the Achaian principality was that the Salic Law did not apply in it, and during the thirteenth and fourteenth centuries there were to be no fewer than six women rulers, which is remarkable for a military society. A number of Greek local rulers, the 'archons', were allowed to retain their estates and serfs, becoming part of the new Frankish feudal organization.

The Franks of Achaia were not particularly respectful to the ecclesiastical order, even that of their own Catholic Church. The old episcopal palace adjoining Patras cathedral was demolished to make way for a castle. Geoffrey de Villehardouin, nephew of the chronicler and the second prince of Achaia, refused to pay tithes, and did not insist on either his Latin or Greek subjects paying them. In criminal cases the clergy were compelled to use the secular courts rather than their own spiritual ones, to the anger of Innocent III. One is struck by the anticlerical attitude of the new feudal lords of the Empire, not only in Achaia but elsewhere, and their determination that the Church should not be too rich or powerful. Thus did the Frankish soldiers repay the clergy for their support in the conquest of Constantinople.

The Achaian princes became accustomed to keeping a fine court, thoroughly French in speech and manner, and famous for its devotion to the ideals of chivalry. Not many years after the conquest, in 1224, Pope Honorius III could say to Queen Blanche of France, with reference to Achaia, that 'as it were a new France has been created'.[19] In the principality of Achaia the Latin Conquest had some of its deepest and most enduring effects.

The first lord of Athens was the Burgundian knight Otto de la Roche, who set up a society less feudalized than that of the Achaian principality, he being surrounded not so much by powerful barons as by members of his own family who came to join him in Attica from their native Burgundy when they heard of his success. Thus a nephew of Otto, a certain Guy, who had undergone all the risks of the campaign, was now obliged to share the lordship of Thebes with an uncle newly arrived from Burgundy. Local Greek 'archons' also seem to have been less evident in Attica than in Achaia. Otto's rule over the indigenous population was not unduly harsh, and many Greek exiles soon returned to Athens, though these did not include the archbishop, Michael Choniates.

Otto's court was held normally in Athens, on the Acropolis, which he fortified, and Athens remained the ecclesiastical centre of Attica, a Frenchman Bérard being installed as archbishop in place of the Orthodox Michael, with the approval of Innocent III. The pope confirmed to Bérard the right to certain markets and gardens, as well as the control of monasteries throughout Attica, such as that of Daphni. There was to be no Greek archbishop resident again in Athens until after the Turkish conquest of the city in 1456. The Parthenon cathedral was plundered by the Franks, and the fine library of Michael Choniates broken up and scattered. Catholic canons were installed, the pope approving the adoption of the Use of Paris in their liturgical rites. In 1208 Innocent took the church of Athens under his personal protection, ordering it to be left secure in its possessions, though Otto, like all the Frankish lords in Greece, actually took what he pleased from the Church and was loath to pay tithes. As for the Latin Church in Greece, this was on the whole a sorry institution, far removed from the higher ideals of Catholic Christendom, and the native Greeks could hardly have been impressed, especially when they thought, with wistful regret, of their own highly respected, exiled archbishop Michael Choniates.

Chapter 15

Some Reactions and Consequences

It has sometimes been assumed that medieval Western Europe was morally shaken by the conquest of Constantinople, and that there was a thrill of horror when the news was received. Did Western Christendom, in fact, during the early years of the thirteenth century, regard the Fourth Crusade and its sequel as offences against humanity? The evidence is to the contrary.

The Fourth Crusade's author, Innocent III, had not been in favour of the original idea of a diversion to Constantinople, and indeed had not even known what happened until he heard of the first capture of the city and the placing of Prince Alexius and his deposed father on the throne. In his anger the pope had written to the Crusaders ordering them to set out immediately for the Holy Land.[1] After the second and decisive capture of Constantinople, however, the new emperor Baldwin wrote to Innocent, formally notifying him of what had taken place, at the same time taking the opportunity to invite others from the West, including members of the clergy, to come and join them. He suggested an ecclesiastical Council, over which the pope himself would preside, in Constantinople; and he was full of praise for the support given to the great venture by the Church. Baldwin declared his intention to introduce the Latin liturgy into Constantinople, and to set out for the Holy Land as soon as he had made his position as emperor secure.

The pope's reaction must have delighted him. Innocent reversed his earlier attitude, and congratulated Baldwin on a feat which had brought glory to God and the apostolic see. The taking of Constantinople was a 'splendid miracle'. He called on all men to support Baldwin, and expressed the hope that the conquest would be a help in the liberation of the Holy Land. Innocent exhorted the new emperor to remain a staunch son of the Catholic Church. The Eastern Church was now under papal protection, and he would ensure that the requested priestly reinforcements were sent out; but the union of the Church, Greek and Latin, under Roman supremacy, must now be made a reality.[2] Shortly afterwards, thinking that he had been over-hasty with these fulsome congratulations, Innocent wrote again, stating that though he was indeed grateful for the subjection of Constantinople to the Catholic Church, he would have been even more pleased at the capture of Jerusalem.[3]

But on receiving details of the sack of Constantinople Innocent was furious, realizing immediately that because of their blatant rapacity and sacrilegious behaviour the Crusaders had perpetrated an offence which would incur the unrelenting hatred of Byzantines for Westerners. He gave vent to his feelings in a powerful letter (addressed to Peter Capuano) in which his whole tone changed.[4] 'These warriors of Christ, who should have wielded their weapons only against infidels, have bathed in Christian blood . . . even virgins vowed to God were subject to their ignominious brutality.' Innocent was angry not only over the reprehensible nature of the sack of the city but because the Empire had been appropriated without reference to his authority; and he was especially bitter towards the Venetians, who had used a splendid Crusading army for their own material gain. Innocent rebuked Cardinal Peter, his own legate, who, after approving both the diversion and the first assault on the capital, had now formally absolved the Crusaders from their vow to fight in Syria. The pope suspected Peter Capuano of being deeply implicated in the whole unfortunate affair. Boniface, who had been official leader of the Crusading army, in fact tried to shift the ultimate blame for the diversion on to Peter though Innocent refused to be moved by this attempt, maintaining that Boniface as commander-in-chief must bear the final responsibility for the sack of the city. Writing to Boniface, he chastized him for fighting Christians rather than Saracens, and placing material gain before spiritual truth. He refused to grant absolution from his vow to go to Syria.[5]

The Crusade, in fact, had been one of Innocent III's most cherished projects, with its aim of delivering and ensuring the future security of the Holy Places. But though he had initially approved neither the attack on Zara nor the diversion to Constantinople, and had condemned the sack, yet on first hearing of the conquest he had expressed his delight with the achievement as such. For this reaction Byzantine churchmen were never to forgive him, being convinced that in some way he was responsible for the outrage of 1204. In writing his congratulatory letters, Innocent had unwittingly committed a blunder which put his seal on the schism between East and West, and made virtually impossible the very reunion project on which he had set his heart. To his tidy, canonical mind, the conquest of the Eastern Empire necessarily entailed the organic union of the Greek and Latin Churches.[6] In the years which followed, Innocent never wavered from his conviction that by virtue of the military victory over Constantinople, unplanned by him and wholly unexpected, the Orthodox Church had been brought back to the fold, and a divine judgement had fallen on men who had created schism.[7]

There were, however, some misgivings in the West over the conquest, these principally arising from a widespread feeling of perplexity that so many attempts to win back the Holy Sepulchre had failed. Why did God so persistently let His warriors down? Earlier, the poet known as the Monk of Montaudon, writing about 1193, had been distressed that the Almighty should have withheld complete success even from so illustrious a soldier of the Cross as Richard Lion-Heart. There were angry protests against the 1204 conquest by the poets

13. Aliense's quite unhistorical picture of Doge Dandolo crowning Baldwin as emperor;
an indication of how later Venetians saw the conquest of Constantinople.

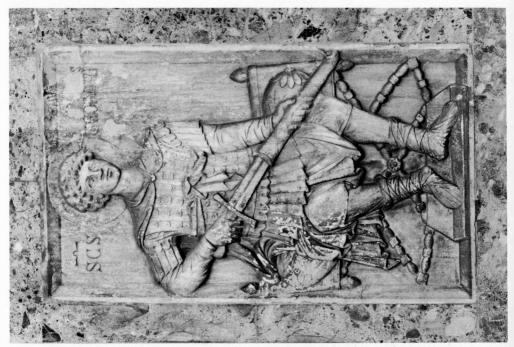

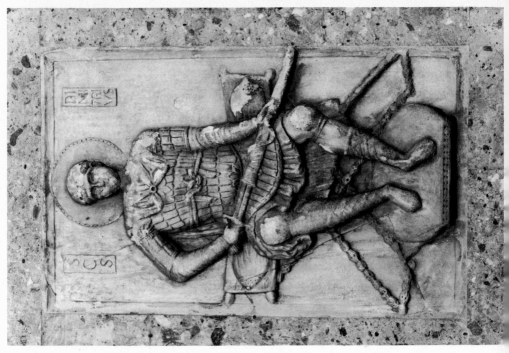

14a. This relief of St. Demetrius, from Constantinople, is in a spandrel of the west façade of St. Mark's. (*Left*)

14b. In another spandrel of the same façade, a relief of St. George, made by Venetian craftsmen half-copying the St. Demetrius relief.

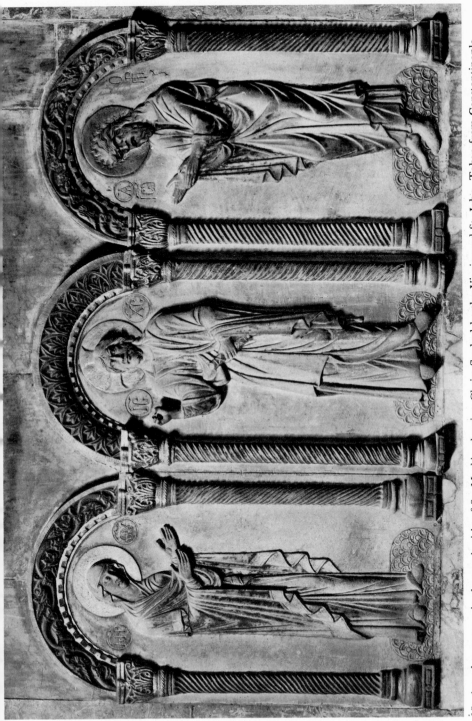

15. A sculpture now in the south aisle of St. Mark's, showing Christ flanked by the Virgin and St. John. Taken from Constantinople.

16. Theodore I Lascaris (1204-22), emperor in Nicaea.

Guy de Provins and Guillaume Figuiera of Toulouse. The former (a Cluniac monk) wrote a satirical attack on the Church called *La Bible*, and asked why Rome had permitted Crusading attacks on the Byzantine Empire. The troubadour Guillaume, a layman who flourished some twenty years after the Fourth Crusade, maintained in his songs that avarice was the root reason for the attack on the Byzantines, and he was unsparing in his criticism of the papacy. 'Why does Rome spare the Muslim and make war on Christians?'[8] The great German lyric poet Walther von der Vogelweide accused Rome of draining Germany of money and suspected that a large part of the funds raised for the Fourth Crusade went into the pockets of the clergy.

In the course of the thirteenth century poetical vernacular literature was to become increasingly scathing about papal leadership of the Crusading movement, the origin of this criticism being the unfortunate role of Rome in the Fourth Crusade. The troubadours of Provence were naturally badly disposed to Innocent III and his memory after the Albigensian Crusade which, in 1208, he unleashed on their rich and civilized land. Unfortunately, too, succeeding popes tended to make increasing use of the Crusades for the furtherance of their political aims. For this misuse of the Crusading idea, or rather abuse of it, Innocent must bear a measure of responsibility. After his death in 1216 most of the old Crusading fervour evaporated even though the Holy War was to remain in being as a Catholic institution, being invoked not only against non-Christians but against heretics and enemies of the papacy. The assault on the Orthodox Empire, in the final analysis approved by Rome, had set a fearful precedent.

Despite the reservations of the Provençal troubadours, the reaction of Western Christendom to the conquest of Constantinople was mostly favourable, and this approval is illustrated especially by the enthusiastic reception given to the relics brought back after the great pillage. There had been many men in the army to whom relics meant as much as money or finery. These not unnaturally included clerics and monks, but pious laymen also figured amongst them, and indeed to obtain tangible memorials of the saints or fragments of the Cross had always been regarded as one of the specific objects of going on crusade, Crusaders being essentially pilgrims in arms rather than soldiers proper.[9] Numerous relics were brought home to the West by the proud victors. Their trophies were solemnly received, many a procession winding its way through the streets of cathedral cities with the ringing of bells, sounding of trumpets, and preaching of sermons. Annual holidays were proclaimed, and during the years following the sack feasts were established for the anniversary of the reception of relics, most of them for churches in France or Venice.[10] Such feasts had their liturgical offices, with appropriate lections and prayers, and the feeling of hostility towards Byzantium behind them can be sensed from the hymn composed for the feast of welcome to the relics at Angers cathedral, in which Constantinople is called 'the long unholy city'.[11] Soissons received its initial reward in 1205. Its bishop Névelon, a prime mover of the Crusade, sent to his cathedral a consignment of relics, including a finger of St. Thomas and a thorn from Christ's Crown. There followed other precious objects, such as the skulls of St. John Baptist, St. Thomas, and St. James, and portions of the True Cross. Some of these relics were handed round to monasteries of the Soissons diocese, amongst them the nunnery of Notre Dame at Soissons, where some of the early conferences had been held and of which the Crusaders must have had poignant memories. Most of the Soissons relics disappeared during the troubles of the Reformation and the French Revolution.

Bishop Garnier, another stalwart whose exertions had helped to make the conquest possible, sent rich gifts to his cathedral of Troyes, enabling its clergy to repair damage caused by fire in 1188. Sens cathedral, which had also recently suffered fire damage, obtained something from the Crown of Thorns. Amiens, like Soissons, received a skull of St. John Baptist (or part of it), the gift of the distinguished soldier Peter d'Amiens who, after being a critic of the diversion, had joined enthusiastically in the assault on Constantinople and in its pillage. All these cathedrals were in northern France, true Crusading territory. Many relics were also brought back as private souvenirs, to be placed in the castle chapels of returned warriors, and there was a brisk trade in the sale and purchase of relics and other valuables.

In these donations and distributions, relics of the Passion and especially Cross-fragments figured largely. Crusaders were soldiers dedicated to the veneration of the Redeemer's death, and medieval men in general had a consuming interest in the sufferings of Christ. It is in connection with the reception of Cross-relics that we have what is virtually our only evidence of any English connection with the Fourth Crusade or its sequel. In 1205 a certain English priest (his name is not given by the chroniclers), returning from pilgrimage in Jerusalem by way of Constantinople, took service as a chaplain in the emperor's palace, where Baldwin appointed him a custodian of the relics. On hearing the reports of Baldwin's death in captivity he hurriedly left the capital, doubtless sharing the fear felt by many that the triumphant Kalojan was about to overrun the whole Empire and assume the throne. The priest carried off with him as many relics and precious objects as he could carry, including a certain piece of the True Cross which the Byzantine emperors had been accustomed to take with them into battle, and he arrived safely with these in his native East Anglia. St. Albans abbey obtained from him two fingers of St. Margaret, and a small and indigent Cluniac priory, Broomholm in Norfolk, received the Cross-fragment, which became the centre of a miracle-working cult, enabling the monks to improve their buildings and amenities.[12]

Another Cross-fragment, originally enshrined by the emperor Constantine VII in 959 in a reliquary decorated with jewels and cloisonné enamels, was taken back to Germany by Heinrich von Ülmen and is now in Limburg-an-der-Lahn. It is one of the best-authenticated of surviving pieces from the loot. Does it matter to us whether or not such relics were genuine? It would be as naïve and uncritical to dismiss them all as fraudulent nonsense as to accept every one as necessarily authentic. For the historian the important point is that the acquiring of such objects was an incentive to the individual medieval soldier. Robert de Clari, as a pious knight, carried home many relics of one kind or another to present to the Benedictine abbey of Corbie, again including pieces of the Cross. A prominent member of the Crusade, Conrad, bishop of Halberstadt near Magdeburg, returned in 1208 to his diocese with a large assortment of relics, amongst which there were not only a Cross-fragment and some drops of Christ's Blood, but also pieces of his burial linens. The bishop was able to enrich his cathedral from the spoils with gold and silver plate, jewels, and altar frontals and chancel hangings of silk. Also in 1208 Cardinal Peter Capuano went back to his native Amalfi, taking with him several relics, of which the prize item was the body of St. Andrew.[13] Relic-hunting continued in Constantinople for many years after 1204, and the ransacking of the imperial city's famous collection of relics must rank as one of the most bizarre episodes in the history of Christianity. We may suspect that the ingenious craftsmen of Constantinople made the most of the opportunity, and plied a good business in forgeries and fabrications, making beautiful reliquaries to contain parts of the human body, which were after all easy to obtain. In 1215 the Fourth Lateran Council was to find it necessary to instruct bishops to ensure that their churches did not receive fraudulent gifts. In Western Europe the Crusades, culminating in the Fourth, gave rise to a large increase in the cult of relics, and great ingenuity was expended on the production of fakes.

Of all the relics which are claimed to have found their way to the West as a result of the sack of Constantinople, the most celebrated is the shroud now in the guardianship of Turin cathedral. This is the grave-covering of a man who had been scourged, crowned with thorns, buffeted about the face, pierced in the right side, and crucified. The image of the sufferer has been left on the shroud, revealing a peculiarly noble and striking face. There are certainly known to have been burial linens of Christ in Constantinople, and when in 1201 there was an attack by a disorderly crowd on the principal Bucoleon chapel and it seemed that its relics might come to harm, an appeal for order had to be made, the crowd being reminded of the presence there of the sacred linens, which were removed soon afterwards to the Blachernae palace. Robert de Clari was apparently referring to these when in his lengthy account of the wonders of Constantinople he said that there was a church 'called my Lady Saint Mary of Blachernae, where they kept the shroud [li sydoines] in which Our Lord had been wrapped, which was put up straight every Friday so that the face [le figure] of Our Lord could be easily seen on it. And nobody, whether Greek or French, ever knew what happened to this shroud after the capture of the city.'[14] After 1204 the shroud just disappeared. It is possible that it was brought to the West and may even be identical with the present Turin Shroud, though there is no documentary evidence to this effect, our earliest specific historical knowledge of the present shroud being that it belonged to Geoffrey de Charny of Lirey, a French knight killed at the battle of Poitiers in 1356.[15]

The Cistercians, to whom the success of the attack on Constantinople owed so much, had their share of the relics. Not only the abbot of Pairis, Martin, took religious trophies back to Western Europe. Later, in 1210, abbot Hugh of St. Ghislain was commissioned by the emperor Henry to take to Clairvaux a consignment of relics, which included an eyelash of St. John Baptist. Even as late as 1263 two Cistercian abbots, of Daphni in Greece and of its mother house Bellevaux, were to be entrusted with carrying an arm of St. John Baptist to Citeaux itself, on behalf of Otto de Cicon, lord of Karystos, who had looted it from a chapel in the Bucoleon. The Cistercian Chapter General was so delighted with the gift that it granted to the abbots of Daphni the concession of attending Citeaux for the annual Chapter (which involved an arduous journey) only once in every seven years.[16]

A principal beneficiary of the conquest, in the matter of relics as in everything else, was Venice. St. Mark's basilica obtained fragments from the Cross and a few drops of the Blood, and the booty also included a thorn from the Saviour's Crown, a portion of the pillar across which he was scourged, an arm of St. George and a piece of St. John Baptist's skull. Venice had long been an avid collector of relics, and as early as 829 there was the famous occasion when two Venetian merchants, Rusticus and Tribunus, prised open the sarcophagus of St. Mark in an Alexandrian church and smuggled the saint from Egypt in a basket filled with pork (which the Muslim customs officials would not touch) to bring it to Venice, where it was received with joy and solemn processions. Early in the twelfth century a rock on which Christ preached was taken from Palestine to be placed in the baptistry of St. Mark's, and there were various acquisitions in the thirteenth century, in the immediate aftermath of 1204.

In 1238 a Venetian banker received from Constantinople the full Crown of Thorns as security for a loan to the hard-pressed Latin emperor Baldwin II, and for a time it was exhibited in St. Mark's. In the next year it was bought by St. Louis, king of France, with some Cross-fragments and the Holy Lance, and to enshrine these treasures he built, around 1245, the marvellous church of Sainte-Chapelle in Paris. The treasure of relics assembled by St. Louis at Sainte-Chapelle was so large that he was able to distribute many to other churches, not only in France, but in Spain, Italy, Germany, and Sicily. In 1273 a feast was established in Bergen for a relic (a thorn from Christ's Crown) obtained from Sainte-Chapelle; and a similar thorn, originally part of the 1204 booty, was also taken from the store of St. Louis and sent to Scotland.

Amongst the spoils which the Venetians took home, besides the famous copper horses, were many chalices and reliquaries, which were deposited in the Treasury of St. Mark's. The gold reredos in the basilica known as the Pala d'Oro, made to order for St. Mark's in Constantinople itself in 1105, was enlarged under Doge Peter Ziani in 1209 to include looted items from the sack. The gems and enamels with which it is studded are of Byzantine work dating from the tenth to the early thirteenth centuries, and the large plaques may well be from either St. Sophia or the Pantocrator church, both of which churches came into Venetian custody. For several years after 1204 the process of pillaging Constantinople by Venice went on remorselessly, many marble slabs and capitals being brought back for the embellishment of the State's great church. Venice was already accustomed to authorized looting, and when Doge Domenico Selvo had been busy with the construction of St. Mark's, towards the end of the eleventh century, his sea-captains had been under permanent instructions to bring back from the East anything likely to be of value for the basilica. After 1204 various clusters of marble columns with Byzantine capitals were added to the fabric, and columns were shipped to Venice to adorn the façades. As a result the church's exterior was transformed. The well-known porphyry group of the Tetrarchs Diocletian, Maximinian, Constantius, and Galerius, set into the south wall of the Treasury, came in the aftermath of the sack.

A good example of the use of Byzantine spoils in the years after 1204 is a series of six reliefs in the spandrels of the arches of the western façade of St. Mark's. A relief of Demetrius, a seated warrior-saint drawing his sword, is the work, classical in character, of a late twelfth-century Byzantine artist and almost certainly came to Venice as part of the loot. To match this relief a Venetian near-copy has been made, again a seated warrior in the act of drawing his sword, the saint this time being St. George, but it is less balanced and shows greater extravagance in the use of space. Again in the series of six reliefs, a Byzantine Hercules is accompanied by a Hercules made in Venice.

It is not always easy to decide what in St. Mark's is genuine Byzantine work or is the product of native Venetians using Byzantine styles or working from Byzantine prototypes. It is also sometimes difficult to judge at what time any particular piece of undoubted Byzantine sculpture or precious jewellery, now in Venice, actually arrived. The four columns of the ciborium of St. Mark's, for example, include reliefs modelled on looted early Byzantine work, and also some of the original work itself. Much must have come through earlier trading or raiding; but a high proportion probably came with the post-1204 spoils. In some cases there is little doubt, as with a triple sculptured marble relief of Christ, the Virgin, and St. John, now set into the wall of the south aisle of St. Mark's. Broadly, the impression which we obtain from St. Mark's is that the conquest gave a great stimulus to Venetian confidence and pride, which expressed itself in a deliberate programme of beautification of the building, before 1204 much plainer and less ambitious than the remarkable church we know today.

Not only was there an influx of artistic booty from Byzantium after 1204 but also of Byzantine artists and craftsmen, who came to join the Venetian workshops. After the middle of the century the Byzantine influence began to lessen, which was perhaps well for Venetian art as the Venetian sculptors were essentially imitators. With the restoration of the Byzantine Empire to Constantinople in 1261 there was to be a renewal of Byzantine influence in Venetian art for a short period; and then Venice in her art began to draw closer to the

Gothic of the West.

By reason of the great spoliation of Byzantium, Venice was now probably the richest and most beautiful city in existence, and this was claimed by a writer of about 1240, Boncompagno da Signa, who said, 'you will not find its match in all the world!'[17] Some indication of how complete was the success of Enrico Dandolo's scheming is the phenomenal growth of Venice's population, which by the fourteenth century was to reach almost 200,000, compared with 80,000 for Paris, 50,000 for Rome, and a mere 35,000 for London.[18]

The most important immediate consequence of the conquest was that the Venetians were able to establish an unshakeable position within the Eastern Empire, a position which all along had been their main objective and which was to be the basis of their future prosperity. After the taking of Constantinople in 1204 commercial privileges previously negotiated were of course maintained. The merchants of Venice took their stipulated three-eighths of the capital, and proceeded to acquire many islands, the most notable of these being Crete, where there was already a Genoese colony to dispute effective possession with the Venetians, who were not to gain real control until 1212. The Venetians then ruled Crete in partly feudal style, fiefs in the island being granted by the homeland Venice commune to individual knights. The Venetian population in Crete during the thirteenth century reached about 3,500, defended by a force of 150 knights.[19] The latter were all Venetian citizens, their new lands in the island being forcibly taken from local nobles, which understandably led to much bitterness, as did the Venetian insistence that the Orthodox Church be subordinate to Rome. The acquisition of Crete was of crucial importance, enabling Venice to dominate the eastern Mediterranean.

A prominent agent in the securing of Venetian ascendancy in the islands was a certain nephew of Dandolo, Marco Sanudo. An able diplomat, it was he who negotiated the purchase of Crete from Boniface. A lawyer by training, he was also an enterprising man of action. Fitting out a small fleet of galleys at his own expense, he sailed with a group of like-minded adventurers and seized the cluster of islands known as the Cyclades, the most fertile of which were Paros and Naxos, noted for their orange and lemon groves. The Byzantine fortress of Naxos was at the time held by Genoese pirates, but Sanudo besieged and took it, and in 1207 established the Duchy of the Archipelago, a political unit destined to endure for about three centuries. The capital was in Naxos itself. In Paros there still survive some remnants of the thirteenth-century fortifications, which the Venetians built from ready-made marble pieces of the ruined temples of Demeter and Apollo.

Another nephew of the doge, Marino Dandolo, took the large island of Andros as a sub-fief of the Duchy, and members of his expedition sailed further north and helped themselves to other islands, including Skyros and Skopelos. The island of Patmos, with its revered religious traditions, the Venetians left to the monks. Had not St. John said that he was 'in the isle that is called Patmos, for the word of God, and was in the Spirit on the Lord's day'?[20] The Venetians were certainly not indifferent to religion, and they often introduced Latin bishops to rule the Church, which may account for the strong Catholic population to be found today in the islands of the Archipelago, especially Naxos. In other Venetian islands, however, such as Crete and Euboea, Catholicism is not today widespread. The Sanudo family were generally tolerant in their Duchy, and they encouraged inter-marriage.[21] Many north European physical types, blue-eyed and fair, are still to be seen amongst the people of the islands, and there are survivals of Ven-etian influence in the architecture of the more substantial houses. Family names of Italian origin, such as Venieri and Crispi, are also still found.

The island of Euboea, virtually part of the Greek mainland rather than of the Archipelago, was first captured in 1205 by the Frankish Crusader Jacques d'Avesnes, and divided by Boniface after Jacques's death into three fiefs, which were granted to men from Verona. In 1209 Venice established the right to trade in the island, with a warehouse and its own church in every town. From now on Venetian authority was to grow in Euboea, Venetian settlers continuing to arrive during the thirteenth century, though the connection of Euboea with Verona was also maintained, immigrants coming from that city as well, making of Euboea a Lombard-Venetian joint colony, of which several ruined castles remain as evidence.

Another result of the 1204 conquest was that Venetian merchants were now able to enter the Black Sea more easily, though it was actually the Genoese rather than the Venetians who were to realize the potentialities of the Crimean trade. Of more immediate importance was the acquisition by Venice of Corfu, a vital link in her projected chain of maritime bases. The Venetians first had to get rid of a Genoese pirate, Leone Vetrano, who had established himself in the island many years before the Crusade. On the Crusaders' approach to Corfu during their voyage to Constantinople the pirates had withdrawn, but Vetrano soon returned to his old headquarters. Vetrano, with the local inhabitants, gave trouble until an imposing Venetian fleet appeared in 1206, when a governor was installed and Vetrano executed. In 1207 the Republic transferred responsibility for Corfu from the commune to a group of ten Venetian nobles, to hold it in hereditary fiefs. The arrangement guaranteed that the native Greeks were to pay no greater taxes than those formerly paid to Byzantium, and that the Orthodox Church would be left undisturbed. Venice retained Corfu until 1214, when it was acquired by Michael Comnenus Ducas, ruler of Epiros.

Amongst Venice's acquisitions were also the ports of Coron and Modon, on the south-western coast of Achaia, which were to prove invaluable as stations for merchant ships on their voyages to the Levant and Constantinople. By such conquests of islands and coastal strong points Venice had practically achieved her objective, the domination of the eastern Mediterranean carrying-trade. The first of the great European colonial empires had been established; and so satisfied was Venice with her gains that she found it unnecessary to take in full the three-eighths of the Byzantine imperial territories to which she was entitled by her agreement with the Franks, though she did assume control of the important city of Adrianople which guarded the approaches to Constantinople from the north.

Chapter 16

Byzantium Survives

Despite the unprecedented disaster which had befallen it, Byzantium refused to be crushed. Politically, it reasserted itself in three interim States which emerged from the general wreck; and to the Empire of Nicaea and the independent State or Principality set up after 1204 in Spiros, as well as to the remote Empire of the Comneni at Trebizond on the southern shores of the Black Sea, there will always be attached a peculiar interest.

Most of the Orthodox bishops refused an oath of obedience to Innocent III and went to Nicaea, though these did not include Michael Choniates of Athens, who wandered in Greece for nearly a year before settling on the island of Keos, where he remained an exile until his death in 1220. He declined an invitation to join the new imperial court in Nicaea itself, and another to settle in Epiros. He found solace in the composition of Greek verse, and prayed for the day when God would drive the Latin barbarians from Athens, the very heart of Hellenism. The Empire of Nicaea, comprising much of western Asia Minor, was founded by Theodore Lascaris (son-in-law of Alexius III), who had fought valiantly in the defence of the capital. After their capture of Constantinople in 1204 the Latins almost immediately tried to conquer the north-westerly regions of Anatolia. But Theodore Lascaris stood firm in his base at Prousa until the Bulgarian defeat of the Latins at Adrianople in March 1205, with its resulting shortage of manpower, made necessary their withdrawal from Asia Minor and thus gave Theodore the opportunity to establish his authority in the region. He was proclaimed emperor in 1206.[1]

Not only the higher clergy but many of the nobility also went to Asia Minor, where they were welcomed by Theodore, though in their sheer despondency some of the Byzantine bureaucracy became monks. Amongst the exiles who went to Nicaea was Nicetas, who arrived in 1206, in due course to become a judge and official court rhetor, besides writing his famous *History*. When Theodore defeated the Seljuk Turks under their sultan Kai-Khusrū at Antioch on the Meander in 1211, so resounding was the success that not only were the western Asia Minor provinces made secure but there were high hopes that Constantinople itself might soon be recovered. In 1211 the erstwhile emperor Alexius III, again at large, fell into Theodore's hands, and because he had been trying (with the sultan's help) to regain his throne, he was accused and convicted of high treason, blinded and sent to spend his remaining years in a monastery. Theodore's hopes of a return to Constantinople were dashed, however, by his defeat at the hands of the Latin emperor Henry. Theodore was succeeded by his son-in-law John III Vatatzes (1222–54), who controlled not only the western regions of Anatolia but secured many islands off the coast, and he made major reconquests on the European mainland itself, in Thrace and Macedonia. In 1235 he was even bold enough to lay siege to Constantinople, which was saved by the arrival of a fleet of Venetian and other Italian vessels and strong forces of Franks from the principality of Achaia. In 1243 Vatatzes allied with the Seljuk Turks to drive off the Mongols, who at this time were threatening Asia Minor and also the whole of Western Europe.

Under the Nicaean emperors western Asia Minor, with its profusion of vineyards and olive groves, became extremely prosperous, Vatatzes being particularly interested in agriculture. With his devout wife Irene he founded hospitals and churches, and undertook charitable work on behalf of the poorer classes of society. Characteristically, the Venetians were soon doing business with the Nicaeans, and Vatatzes was to maintain good relations also with the papacy and with the Hohenstaufen emperor Frederick II. The emperors of Nicaea were able rulers and well served by their government officials, though the armed forces continued to depend largely on Latin recruits, including Varangians, whose special trust was to guard the emperor's central treasury at Magnesia. Cuman horse-archers were also employed, and the army was kept up to strength by an economy run more efficiently than Constantinople's had been during the disastrous closing years of the twelfth century.

Certainly the political achievement of the Nicaeans must not be exaggerated. In terms of the overall balance of power, the Nicaean Empire was of relatively small importance, but it did maintain the continuity of the Byzantine imperial traditions. John III Vatatzes may be called the last of the great Byzantine emperors, and despite the decline of Byzantium from its former power and influence his Empire retained its fascination for Westerners. This is shown, for example, by the frequency of mixed marriages during the thirteenth century, it still being considered advantageous for a Latin nobleman to obtain the hand of a Byzantine princess.

The Byzantine successor State later to be known as the Despotate of Epiros was founded by Michael I Comnenus Ducas, a cousin both of Isaac II and Alexius III.[2] After Constantinople's collapse in 1204 he prudently attached himself to Boniface, but seceded during the Latin invasion of northern Greece and set himself up as independent ruler of Epiros. He had no official title, but the local inhabitants accepted his authority and regarded him as their saviour from the Latins. An outstanding success of his reign was the recapture of Durazzo (with its fine harbour) and Corfu from Venice. His dominion came to extend from Durazzo in the north to Naupaktos in the south, an area corresponding to southern Albania and the modern provinces of Epiros and Acarnania in north-western Greece. Like Nicaea, Epiros harboured many refugee immigrants from Constantinople after 1204, including artists and craftsmen who maintained the traditions of Byzantine art.

During the rule of Michael's brother Theodore I Comnenus Ducas (1215-30) the principality became increasingly self-assured. Theodore seized Thessalonica in 1224 from its Latin king Demetrius of Montferrat, son of Boniface by his Hungarian wife Margaret, and this was the end of the kingdom founded by the ambitious Crusading commander-in-chief. Proclaimed and crowned emperor at Thessalonica, Theodore was for a time a serious threat to Constantinople itself, and the jealousy of Nicaea was aroused. In fact, the antagonism of the two Byzantine States, Nicaea and Epiros, towards each other was a principal reason for the continued existence of the ineffective Latin Empire in Constantinople after the death of the able Henry of Flanders.

Theodore Comnenus, however, became over-confident and was defeated by the Bulgarians in 1230, and the Thessalonian 'empire' collapsed – though Epiros itself remained independent. During this time the Bulgarian king was John Asen, nephew of Kalojan, as forceful as his uncle but more humane. With the Latin Empire by now clearly doomed, Asen saw himself as the potential restorer of the Eastern Empire, but there followed a conquest of Thessalonica by the second Nicaean emperor Vatatzes in 1246. He obtained the allegiance of many prominent Albanians, and Epiros, now ruled by Theodore's nephew, Michael II Ducas, came under the influence of Nicaea.

The Empire of Trebizond is connected rather more loosely with the historical process which ensured the survival of Byzantinism.[3] When in 1185 the emperor Andronicus had perished, his son Manuel had been murdered with him, but Manuel's infant sons Alexius and David were smuggled from the capital and taken to Georgia, at the time ruled by Tamara (1184-1212), a famous queen who maintained a strong and prosperous Christian State in the face of the Seljuk Turks. After their escape we hear no more of the princes until 1204, when the young Alexius seized Trebizond. His brother David advanced westwards and occupied Pontus and Paphlagonia, but was brought to a halt by Theodore Lascaris of Nicaea. Eventually David was killed fighting the Turks, and Alexius died in 1222. The Trapezuntine Empire, whose official language was Greek, was to survive as a distant outpost of Byzantinism and Orthodoxy until some years after the final conquest of Constantinople by the Ottoman Turks in 1453.

Meanwhile, in the Nicaean Empire the second emperor John III Vatatzes was succeeded in 1254 by his son Theodore II Lascaris. Theodore's infant son John followed him in 1258, to be pushed aside almost immediately by an ambitious general, Michael VIII Palaeologus. First consolidating his position, and defeating the Greeks of Epiros, Michael then opened a direct assault aimed at the recapture of Constantinople. By now the Latin Empire was in a pitiable condition, almost bankrupt and desperately appealing for reinforcements from the West. There was an abortive attempt to take Constantinople in 1260, and then in the following year a small Nicaean force gained entry into the city through an underground passage at a moment when the main Latin garrison and the Venetian fleet were campaigning on the Black Sea coast. The emperor, Baldwin II, and the Latin patriarch fled ignominiously. On 15 August 1261 the Byzantines officially entered the city in triumph, led by Michael Palaeologus, who with his wife Theodora was formally crowned in St. Sophia. Although Frankish rule in Greece, and Venetian dominance of the islands, was to continue for generations to come, the Latin Empire, one of the most useless political creations in history, was at an end.

The young Prince John, a child of ten, was blinded on Christmas Day 1261. The Byzantine patriarch Arsenius, now in possession of St. Sophia, indignantly excommunicated Palaeologus for this atrocious deed, but after some bitter recriminations was himself deposed.

To secure his usurpation of power, Palaeologus was obliged to make concessions to the nobility, and the result was a growth in the number of large landed estates and an increasing development of society along lines similar to those of Western feudalism. Despite energetic attempts Michael Palaeologus (who reigned until 1282) did not succeed in restoring the Byzantine Empire to its former extent, and there was never to be a real recovery of the old imperial authority. From now on the capital had a much smaller population, and failed to regain the ancient glory extinguished for ever by Christ's soldiers in 1204. The important achievement of the Nicaean Empire was not that in 1261 it overthrew a foredoomed Latin regime in Constantinople, but that for over a critical half-century it upheld and indeed strengthened the conception of Hellenism, and handed this on to posterity. If the Latin Empire had succeeded, and Innocent III's dream of a united Christendom had been realized, the idea of Hellenism might have been lost, though Europe could have been perhaps spared its fatal destiny of division into Western and Eastern spheres.

The ecclesiastical significance of the conquest of Constantinople by the Latins in 1204 is that this marked the decisive separation of the Greek and Latin Churches. A reunion was indeed negotiated at the Council of Lyons in 1274, though it came to nothing; and popular Orthodox opinion also failed to confirm the reunion concluded by the respective hierarchies at Florence in 1438–9. By this time it was anyhow too late. The Ottoman Turks were at the gates of a fatally weakened Constantinople, and large areas of Europe were soon to be open to successive waves of Oriental invasion. The Crusaders, largely responsible for the progressive weakening and disruption of the Empire which was the marvel of the world, had thus ensured the survival and extension of the power of Islam, against which they had pledged themselves to fight. It is one of the strangest paradoxes in history.

Appendix 1

The Byzantine Emperors 1081–1282

Comnenian Dynasty

1081–1118   Alexius I Comnenus
1118–43   John II
1143–80   Manuel I
1180–3   Alexius II (with Maria of Antioch and Manuel's nephew Alexius
          Comnenus as co-regents)
1183–5   Andronicus I

Angelus Dynasty

1185–95   Isaac II (deposed)
1195–1203   Alexius III
1203–4   Isaac II (restored, ruling jointly with Alexius IV)
1204   Alexius V Mourtzouphlos

Lascarid Dynasty (Nicaean Empire)

1204–22   Theodore I Lascaris
1222–54   John III Vatatzes
1254–8   Theodore II Lascaris
1258   John IV Lascaris

Palaeologan Dynasty

1258–82   Michael VIII Palaeologus (in Constantinople from 1261)

Appendix II

The Latin Emperors of Constantinople

1204–5	Baldwin I
1206–16	Henry (regent 1205–6)
1216–21	Peter de Courtenay (his wife Yolande regent 1217–19, Conon de Béthune 1219–20)
1221–8	Robert de Courtenay
1228–61	Baldwin II (deposed, died 1273)

Appendix III

Twelfth-Century Doges of Venice

1101	Ordelafo Faliero
1118	Domenico Michiel
1129	Peter Polani
1148	Domenico Morosini
1155	Vitale II Michiel
1172	Sebastiano Ziani
1178	Orio Malipiero
1193–1205	Enrico Dandolo

The House of Comnenus

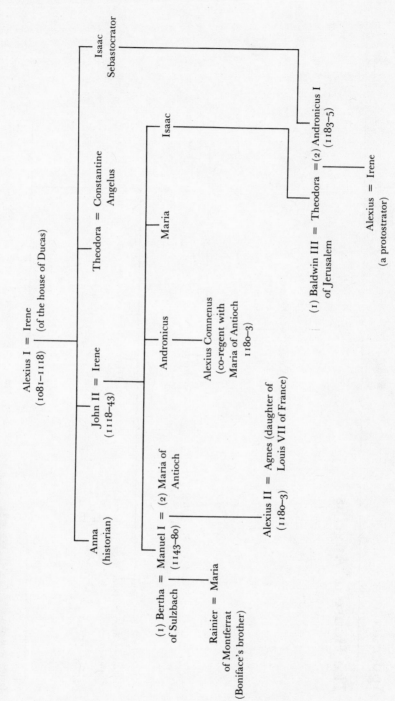

Appendix v

The House of Angelus

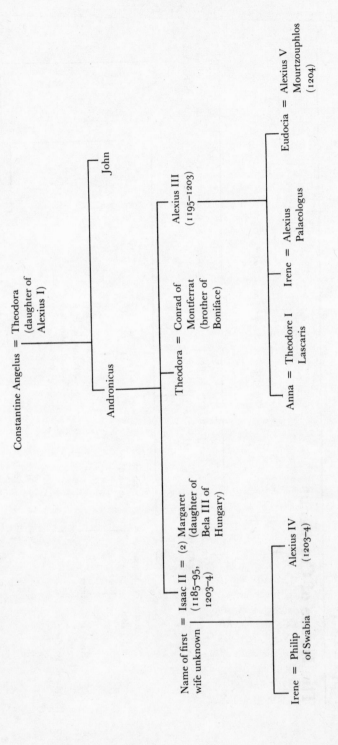

Notes

The following abbreviations are used in the Notes:

MGH   Monumenta Germaniae Historica
PG   J. P. Migne, Patrologia Graeca
PL   J. P. Migne, Patrologia Latina
RS   Rolls Series

Chapter 1 Soldiers of the Cross

1   Eusebius, *Life of Constantine*, I. 28, in *A New Eusebius*, ed. J. Stevenson (London, 1960), p. 299.

2   Augustine, *The City of God*, i. 20.

3   Tacitus, *Germania*, xiv.

4   Bede, *Historia Ecclesiastica*, v. 23.

5   Cf. D. Douglas, *The Norman Achievement* (London, 1969), chap. 5, for the theme of the Holy War.

6   Cyril, *Catechetical Lectures*, iv. 10, x. 19, xiii. 4. The feast of the Invention of the Cross on 3 May, abolished in the Roman Catholic Church in 1960, still appears in the official Calendar for the Church of England.

7   F. J. E. Raby, *A History of Christian Latin Poetry* (2nd edn. Oxford, 1953), pp. 88–91. The *Pange lingua* was 'written in the metre of the Roman soldiers' songs, the trochaic tetrameter'.

8   For the Cross-cult and its relationship to the Crusading movement, cf. A. Frolow, *Recherches sur la Déviation de la IVe Croisade* (Paris, 1955), pp. 59–71.

9   The actual text of the speech has not survived, though various chroniclers report it. See D. C. Munro, 'The Speech of Pope Urban II at Clermont' (*American Historical Review*, XI, 1906).

10   Cf. S. Runciman, *A History of the Crusades* (Cambridge, 1952), II. 149–51.

11   The Crusade as it appeared from the ranks is illustrated by Rosalind Hill, 'Crusading Warfare: a Camp-Follower's View, 1097–1120' (*Proceedings of the Battle Conference of Anglo-Norman Studies*, I, 1979, ed. R. Allen Brown, pp. 75–83).

12   Anna Comnena, *Alexiad*, xiii. 10. For Anna herself see Rae Dalven, *Anna Comnena* (New York, 1972), a general survey.

13   Fulcher, *Chronicle of the First Crusade* (English translation by Martha E. McGinty, Philadelphia, 1941), pp. 27–8.

14   *Gesta Francorum*, ed. Rosalind Hill (Nelson, 1962), p. 7.

15   Fulcher, op. cit. pp. 55–8.

16 They would be well aware too that some years before, in 1083, Alexius had hired 7,000 Seljuk Turks to fight in his army: *Alexiad*, v. 5.

17 For the military religious Orders see Desmond Seward, *The Monks of War* (London, 1972); for the Syrian Franks, J. L. La Monte, 'The Significance of the Crusaders' States in Medieval History' (*Byzantion*, XV, 1941, pp. 300–15).

18 Nicetas, *Historia*, 85. All references are to the Bonn edition by I. Bekker.

19 Odo de Deuil, *De profectione* (Latin text and English translation by Virginia G. Berry, Columbia, 1948), p. 57.

20 ibid. pp. 66–71.

Chapter 2   Byzantium and Western Europe

1   Isolated local communities in southern Italy, however, continued for several years to protest their allegiance to Byzantium: G. Every, *The Byzantine Patriarchate, 451–1204* (London, 1947), p. 175.

2   M. J. Kyriakis, 'Poor Poet and Starving Literati in Twelfth Century Byzantium' (*Byzantion*, XLIV, 1974, p. 291).

3   These gifts are described by John Phocus in an account of the Syrian monasteries in 1185: PG, 133, cols. 927–62.

4   Cf. H. St. L. B. Moss, in *Byzantium* (ed. N. H. Baynes and H. St. L. B. Moss, Oxford, 1948), p. 31.

5   Cf. Anthony Bryer, 'Cultural Relations between East and West in the Twelfth Century' in *Relations between East and West in the Middle Ages*, ed. D. Baker (Edinburgh, 1973), p. 87.

6   Roger of Hovedon, *Chronica* (ed. W. Stubbs, RS 1868–71), II. 102.

7   The fullest account of the 1182 massacre is by William of Tyre, *A History of Deeds done beyond the Sea* (English translation by E. A. Babcock and A. C. Krey, Columbia, 1943), II. 464–7; cf. Nicetas, 325.

8   Nicetas, 462.

9   Quoted by A. A. Vasiliev, *A History of the Byzantine Empire* (2nd ed. Wisconsin, 1952), II. 433, though Vasiliev's reference to Michael Choniates should read Lambros I. 163, not I. 157.

10   There are different accounts of the closing stages of Andronicus's career. The details vary, but there is general agreement that he was put to death in a most vindictive way: see Edgar H. McNeal, 'The Story of Isaac and Andronicus' (*Speculum*, IX, 1934, pp. 324–9), and Charles M. Brand, *Byzantium Confronts the West* (Harvard, 1968), pp. 71–3. Cf. Robert de Clari, pp. 54–6.

11   Nicetas, 481.

12   Cf. Charles M. Brand, 'The Byzantines and Saladin, 1185–92' (*Speculum*, XXXVII, 1962, p. 170).

13   Frederick's letter to his son is quoted at length in translation by Edgar N. Johnson, 'The Crusades of Frederick Barbarossa and Henry VI', in *A History of the Crusades*, II (ed. Kenneth W. Setton, Wisconsin, 1969).

14   Nicetas refers to the capture of Cyprus: 547–8.

15   S. Runciman, *A History of the Crusades* (Cambridge, 1954), III. 53.

16   Nicetas, 499, 582–4.

17   ibid. 600.

18 Kalojan is the proper name of the king usually called by the bogus form of Ioannitsa. He is still known as Kalojan in Bulgaria.

Chapter 3 Byzantium and Islam

1 Of particular value is John L. La Monte's contribution 'Crusade and Jihād' to the collection of essays, *The Arab Heritage*, ed. Nabih A. Faris (Princeton, 1946), pp. 159–98.
2 Cf. S. Runciman, *Byzantine Civilisation* (London, 1948), p. 291.
3 Cf. D. C. Douglas, *The Norman Achievement*, p. 150; and S. Runciman, *The Eastern Schism* (Oxford, 1955), p. 69.
4 Koran, Sura 112.
5 For this controversy see John Meyendorff, 'Byzantine Views of Islam' (*Dumbarton Oaks Papers*, XVIII, 1964, pp. 124–5).
6 A. Guillaume, *Islam* (Penguin, 1954), pp. 74–6.
7 Rābi'ah al-'Adawīyah, quoted by Gustave von Grunebaum, 'The Growth and Structure of Arabic Poetry', in *The Arab Heritage*, ed. Faris, p. 139.

Chapter 4 The Church Militant but Divided

1 S. Runciman, *The Eastern Schism*, p. 13.
2 W. Levison, *England and the Continent in the Eighth Century* (Oxford, 1946), p. 159.
3 For the bull: PL, 143, cols. 1002–4.
4 As recent a book as Friedrich Heer's *The Medieval World* (first published in 1962) can declare that 'the separation of the Eastern and Western Churches had become complete in 1054' (p. 124 in 1974 edition).
5 G. Every, *The Byzantine Patriarchate, 451–1204* (London, 1947), pp. 130–1.
6 PL, 189, col. 262.
7 Cf. Donald Nicol, 'The Papal Scandal' (*Studies in Church History*, XIII, 1976, p. 144).
8 Odo de Deuil, *De profectione* . . . , p. 69.
9 G. Every, op. cit. p. 168; PL, 214, col. 772. The point is that in the Latin Church only bishops can confirm, not parish priests as in the Orthodox.
10 PL, 217, col. 658.
11 ibid. 214, col. 21.
12 ibid. col. 377.
13 Cf. J. Gill, 'Innocent III and the Greeks: Aggressor or Apostle?' in Baker (ed.), *Relations between East and West in the Middle Ages*, pp. 96–7.
14 PL, 214, cols. 1082–3.
15 ibid. col. 764.
16 Donald Nicol, op. cit. p. 146.
17 Cf. D. J. Geanakoplos, in *The Byzantine East and Latin West* (Oxford, 1966), pp. 55–83.
18 PL, 214, cols. 308–12.
19 *Selected Letters of Pope Innocent III*, ed. C. R. Cheney and W. H. Semple (Edinburgh, 1953), p. 38.
20 See James A. Brundage, 'The Problem of the Crusading Monk', pp. 57–62, and Daniel S. Buczek, 'The French Cistercians and their Enemies', pp. 90–1 (*Studies in Medieval Cistercian History*, XIII, Massachusetts, 1971).

Chapter 5   The Gathering of the Host

1   Roger of Hoveden, *Chronica*, IV. 76.

2   Ralph of Coggeshall, *Chronicon Anglicanum* (ed. J. Stevenson, RS, 1875), p. 130.

3   E. John, 'The Preliminaries of the Fourth Crusade' (*Byzantion*, XXVIII, 1958, p. 97), has argued in favour of putting the tournament a year earlier, in November 1198, but I prefer the later date.

4   Villehardouin, I. 4. All references are to the 2-volume edition by Faral.

5   On this see Edgar H. McNeal, 'Fulk of Neuilly and the Tournament of Écry' (*Speculum*, XXVIII, 1953, pp. 371–5). For Fulk see also M. R. Gutsch, 'A Twelfth Century Preacher – Fulk of Neuilly', in *The Crusades and other Historical Essays*, ed. L. J. Paetow (New York, 1928), pp. 183–206; and Paul Alphandéry, *La Chrétienté et l'idée de Croisade*, 2 vols. (Paris, 1954), II. 45–64.

6   Fulcher, *Chronicle* . . . , p. 32.

7   For details of the Ely pontifical see J. Brückmann, 'Latin Manuscript Pontificals and Benedictionals in England and Wales' (*Traditio*, XXIX, 1973, pp. 411–12).

8   On the question of Crusading vows the indispensable work is James A. Brundage, *Medieval Canon Law and the Crusader* (Wisconsin, 1969).

9   Villehardouin, I. 10–12. There is useful information about Baldwin in Robert L. Wolff, 'Baldwin of Flanders and Hainaut, First Latin Emperor of Constantinople' (*Speculum*, XXVII, 1952).

10   *Les Chansons de Conon de Béthune*, ed. A. Wallensköld (Paris, 1921), pp. 6–9.

11   On the Compiègne shroud, see Maurus Green, 'Enshrouded in Silence' (*Ampleforth Journal*, LXXIV, pt 3, 1969, pp. 329–30). This shroud held its awe for the Catholic mind throughout the Middle Ages and until its destruction in the French Revolution.

12   Villehardouin, I. 14.

13   ibid. 18.

14   ibid.

15   The list is given by Villehardouin, II. 168.

16   ibid. I. 18.

17   ibid. 22.

18   Cf., however, Donald E. Queller, *The Fourth Crusade* (Leicester, 1978), p. 15, where it is maintained that the task of constructing the necessary transports would be formidable. The Arsenal was founded in 1104.

19   Villehardouin, I. 22.

20   ibid. 26.

21   For all this see Villehardouin, I. 26–30.

22   On Egypt as the intended destination, cf. A. Luchaire, *Innocent III, la Question d'Orient* (Paris, 1911), pp. 86–92. See also Donald Nicol, 'The Fourth Crusade and the Greek and Latin Empires' (*Cambridge Medieval History*, IV, pt i, 1966), pp. 276–7; and D. E. Queller, op. cit. pp. 13–14.

23   PL, 214, col. 121; Villehardouin, I. 32.

24   Cf. D. E. Queller, 'Innocent III and the Crusader-Venetian Treaty of 1201' (*Medievalia et Humanistica*, XV, 1963, pp. 31–4), and *The Fourth Crusade*, pp. 16–17.

25   Roger of Hoveden, op. cit. IV. 165–7.

26   Villehardouin, I. 32.

27   Robert de Clari, p. 37. Robert, however, is not at his most reliable for events
     preceding the assembling of the host at Venice. All references to Robert de Clari are
     to the English translation by McNeal.
28   Villehardouin, I. 34.
29   Cf. Jonathan Sumption, *The Albigensian Crusade* (London, 1978), p. 78.
30   Villehardouin, I. 42.
31   Queller, rather unconvincingly, argues otherwise – 'Boniface was a choice agreeable
     also to Pope Innocent III': *The Fourth Crusade*, pp. 24–5.
32   Villehardouin, I. 42–4.
33   ibid. 46.
34   On the place of the Cistercians in the Fourth Crusade see Elizabeth A. R. Brown,
     'The Cistercians in the Latin Empire of Constantinople and Greece, 1204–76'
     (*Traditio*, XIV, 1958, pp. 63 ff.); and Brenda Bolton, 'A Mission to the Orthodox:
     Cistercians in the Latin Empire' (*Studies in Church History*, XIII, 1976, pp. 169 ff.).

Chapter 6   Venice Looks to the East

 1   William McNeill, *Venice, the Hinge of Europe, 1081–1797* (Chicago, 1974), contains a
     critical survey of Venice covering the Crusading period. Two works by Gino
     Luzzatto are also useful: *Studi di Storia Economica Veneziana* (Padova, 1954) and
     Storia Economica di Venezia dall' XI and XVI Secolo (Venezia, 1961).
 2   Quoted in Pompeo Molmenti, *Venice*, trans. H. F. Brown (London, 1906), I. 14.
 3   Cf. P. Molmenti, ibid. p. 163.
 4   For the growth of trade in Venice and the other Italian cities, see Gerald Hodgett,
     A Social and Economic History of Medieval Europe (London, 1972), chap. 6.
 5   For Venetian naval and maritime strength, see G. Luzzatto, *Studi di Storia Economica
     Veneziana*, pp. 146 ff.
 6   There are several photographs of Venetian sculptures depicting tradesmen and
     craftsmen in Luzzatto, *Storia Economica di Venezia dall' XI al XVI Secolo*.
 7   Edwin Pears, who knew Constantinople and its waters well, stressed this fatal
     neglect very strongly: *The Fall of Constantinople* (London, 1885), pp. 173–4.
 8   Nicetas, 713–14.
 9   *Rerum Italicarum Scriptores*, XXII, 4, p. 527.
10   *Novgorod Chronicle* (*Byzantion*, XLIII, 1973, p. 311).
11   Villehardouin, I. 174–6.
12   For the Venetian quarter: H. F. Brown, 'The Venetians and the Venetian Quarter in
     Constantinople to the close of the Twelfth Century' (*Journal of Hellenic Studies*, XL,
     1920, pp. 68–88).

Chapter 7   The Affair Goes Awry

 1   Nicetas, 595.
 2   ibid. 710–12.
 3   All references to the *Novgorod Chronicle* henceforth will be to the short section relevant

to the Fourth Crusade, for which see the concluding passages of J. Gordon, 'The Novgorod Account of the Fourth Crusade' (*Byzantion*, XLIII, 1973, pp. 297–311).

4 On the problem of the prince's escape: H. Grégoire, 'The Question of the Diversion of the Fourth Crusade' (*Byzantion*, XV, 1941, pp. 158–66).

5 Robert de Clari, pp. 45–6.

6 *Gesta Innocentii*, PL, 214, col. 132.

7 J. Folda, 'The Fourth Crusade' (*Byzantinoslavica*, XXVI, 2, Prague, 1965, pp. 285–6).

8 PL, 214, cols. 1123–4.

9 Queller firmly repudiates the idea of a plot at the Swabian court to unseat Alexius III (Preface, p. x), but a careful reading of his *Fourth Crusade*, pp. 30–5, has had the effect of reinforcing my own conviction that there was indeed such a 'plot'.

10 Villehardouin, I. 70–4.

11 ibid. 50.

12 ibid. II. 28.

13 ibid. I. 58. Queller's estimate of the total number who went direct to the Holy Land is about 2,100: *Fourth Crusade*, p. 43.

14 Villehardouin, I. 58.

15 ibid.

16 ibid. I. 60–2.

17 Robert de Clari, p. 41.

18 S. Runciman, *A History of the Crusades*, II. 258–9.

19 *Gesta Innocentii*, PL, 214, col. 138.

Chapter 8   The Crusade at Zara

1 Villehardouin, I. 66.

2 ibid. 74.

3 ibid. 76–8; Robert de Clari, pp. 42–3.

4 Villehardouin, I. 80.

5 'Je vos deffent de par l'apostoille de Rome que vos ne assailliez ceste cité': ibid. I. 84.

6 PL, 214, col. 1178.

7 ibid. cols. 1123–5.

8 ibid. cols. 1179–82.

9 ibid. 215, cols. 103 ff.

10 ibid. cols. 106–7.

11 Queller, *The Fourth Crusade*, pp. 56, 183 n. 31.

12 Villehardouin, I. 90.

13 ibid. 96–8.

14 Roger of Hoveden, *Chronica*, IV. 111.

15 Villehardouin, I. 98.

16 S. Runciman, *A History of the Crusades*, III (1954), p. 116, assumes that there was enthusiasm for the attack on Constantinople by the 'average crusader'. But both A. Frolow, *Recherches sur la Déviation de la IVᵉ Croisade* (Paris, 1955) and W. A. Daly, 'Christian Fraternity, the Crusaders, and the Security of Constantinople, 1097–1204' (*Medieval Studies*, XXII, 1960) emphasize the considerable opposition within the army to the diversion.

17 *Selected Letters of Pope Innocent III*, ed. C. R. Cheney and W. H. Semple (Edinburgh, 1953), p. 38.
18 Villehardouin, I. 118.

Chapter 9 City of the World's Desire

1   Eadmer, *De Vita Anselmi*, ed. R. W. Southern (London, 1962), p. 133.
2   Benjamin of Tudela, *Oriental Travels*, trans. M. N. Adler (London, 1907), p. 13.
3   A. A. Vasiliev, *A History of the Byzantine Empire*, II. 482.
4   A. Frolow, *Recherches sur la Déviation* . . . , p. 64.
5   Jonathan Shepard, 'The English and Byzantium' (*Traditio*, XXIX, 1973, p. 79). One relic, an arm of St. John Chrysostom, was presented to Abingdon abbey: *Historia Monasterii de Abingdon*, ed. J. Stevenson (RS, 1858), pp. 46–7.
6   Villehardouin, I. 194.
7   M. Ehrhard, Le Livre du Pèlerin d'Antoine de Novgorod' (*Romania*, LVIII, Paris, 1932, pp. 44–65).
8   On this see P. Magdalino, 'Manuel Komnenos and the Great Palace' (*Byzantine and Modern Greek Studies*, IV. Essays presented to Sir Steven Runciman, Oxford, 1978, pp. 101–14).
9   C. Mango and J. Parker, 'A Twelfth-Century Description of St. Sophia' (*Dumbarton Oaks Papers*, XIV, 1960, pp. 233–45. Greek text with English translation and commentary).
10 For Byzantine monks see Peter Charani, 'The Monk as an Element in Byzantine Society' (*Dumbarton Oaks Papers*, XXV, 1971, pp. 63–84).
11 Cf. R. Guilland, 'Études sur l'Hippodrome de Byzance' (*Byzantinoslavica*, XXVI, 1, Prague, 1965, p. 30).
12 M. Angold, *A Byzantine Government in Exile* (Oxford, 1975), p. 30.
13 For Michael Choniates (formerly usually called Michael Acominatus) see the illuminating article by K. M. Setton, 'Athens in the Later Twelfth Century' (*Speculum*, XIX, 1944, pp. 179–207).
14 Nicetas, 265–8.
15 J. Brondsted, *The Vikings* (London, 1960), p. 193; cf. H. R. Ellis Davidson, *The Viking Road to Byzantium* (London, 1976), p. 238.
16 *Alexiad*, iv. 10.
17 Cf. *The Ecclesiastical History of Ordericus Vitalis*, ed. M. Chibnall (Oxford, 1969), pp. 202–4.
18 Nicetas, 323, 547.
19 For the Varangians see further Sigfús Blöndal, *The Varangians of Byzantium*, translated revised, and rewritten by Benedikt Benedikz (Cambridge, 1978); and J. Godfrey, 'The Defeated Anglo-Saxons take service with the Eastern Emperor' (*Proceedings of the Battle Conference of Anglo-Norman Studies*, I, 1979, ed. R. Allen Brown, pp. 63–74).
20 Nicetas, 75.
21 William H. McNeill, *Venice, the Hinge of Europe, 1081–1797*, pp. 8–9.
22 For the fleet: M. Sesan, 'La flotte byzantine à l'époque des Comnènes et des Anges, 1081–1204' (*Byzantinoslavica*, XXI, 1, Prague, 1960, pp. 48–53); and Hélène Ahrweiler, *Byzance et la Mer* (Paris, 1966).
23 Cf. S. Runciman, *Byzantine Civilisation*, p. 162.

Chapter 10 The First Siege

1 Villehardouin, I. 124.
2 ibid. 130.
3 Nicetas, 718; cf. Villehardouin, I. 138.
4 Villehardouin, I. 148.
5 According to a subsequent letter of Baldwin, Louis, and Hugh de St. Pol: Arnold of Lübeck, *Chronica Slavorum*, ed. J. M. Lappenberg (MGH, 1868), p. 242.
6 Villehardouin, I. 148.
7 ibid. 158.
8 Nicetas, 719; Robert de Clari, pp. 69–70.
9 Villehardouin, I. 160–2.
10 Perhaps as a protection against Greek fire, though there is doubt as to whether this weapon was really used in 1203–4.
11 Villehardouin, II. 54.
12 Charles Brand, *Byzantium Confronts the West*, p. 234, suggests 10,000, including fewer than 2,000 knights.
13 Villehardouin, I. 164.
14 Nicetas, 722–3.
15 Villehardouin, I. 172–4. Queller writes in somewhat derogatory fashion of the 'savagery of the Varangians', who 'fought bloodily': *The Fourth Crusade*, p. 102.
16 Villehardouin, I. 174–6.
17 ibid. 278.
18 M. H. Keen, *The Laws of War in the late Middle Ages* (London, 1965), pp. 64–5.
19 Villehardouin, I. 180; cf. Robert de Clari's eye-witness description, pp. 71–6.
20 Robert de Clari, pp. 45–51, for the engagement.
21 Nicetas, 723.

Chapter 11 The Die is Cast

1 Nicetas, 727.
2 Villehardouin, I. 188–92.
3 ibid. 196; PL, 215, col. 239.
4 PL, 215, cols. 236 ff.
5 ibid. cols. 260–2. According to Hugh of St. Pol, *Chronica Regia Coloniensis*, ed. G. Waitz (MGH), p. 208, and Robert of Auxerre, *Chronicon* (MGH), p. 270, the patriarch had promised in March 1203 to submit to Rome and go there to collect his pallium. But this story is strongly questioned by Donald Nicol, 'The Papal Scandal' (*Studies in Church History*, XIII, 1976, p. 147n.).
6 Cf. J. Gill, in *Relations between East and West in the Middle Ages*, ed. D. Baker, p. 97.
7 Robert de Clari, p. 81.
8 Villehardouin, I. 196.
9 ibid. 202.
10 ibid. 205.
11 For the fire, ibid. 206–12.
12 ibid. II. 8.

13 Nicetas, 735–6.
14 Charles M. Brand, 'A Byzantine Plan for the Fourth Crusade', with an English translation of the speech (*Speculum*, XLIII, 1968, pp. 462–75). The strong emphasis on the need for conciliation would seem to rule out its actually having been delivered on 6 January, as by then the Empire and the Latins were to be virtually at war.
15 Villehardouin, II. 14.
16 ibid. 16–18.
17 ibid. 22.
18 ibid. 24.
19 ibid. 24–8.
20 Robert de Clari, p. 92.

Chapter 12   The Storming of Constantinople

1 Villehardouin, II. 48.
2 ibid. 36–8.
3 PL, 215, col. 450.
4 Villehardouin, II. 40.
5 Robert de Clari, p. 94.
6 Nicetas, 755.
7 Alexius V became husband of Eudocia later. Cf. Donald Nicol, 'The Fourth Crusade and the Greek and Latin Empires' (*Cambridge Medieval History*, IV, pt i, 1966, pp. 283–4), and D. E. Queller, *The Fourth Crusade*, pp. 147, 216. Villehardouin, II, 78.
8 Villehardouin, II. 46.
9 Gunther of Pairis, *Historia Constantinopolitana*, in P. Riant, *Exuviae*, I. 101.
10 Villehardouin, II. 50.
11 Nicetas, 726.
12 Cf. E. Frances, 'Sur la conquête de Constantinople par les Latins' (*Byzantinoslavica*, XV, 1, Prague, 1964, pp. 21–6).

Chapter 13   The Great Sack

1 Robert de Clari, p. 100.
2 ibid. p. 79; cf. Villehardouin, I. 186–96.
3 Gunther of Pairis, op. cit. I. 104–8.
4 Nicetas, 759–62.
5 ibid. 757.
6 ibid. 759.
7 Charles M. Brand, *Byzantium Confronts the West*, p. 121.
8 Villehardouin, II. 52.
9 Robert de Clari, p. 101.
10 So Robert, his brother, tells us: pp. 117–18.
11 Gunther of Pairis, op. cit. I. 104–8. Cf. Riant, *Des Dépouilles Religieuses*, p. 6.
12 For the statues: Nicetas, 687–8, 856–68.
13 Robert de Clari, pp. 108–10. For the horses, see *The Horses of San Marco, Venice* (Procuratoria di S. Marco and Olivetti, 1979), translated by John and Valerie Wilton-Ely.

14 Nicetas, 759.
15 ibid. 763.

Chapter 14 A New Empire

1 Villehardouin, II. 62.
2 Robert de Clari, p. 116.
3 Villehardouin, II. 124–6; Nicetas, 790; R. L. Wolff, 'Baldwin of Flanders and Hainaut' (*Speculum*, XXVII, 1952, pp. 288–9).
4 Villehardouin, II. 62.
5 The pope wrote to congratulate her for returning to the Catholic faith: PL, 215, col. 714.
6 On Margaret's marriage to Boniface: Donald Nicol, 'Mixed Marriages in Byzantium in the Thirteenth Century' (*Studies in Church History*, I, 1964, pp. 162–3).
7 PL, 215, cols. 512–17.
8 Emerson H. Swift, 'The Latins at Hagia Sophia' (*American Journal of Archaeology*, XXXIX, 1935, p. 460).
9 Villehardouin, II. 80.
10 ibid. 110.
11 ibid. 122–4, for this migration.
12 Robert de Clari, pp. 86–8.
13 Nicetas, 808–9. Villehardouin does not mention Kalojan's offer.
14 Cf. R. L. Wolff, 'The Second Bulgarian Empire' (*Speculum*, XXIV, 1949, p. 202).
15 Villehardouin, II. 184.
16 The office of *podestà* was peculiar to the Italian city-republics. It was held for a limited period, generally a year at a time, and combined military and civic responsibilities.
17 Nicetas, 847; Villehardouin, II. 252; R. L. Wolff, 'Baldwin of Flanders and Hainaut', loc. cit., p. 290.
18 A. Wallensköld (ed.), *Les Chansons de Conon de Béthune*, p. vii. For the more constructive side of the Crusaders' work, see also Andrea van Arkel and Krijnie Ciggaar, 'St. Thorlac's in Constantinople, built by a Flemish emperor' (*Byzantion*, XLIX, 1979, pp. 428–46).
19 Cf. A. A. Vasiliev, *A History of the Byzantine Empire*, II. 465.

Chapter 15 Some Reactions and Consequences

1 PL, 225, cols. 260–2.
2 ibid. 215, cols. 454–5.
3 ibid. 225, cols. 957–8.
4 ibid. 215, cols. 699–702.
5 ibid. cols. 710–14.
6 Donald Nicol, 'The Papal Scandal' (*Studies in Church History*, XIII, 1976, p. 145).
7 Freddy Thiriet, *La Romanie Vénitienne au Moyen Age* (Paris, 1959), p. 74.
8 See further P. A. Throop, 'Criticism of Papal Crusade Policy in Old French and

Provençal' (*Speculum*, XIII, 1938, pp. 379–412); and his *Criticism of the Crusade* (Amsterdam, 1940), pp. 30 ff.

9   For the acquisition of relics as a Crusade motive, see A. Frolow, *Recherches sur la Déviation de la IVe Croisade*, pp. 51 ff.; for relics generally, H. Leclercq, 'Reliques et Reliquaires' (*Dictionnaire d'Archéologie Chrétienne et de Liturgie*, ed. F. Cabrol and H. Leclercq, XIV B, Paris, 1948, pp. 2294–359).

10 For a list of feasts of reception of relics see P. Riant, *Des Dépouilles Religieuses*, pp. 76–8.

11 P. Riant, *Exuviae*, II. 45: 'Constantinopolitana civitas diu profana'.

12 Ralph of Coggeshall, *Chronicon Anglicanum*, ed. J. Stevenson (RS, 1875), pp. 201–3; Roger of Wendover, *Flores Historiarum*, ed. H. G. Hewlett (RS, 1886–9), II. 274–6, III. 77. Ruins of the north transept, chapter-house, and refectory remain at Broomholm priory.

13 In a private communication from Parrocchia di S. Andrea Ap., Amalfi, the author is told that these relics are to this day 'kept and venerated in the crypt of the cathedral'.

14 Robert de Clari, p. 112.

15 For other views of the Shroud see Maurus Green, 'Enshrouded in Silence' (*Ampleforth Journal*, LXXIV, pt 3, 1969, pp. 321–45) and Iam Wilson, 'Tomb to Turin' (*Ampleforth Journal*, LXXXIII, pt 1, 1978, pp. 9–23).

16 Brenda Bolton, 'The Cistercians in Romania' (*Studies in Church History*, XIII, 1976, pp. 177–8).

17 Boncompagno's *De Malo Senectutis*, in *Rendiconti delle R. Accademia dei Lincei*, serie V, vol. 1 (1892), pp. 46–67: '. . . ex eo quod in orbe terrarum simile regnum non potest nec poterit inveniri'.

18 Gerald Hodgett, *A Social and Economic History of Medieval Europe*, p. 59.

19 William H. McNeill, *Venice, the Hinge of Europe*, p. 248.

20 Revelation of St. John, 1: 9.

21 Gerald Hodgett, op. cit. pp. 75–6.

Chapter 16   Byzantium Survives

1   For the Nicaean Empire see especially Michael Angold, *A Byzantine Government in Exile* (Oxford, 1975); and there is a full discussion in A. Gardner, *The Lascarids of Nicaea: the Story of an Empire in Exile* (London, 1912).

2   The whole subject is reviewed by Donald Nicol, *The Despotate of Epiros* (Blackwell, 1957).

3   For Trebizond, see A. A. Vasiliev, 'The Foundation of the Empire of Trebizond, 1204–22' (*Speculum*, XI, 1936, pp. 3–37) and W. Miller, *Trebizond, the Last Greek Empire* (London, 1926).

Select Bibliography

Paul Alphandéry, *La Chrétienté et l'idée de Croisade*, 2 vols. (Paris, 1954).

Michael Angold, *A Byzantine Government in Exile* (Oxford, 1975). A study of government and society under the Lascarids of Nicaea.

N. H. Baynes and H. St. L. B. Moss (eds.), *Byzantium* (Oxford, 1948).

John Beeler, *Warfare in Feudal Europe, 730–1200* (Cornell, 1971).

Charles M. Brand, *Byzantium Confronts the West, 1180–1204* (Harvard, 1968).

James A. Brundage, *Medieval Canon Law and the Crusader* (Wisconsin, 1969).

Cambridge Medieval History, IV, pt. i (1966), especially for Donald Nicol, 'The Fourth Crusade and the Greek and Latin Empires, 1204–61' (pp. 275–330).

Otto Demus, *The Church of San Marco in Venice* (Washington, D.C., 1960).

George Every, *The Byzantine Patriarchate, 451–1204* (London, 1947).

A. Frolow, *Recherches sur la Déviation de la IVe Croisade* (Paris, 1955).

Fulcher of Chartres, *Chronicle of the First Crusade* (English translation by Martha E. McGinty, Philadelphia, 1941).

Geoffrey de Villehardouin, *La Conquête de Constantinople*, ed. E. Faral, 2 vols. (Paris, 1961). There is an English translation by M. R. B. Shaw in Penguin Books, 1963.

M. H. Keen, *The Laws of War in the Late Middle Ages* (London, 1965).

Michael Maclagan, *The City of Constantinople* (London, 1965).

William H. McNeill, *Venice, the Hinge of Europe, 1081–1797* (Chicago, 1974).

William Miller, *The Latins in the Levant* (London, 1908).

Nicetas Choniates, *Historia*, ed. Immanuel Bekker (Bonn, 1835), Greek text, with Latin translation.

Donald Nicol, *The Despotate of Epiros* (Blackwell, 1957).

Novgorod Chronicle. English translation by J. Gordon, accompanied by an article, 'The Novgorod Account of the Fourth Crusade', in *Byzantion*, XLIII, 1973, pp. 297–311; and an English translation in Camden Series, 3rd series, 1914, pp. 43–8.

Odo of Deuil, *De profectione Ludovici VII in orientem* (English translation by Virginia G. Berry, Columbia, 1948).

George Ostrogorsky, *A History of the Byzantine State* (English translation by Joan Hussey, Blackwell, 2nd edn. 1968).

Edwin Pears, *The Fall of Constantinople* (London, 1885).

Donald E. Queller, *The Fourth Crusade: the Conquest of Constantinople, 1201–1204* (Leicester, 1978).

Donald E. Queller and Susan J. Stratton, 'A Century of Controversy on the Fourth Crusade' (*Studies in Medieval and Renaissance History*, VI, 1969, pp. 235–77). A review of studies over the past century.

P. E. D. Riant, *Des Dépouilles Religieuses enlevées à Constantinople au XIIIe siècle par les Latins* (Paris, 1875). The best book on the pillage of relics from Constantinople.

P. E. D. Riant, *Exuviae Sacrae Constantinopolitanae*, 3 vols. (Geneva, 1877–1904; 3rd volume by F. de Mely).

Robert de Clari, *The Conquest of Constantinople*, English translation by Edgar H. McNeal (Columbia, 1936); and the edition by Philippe Lauer, *La Conquête de Constantinople* (Paris, 1924).

Steven Runciman, *A History of the Crusades*, 3 vols. (especially vol. III, Cambridge, 1954).

Steven Runciman, *The Eastern Schism* (Oxford, 1955).

Steven Runciman, *Byzantine Civilisation* (London, 1933).

J. J. Saunders, *Aspects of the Crusades* (Christchurch, New Zealand, 1962), especially for chap. IV, on the significance of Egypt.

Kenneth M. Setton (ed.), *A History of the Crusades*, 2 vols. (Wisconsin, 1969).

Philip Sherrard, *Constantinople: Iconography of a Sacred City* (London, 1965).

R. C. Smail, *Crusading Warfare* (Cambridge, 1956).

P. A. Throop, *Criticism of the Crusade* (Amsterdam, 1940).

A. A. Vasiliev, *A History of the Byzantine Empire, 324–1453*, 2 vols. (2nd edn. Wisconsin, 1952).

A. A. Vasiliev, 'The Foundation of the Empire of Trebizond, 1204–22' (*Speculum*, XI, 1936, pp. 3–37).

J. F. Verbruggen, *The Art of Warfare in Western Europe during the Middle Ages*, translated by S. Willard and S. C. M. Southern (North Holland, 1977).

William of Tyre, *A History of Deeds done beyond the Sea* (English translation by E. A. Babcock and A. C. Krey, Columbia, 1943).

Robert L. Wolff, *Studies in the Latin Empire of Constantinople* (Variorum Reprints, London, 1976).

Index

Abbasids, of Baghdad, 26.
Achaia, principality of, 144–5.
Acre, 71, 84, 135.
Adhémar, bishop of Le Puy, 5, 6.
Agnes, 13, 126.
al-Adil, 28.
al-Afdal, 27.
al-Aziz, 27.
al-Hakim II, caliph, 25.
al-Harawy, 89.
al-Zahir, 27.
Alamanikon, 23.
Alard Maquereau, 48, 52.
Aleaumes de Clari, 45, 123, 130.
Alexander III, pope, 15, 58.
Alexius, of Trebizond, 159.
Alexius I Comnenus, Byzantine emperor, 4, 6,
    9, 12, 22, 166.
Alexius II, Byzantine emperor, 15.
Alexius III, Byzantine emperor, accession,
    22, 67; campaigns in Balkans, 23; ill
    disposed to Philip of Swabia, 34; worsening
    of relations with Venice, 63; 81, 102,
    104–5; flight, 109; in exile, 114; in Thrace,
    137; captured, 138; ends his days in a
    monastery, 157–8.
Alexius, prince, in custody, 67; at Swabian
    court, 67; visits pope, 69; proposes pact, 82;
    arrives in Zara, 85; confirms agreement at
    Corfu, 85; appears before Constantinople,
    104; becomes Alexius IV, 110–12; tours his
    Empire, 113; fails to satisfy Crusaders, 115;
    attacks Venetian fleet, 116; murdered, 117.
Alexius V Ducas Mourtzouphlos, Byzantine
    emperor, takes throne, 116–17; final breach
    with Crusaders, 118; his rule, 118–19;
    defeated by Henry, 119; defends the capital,
    121–3; flight, 123–34; in Thrace, 137;
    blinded, 137; executed, 138.
'Alī, caliph, 26.
Alp Arslan, 4.
Amalfi, merchant quarter in Constantinople,
    65; Latin monastery on Mt. Athos, 32;
    relics of St. Andrew, 151.

Amalric I, king of Jerusalem, 3, 12–13.
Andravida, 144.
André d'Ureboise, 123.
Andrew II, king of Hungary, 36.
Adrianople, 138; battle of, 141.
Andronicus I Comnenus, Byzantine emperor,
    15–17; death, 18, 166.
Angelo Partecipazio, doge, 56.
Angers, cathedral, 149.
Anna Comnena, 6, 98.
Anna Delassena, 121.
Anna, wife of Theodore I Lascaris, 109.
Anthony of Novgorod, 89–90.
Antioch, capture of, 6; principality of, 7.
Aquileia, 45.
Archipelago, duchy of the, 154.
arengo, 50, 57.
arms, borne by clergy, 5, 31; contemporary
    weapons and armour, 45–6.
Arnulf, bishop of Lisieux, 9.
Arsenius, patriarch of Constantinople, 160.
Artandus, Cistercian monk, 54.
Asen, mountain chieftain, 22.
Assizes of Romania, 137.
Athena, statue destroyed, 117.
Athens, lordship of, 145–6.
Aymar, Latin patriarch of Jerusalem, 35.
Ayyubid Empire, 27.

Baldwin, count of Flanders, takes Cross, 44;
    in Venice, 72, 74; in Zara, 83; at first siege,
    104, 107, 108; at second siege, 124, 132;
    elected emperor, 134–5; quarrel with
    Boniface, 138; captured by Kalojan, 141;
    death, 143.
Baldwin II, Latin emperor, 152, 160.
Baldwin, brother of Godfrey, 5, 7.
Baldwin III, king of Jerusalem, 9.
Basil of Caesarea, 24.
Bela III, king of Hungary, 36, 74.
Benjamin of Tudela, 88.
Bérard, Latin archbishop of Athens, 145.
Bernard, preaches Crusade, 9.
Berthold, count of Katzenellenbogen, 77, 137.

Blachernae, palace, 91, 110; assigned to Latin emperor, 120; 127, 132; taken by Crusaders, 126; looted, 129.
Blanche of Navarre, 40.
Bloody Field, 5.
Bohemond, 5, 6, 7, 11–12.
'Bohemond's castle', 106.
Boncompagno da Signa, 154.
Boniface, marquis of Montferrat, interested in Crusade, 52; appointed leader, 53; at Cistercian Chapter General, 54; at Swabian court, 55, 68; visits pope, 69; at Zara, 82–3; at first siege, 104, 107, 113; at second siege, 124; occupies Bucoleon, 126; 131, 134, 135; marries Margaret, 136; king of Thessalonica, 136; quarrel with Baldwin, 137–8; death, 143–4.
Broomholm priory, 150, 175.
Bruges, a recruiting centre, 44.
Bucoleon, palace, 87; assigned to Latin emperor, 120; taken by Crusaders, 126; looted, 129; occupied by Baldwin, 135.
Byzantine Empire, administration, 96; army, 96–9; navy, 23, 62–3, 99–100; diplomacy, 100; contacts with Islam, 24.

caesaro-papism, 35.
Canabus, 117.
Cassiodorus, 56.
Celestine III, pope, 32.
Chagri Beg, 3.
Chalcedon, 102.
Charlemagne, 2.
Charles Martel, victor of Tours, 2.
Chrétien de Troyes, 40.
Christ Euergetes, church, 108.
Christ Pantepoptes, church, 121, 136.
Cistercians, 37–8, 152; Chapters General, 38, 152.
Cluniac revival, 2.
Compiègne, conference at, 47; shroud, 168.
Conon de Béthune, takes Cross, 44; member of Committee of Six, 48; 102, 116, 142; regent, 144.
Conrad, bishop of Halberstadt, 122, 134, 151.
Conrad of Montferrat, 18, 53.
Conrad III, western emperor, 9, 12.
'conservator', 37.
Constantine Ducas, 124.
Constantine the Great, vision of Cross, 1.
Constantine Lascaris, 123, 124, 125.
Constantine of Rhodes, 89.
Constantine, finance minister, 110.
Constantinople, foundation of, 88; its riches, 89; walls, 90, 106; palaces, 91; churches and monasteries, 91–3; scholarship, 93–5; attitude of First Crusaders, 6, of Second

Crusaders, 9; Normans advance on, 11; William I of Sicily threatens the city, 12; in danger from Henry VI, 22–3.
Corfu, Crusaders at, 85–7; acquired by Venice, 155; by Epiros, 158.
Coron, 155.
Crete, 136, 154.
Cross-taking, 36–7, 42–3.
Crown of Thorns, relic, 152.
Cumans, 22, 141, 158.
Cyril, bishop of Jerusalem, 3.

Damatrys, 102.
David, of Trebizond, 159.
Demetrius of Montferrat, king of Thessalonica, 159.
Demotica, 138, 140.
Dijon, assembly of bishops, 35–6.
diversion of Crusade to Constantinople, formally proposed, 82.
Domenico Michiel, doge, 61.
Domenico Sanudo, 62.
Domenico Selvo, doge, 60, 153.
Dorylaeum, battle of, 6.
Dositheus, patriarch of Constantinople, 19.
Durazzo, 7, 11, 85, 158.

Eadmer, 88.
Écri, tournament at, 40–2.
Edessa, county of, 7; fall of, 9.
Egypt, importance to Crusaders, 26–7, 48, 72.
Eleanor of Aquitaine, 40.
Ely Pontifical, 42.
Emeric, king of Hungary, 36, 75.
Englishmen, not participants in Fourth Crusade, 51, 150.
Enguerrand de Boves, 85.
Enrico Dandolo, missions to Constantinople, 62; enmity to Byzantium, 64; age, 64; becomes doge, 57, 63; receives Committee of Six, 48–9; takes Cross, 77; at Zara, 78ff.; excommunicated, 81; at first siege, 107, 109; extends his support, 113; at second siege, 122; occupies a palace, 126; his debt finally settled, 130; death, 142.
Epiros, Despotate of, 158–9.
Ernald, abbot of Rievaulx, 38.
'Espousal of the Sea', 58.
'essoin', 19, 127.
Estanor, 105, 111, 114, 122.
Étienne du Perche, 78, 138, 141.
Euboea, 155.
Eudes, duke of Burgundy, 53.
Eudocia, 109, 123, 137.
Eugenius III, pope, 9.
Euphrosyne, empress, 109, 112, 123.

Eustathius, archbishop of Thessalonica, 26, 94.

'filioque' clause, 30.
First Crusade, beginning of, 5; founding of Latin States, 7, 8.
Florence, council of, 160.
Fourth Lateran Council, 27, 151.
Francis of Assisi, 52.
Frederick Barbarossa, western emperor, on Second Crusade, 9; quarrel with Alexander III, 58; on Third Crusade, 19; death, 20.
Fulcher of Chartres, 6, 7, 46, 89.
Fulk of Neuilly, preaches the Crusade, 39; rebukes Richard I, 39–40; not at Écri, 42; present at Soissons, 54; at Citeaux, 54; death, 77.

Galata tower, 105.
Garnier von Borlande, 77, 84.
Garnier, bishop of Troyes, takes Cross, 43; 78, 119, 123, 134, 150.
Gautier, bishop of Autun, 54, 71.
Gautier de Brienne, 43, 52, 56.
Gautier de Gaudonville, 48.
Genoa, 4, 8, 25, 52, 61.
Geoffrey de Joinville, 43.
Geoffrey de Villehardouin, 39; early career, and Cross-taking, 43; member of Committee of Six, 48; returns to France, 52; his account of prince Alexius, 69–70; in Venice, 72; in Constantinople, 110–11, 114, 141, 142, 144.
Geoffrey de Villehardouin, nephew, 140, 145.
Gerald of Wales, 37.
Gilles de Landas, 80.
Gilles de Trasignies, 72, 84.
Glanville, English Crusader, 75.
Godfrey, bishop of Langres, 9.
Godfrey, duke of Lorraine, 5; death, 7.
Greek fire, 99–100, 172.
Gregory VII, pope, 4, 11, 30.
Guido Pallavicini, 140.
Guigues, count of Forez, 71.
Guillaume Figuiera, 149.
Guy de Coucy, 17.
Guy de Lusignan, 20.
Guy de Provins, 149.
Guy de la Roche, 145.
Guy, abbot of Vaux-de-Cernay, at Citeaux, 54; at Zara, 79, 82–3; he defects, 85.

Hagenau, 55.
Harald Hardrade, 98.
Hattin, battle of, 27.
Helena, 2.
Heinrich von Ülmen, 77, 150.

Henry de Champagne, 40.
Henry II, king of England, 13.
Henry of Flanders, takes Cross, 44; at first siege, 107, 108; raids Phileas, 119; at second siege, 124; occupies Blachernae, 126; gains Adramyttium, 140; crowned, 143; death, 144.
Henry, count of Nevers, 43.
Henry IV, western emperor, 11.
Henry VI, western emperor, 22–3, 32.
heresy, spread of, 37.
Hippodrome, 93.
Holy Sepulchre church, 2, 21, 42, 128.
Holy War, 1, 4, 9, 12, 24, 25, 32, 35, 54.
Honorius III, pope, 127, 145.
Horses of St. Mark's basilica, 93, 131–2.
Hubert Walter, 21, 36.
Hugh de Boves, 85.
Hugh, Cistercian monk, 54.
Hugh, abbot of St. Ghislain, 152.
Hugh, count of St. Pol. takes Cross, 44; 69, 72, 73, 83, 86; at first siege, 104, 107, 108, 113; 129, 130, 135; gains Demotica, 140; death, 140.

Iconium, sultanate of, 25.
icons, 29.
Ingeborg, queen, 36.
Innocent III, pope, birth and early career, 32; his spiritual character, 33; election as pope, and his view of papal authority, 32–4; writes to Latin clergy of Constantinople, 32; writes to Alexius III, 34; launches his Crusade project, 35ff.; approaches John of England, 36; money-raising campaign, 36–7; quarrels with Cistercians, 37–8; authorizes Fulk, 39–40; qualified approval of Franco-Venetian treaty, 51; disturbed at developments, 75; anger at sack of Zara, 80; writes to Philip Augustus, 86; reaction to first siege, 112; in correspondence with Kalojan, 140; the Church in Greece, 145–6; reaction to conquest of Constantinople, 147–8.
Ioannitsa, see Kalojan.
Irene, 22, 66, 104.
Isaac II Angelus, Byzantine emperor, 18; negotiations with Saladin, 19; general policy, 21; overthrown, 22; restored, 110; death, 117.
Islam, relations with Byzantium, 24–5; schisms within, 26; Fatimids, 27; Ayyubids, 27–8; Isma'ilism, 26–7.

Jacques d'Avesnes, 44, 86, 105, 138, 155.
Jacques St. Omer, 140.
Jean de Friaize, 48, 80.

Jean de Nesles, 44; defection of, 71, 84.
Jean de Noyon, 80, 134, 138.
Jerusalem, captured by Crusaders, 7; falls to Saladin, 18.
jihad, 24.
John Asen, king of Bulgaria, 159.
John Camaterus, patriarch of Constantinople, 34, 123, 125.
John II Comnenus, Byzantine emperor, 12.
John of Damascus, 25.
John III Vatatzes, Byzantine emperor, 158.
John, cardinal, 15.
John, king of England, 36.

Ka'aba, 26.
Kai-Khusrū, sultan, 157.
Kalojan, 23, 113.
Kilij Arslan, sultan, 12.
Krak des Chevaliers, 7.

La Cour-Dieu, abbey, 54.
Latin Massacre, 15, 17, 22, 32, 62.
Leo IX, pope, 30.
Leone Vetrano, 155.
Lerici, 69.
Limburg-an-der-Lahn, 150.
Louis, count of Blois, takes Cross, 40–2; arrives in Venice, 72; at Zara, 83; at first siege, 104; illness, 120; at coronation, 135; gains Nicaea, 140; death, 141.
Louis VII, king of France, 9, 31, 40, 48.
Louis IX, king of France, saint, 152.
Lyons, council of, 160.

Malik Shah, sultan, 5.
Manganean poet, 12.
mangonels, 79, 106.
Manuel I Comnenus, Byzantine emperor, treaty with Seljuks, 9; his reign, 12–15; marries Bertha, 12; marries Maria, 12; seizes Venetian property, 13, 61; clashes with Church, 26; fights Normans, 61; building work, 91, 93; encourages feudalism, 96; neglects fleet, 99.
Manuel, son of Andronicus, 159.
Manzikert, battle of, 4, 97.
Marco Sanudo, 154.
Margaret of Hungary, marries Isaac, 18; marries Boniface, 111, 126.
Marino Dandolo, 154.
Marino Zeno, 142.
Martin, abbot of Pairis, preaches Crusade, 38, 42; 76, 80; arrives in Constantinople, 118; participates in sack, 130–1.
Mary, countess of Champagne, 40.
Mary, countess of Flanders, takes Cross, 44; dies in Acre, 135.

Matthew de Montmorency, 43, 110.
Melisende, queen, 9.
Michael Cerularius, patriarch of Constantinople, 30.
Michael Choniates, archbishop of Athens, 94, 99, 145, 157.
Michael I Comnenus Ducas, ruler of Epiros, 155, 158–9.
Michael II Ducas, ruler of Epiros, 159.
Michael VIII Palaeologus, Byzantine emperor, 159–60.
Michael Stryphnos, 23, 102, 104, 112.
Milon de Brébant, 48.
Mistra, 144.
Modon, 155.
Monophysitism, 26.
Montaudon, monk of, 148.
mosque, in Constantinople, 114.
Mosynopolis, 137.
Muhammad, 3, 24, 26.
Myriokephalon, battle of, 13, 48, 62.

Névelon, bishop of Soissons, takes Cross, 43; 54; at Zara, 78, 80; at second siege, 123; elector, 134; 142, 149.
Nicaea, Empire of, 156–60.
Niccolò dei Barattieri, 60.
Nicephorus Chrysoberges, oration of, 115.
Nicephorus II Phocas, Byzantine emperor, 24.
Nicetas Choniates, 21, 94–5, 117, 118, 123, 132, 157.
Nicholas de Jenlain, 105.
Nicholas Mesarites, archbishop of Ephesus, 89, 132.
Nicholas Mysticus, patriarch of Constantinople, 25.
Nicholas Rosso, 102.
Nicholas St. Omer, 140.
Nizamiyah universities, 4.
Novgorod Chronicle, 67, 110, 117, 118, 125, 129.
numbers of Fourth Crusaders, 46, 72, 106, 121, 125.

oath, sanctity of, 42, 73.
Odo de Champlitte, 77.
Odo de Deuil, 9, 31.
Ordelafo Faliero, doge, 74.
Orio Malipiero, doge, 62.
Otto de Cicon, 152.
Otto de la Roche, 145–6.
Otto I, Saxon emperor, 2.
Outremer, 7–8, 24.

pacifism, 1–2.
'Pactum' of Venice, 58.
Pala d'Oro, 152.

papacy, claim to supremacy, 29, 31; Innocent's view of, 33–4.
Paradise, ship, 78, 123.
Paschal II, pope, 12.
Patmos, 154.
Paulo Lucio Anafesta, doge, 56.
Peter, count of Amiens, takes Cross, 44; his contingent, 46; 86; at first siege, 104, 108; at second siege, 123–4; 150; death, 138.
Peter de Bracieux, 123.
Peter Capuano, cardinal, oversight of Crusade project, 35, 40; arrives in Venice, 75; sanctions assault on Zara, 76, 80; sails to Syria, 81; in Constantinople, 134, 142; rebuked by pope, 148; returns to Amalfi with relics, 151.
Peter de Courtenay, Latin emperor, 144.
Peter, abbot of Lucedio, 54, 75, 79, 134.
Peter, mountain chieftain, 22.
Peter Orseolo II, doge, 58.
Peter the Venerable, 10, 31.
Peter Ziani, doge, 62, 142, 152.
petraries, 79, 106.
Phileas, raided by Henry of Flanders, 119.
Philip Augustus, king of France, 13; on Third Crusade, 19; returns to France, 21; 36, 39; meets Boniface, 53.
Philip, duke of Swabia, king of Germany, marries Irene, 22–3; quarrel with Otto IV, 34, 36; 55, 67–8, 82, 111, 131.
Pilgrim, ship, 78, 123.
pilgrimage, 2, 4.
Pisa, 5, 8, 52, 61.
Princes' Islands, 102.
pronoia, 96.

Rainier Dandolo, 142.
Rainier of Montferrat, 13, 15, 52, 53.
Ralph of Coggeshall, 40.
Raymond, count of Toulouse, 5, 6, 136.
relics, 3, 6; in Constantinople, 89, 131; acquisition of, 149ff.
reliefs of St. Demetrius and St. George, 153.
Renaud de Dampierre, 72, 84.
Renaud de Montmirail, 43, 84, 138, 141.
Renier de Trit, 44, 140, 141.
Richard I, king of England, on Third Crusade, 19; occupies Cyprus, 20; besieges Acre, 21; truce with Saladin, 21; death, 36.
Robert de Boves, 79, 80, 85.
Robert de Clari, takes Cross, 45; at second siege, 123; describes bronze horses and other animals, 132; describes coronation, 135; describes Christ's shroud, 151.
Robert Curthose, duke of Normandy, 5.
Robert Guiscard, invades Byzantium, 11, 59.
Robert de Joinville, 43, 52.

Roger II, king of Sicily, 12, 61.
Rognvald, 89.
Romanus III, Byzantine emperor, 25.

Sainte-Chapelle, Paris, 152.
Saladin, sultan, his rise to power, 27; takes Jerusalem, 18; fights Richard and Philip, 21; death, 27; 'Saladin' tithe, 37.
Santo Spirito in Sassia, 33.
Schism, the 1054 quarrel, 30–1; complete by close of twelfth century, 32.
Sebastiano Ziani, doge, 58, 60.
Second Crusade, 9; failure of, 3.
Seljuk Turks, emergence of, 3.
Sens, cathedral, 150.
Simon, abbot of Loos, 44, 54, 83.
Simon, count of Montfort, takes Cross, 43; at Zara, 79; defects, 85.
Soffredo, cardinal, 35, 75.
Soissons, conferences at, 46–7, 53; relics at, 149–50.
statues, destruction of, 131.
Stephen, count of Chartres and Blois, 42.
Stephen du Perche, 78.
Suger of St. Denis, 10.
St. Albans, abbey, 150.
St. Elizabeth of Hungary, 36.
St. Mark's, Venice, 59–60; relics of, 152; embellishment of, 152–3.
St. Nicholas monastery, Venice, 70.
St. Sophia, basilica, 90, 91–2, 114, 117, 120, 124, 128–9, 135, 136.
St. Stephen, monastery, 101.

Tamara, queen of Georgia, 159.
Tancred, 5, 7.
tetrarchs, porphyry group, 153.
Theodore I Comnenus Ducas, ruler of Epiros, 159.
Theodore I Lascaris, Byzantine emperor, 109, 125, 140, 143, 157.
Theodore II Lascaris, Byzantine emperor, 159.
Thessalonica, sack of, 17–18, 127.
Thierry of Flanders, 44.
Third Crusade, 19–21.
Thomas, canon of Amiens, 45.
Thomas d'Autremencourt, 140.
Thomas Morosini, Latin patriarch of Constantinople, 136.
Tibald, count of Bar-le-Duc, 53.
Tibald, count of Champagne, 43; takes Cross, 40–2; death, 52–3.
Torre dei Conti, 33.
Trebizond, 12; Empire of, 159.
True Cross, finding and veneration of, 2–3, 165; relics of, 131, 150–1.

Tughril Beg, 3.

Turcoples, 138.

Turin Shroud, 151.

Tzurulum, 137.

Ulfric, 89.

'Ummayads, 25.

Urban II, pope, at Clermont, 1; at Piacenza, 4; council at Bari, 31.

Varangian Guard, origin of, 97–8; Englishmen serving in, 11, 13, 89, 98; defence of Constantinople, 107, 108; palace guards, 110, 117, 119, 126, 135; in Nicaean Empire, 158.

Venice, origins of, 56; maritime power, 8, 11, 48, 57; dogeship, 57, 61; population, 13, 154; active in Byzantium, 13, 58ff.; mass arrests by Manuel, 61; St. Mark's basilica, 59–60; columns in Piazzetta, 60; treaty with Franks, 49–50; Crusaders arrive in, 70; transports completed, 73; imperial electors, 134.

Vilain de Neuilly, 72.

Viola, ship, 78.

Vitale Michiel II, doge, 61.

Vlachs, 22, 47, 140.

Walther von der Vogelweide, minnesinger, 37, 86, 149.

William de Béthune, 44.

William de Champlitte, 137–8, 144.

William I, king of Sicily, 12.

William II, king of Sicily, 17, 62.

William, later Grand Master of Templars, 84.

World, ship, 78.

Yolande, 144.

Zangi, 9.

Zara, 57, 58, 74, 75; recapture of, 78ff.; fleet sails from, 87.